CRIME UNLIMITED?
QUESTIONS FOR THE 21st CENTURY

Also by Pat Carlen

ALTERNATIVES TO WOMEN'S IMPRISONMENT (*editor with Anne Worrall*)
CRIMINAL WOMEN (*with D. Christina, J. Hicks, J. O'Dwyer and C. Tchaikowsky*)
GENDER, CRIME AND JUSTICE (*editor with Anne Worrall*)
JIGSAW: A Political Criminology of Youth Homelessness
MAGISTRATES' JUSTICE
OFFICIAL DISCOURSE (*with F. Burton*)
PAYING FOR CRIME (*editor with D. Cook*)
RADICAL ISSUES IN CRIMINOLOGY (*editor with M. Collison*)
SLEDGEHAMMER: Women's Imprisonment at the Millennium
SOCIOLOGICAL REVIEW MONOGRAPH (No. 23) ON LAW
TRUANCY: the Politics of Compulsory Schooling (*with D. Gleeson and J. Wardhaugh*)
WOMEN, CRIME AND POVERTY
WOMEN'S IMPRISONMENT

Also by Rod Morgan

A TASTE OF PRISON: a Study of Trial and Remand (*with R. D. King*)
CRISIS IN THE PRISONS: the Way Out (*with R. D. King*)
FORMULATING PENAL POLICY: the Future of the Advisory Council on the Penal System
THE FUTURE OF THE PRISON SYSTEM (*with R. D. King*)
NO MORE PRISON BUILDING (*with A. Rutherford*)
HANDBOOK FOR PRISON BOARDS OF VISITORS
FOLLOWING SCARMAN: a Survey of Police Community Consultation Arrangements in Provincial Police Authorities in England and Wales (*with C. Maggs*)
PRISONS AND ACCOUNTABILITY: Opening up a Closed World (*with M. Maguire and J. Vagg*)
COMING TO TERMS WITH POLICING: Questions of Policy (*editor with D. Smith*)
THE OXFORD HANDBOOK OF CRIMINOLOGY (*editor with M. Maguire and R. Reiner*)
THE POLITICS OF SENTENCING REFORM (*editor with C. Clarkson*)
THE FUTURE OF POLICING (*with T. Newburn*)
THE OXFORD HANDBOOK OF CRIMINOLOGY, 2nd edition (*editor with M. Maguire and R. Reiner*)
PREVENTING TORTURE: the Origins and Work of the European Committee for the Prevention of Torture and Inhuman or Degrading Treatment or Punishment (*forthcoming, with M. Evans*)

Crime Unlimited?
Questions for the
21st Century

Edited by

Pat Carlen
Professor of Sociology
University of Bath

and

Rod Morgan
Professor of Criminal Justice
University of Bristol

First published 1999 by
MACMILLAN PRESS LTD
Houndmills, Basingstoke, Hampshire RG21 6XS
and London
Companies and representatives
throughout the world

ISBN 0–333–72502–6

A catalogue record for this book is available
from the British Library.

This book is printed on paper suitable for recycling and
made from fully managed and sustained forest sources.

10   9   8   7   6   5   4   3   2   1
08   07   06   05   04   03   02   01   00   99

Printed and bound in Great Britain by
Antony Rowe Ltd, Chippenham, Wiltshire

Contents

List of Contributors

GARY ARMSTRONG is Lecturer in Criminology, University of Reading.

MICHAEL BLOOR is Professor of Sociology at the University of Cardiff.

PAT CARLEN is Professor of Sociology at Bath University.

REBECCA DOBASH is Professor of Social Policy at Manchester University.

RUSSELL DOBASH is Professor of Criminology at Manchester University.

CLIVE DUNNIGHAN is Lecturer in Criminology at Teesside University.

EVI GIRLING is Research Fellow in the Department of Criminology at Keele University.

CHRIS HALE is Professor of Criminology at the University of Kent.

DICK HOBBS is Reader in Sociology at the University of Durham.

TREVOR JONES is Lecturer in Criminology at the University of Edinburgh.

IAN LOADER is Lecturer in the Department of Criminology at Keele University.

LEE MONAGHAN is a postgraduate student in sociology at the University of Cardiff.

ROD MORGAN is Professor of Criminal Justice at Bristol University.

TIM NEWBURN is Professor of Urban Studies at Goldsmiths College, University of London.

CLIVE NORRIS is Lecturer in Criminology at the University of Hull.

HOWARD PARKER is Professor of Social Policy at Manchester University.

RICHARD SPARKS is Professor of Criminology at Keele University.

IAN TAYLOR is Professor of Sociology at the University of Salford.

Introduction: Crime at the Millennium – New Anxieties and Old Issues

Pat Carlen and Rod Morgan

We stand on the threshold of the twenty-first century with all its promise of new opportunities, new technologies and presently unthought-of discourses and discoveries. Yet, despite the appetite for novelty, innovation and change which a millennium assuredly provokes, many of the recurring social problems of the twentieth century seem, today, to be as unamenable to the most modern remedies as they have ever been. They remain with us, unresolved, blots on the horizon of the twentieth-first century. Nowhere are these challenges to the concept of 'social progress' more evident than in the continuing debates about distributive justice (in recent years given an even sharper edge by mass long-term unemployment and the accompanying crises of western welfare systems); and in equally heated debates about crime and punishment; legitimate modes of social regulation, policing and penality; and the ever-problematic relationships between social justice and criminal justice.

In 1992 the UK Economic and Social Research Council, mindful of the rapidly changing nature and intergenerational (and other) tensions of late or postmodern societies, initiated a Research Programme designed to investigate a range of these issues under the broad heading of 'Crime and Social Order'. The Programme had a particular focus on the new types of citizen-insecurities endemic in what has been called the 'risk society': a society characterised by a 'postmodern condition' of increasing individualism and narcissism, bewildering rates of technological and cultural change, and the breakdown of many of the old philosophical, economic and political certainties which were supposed to have characterised the rampant modernism of the first half or so of this century. Under that timely and imaginative Programme, 22 projects were funded. Now, in this book, selected findings of seven of those projects are presented and discussed, together with two other new articles specially written to

1

complement them. Overall, the collection of nine essays identifies, analyses and discusses some persisting dilemmas of crime and social regulation, old problems which have taken on a new urgency because of their rapidly changing nature, their continuing intractability, and their capacity to generate (or sharpen) social conflict. The major topics examined include: neighbourhood anxieties about crime and policing (Ian Loader, Evi Girling and Richard Sparks in Chapter 1); ecologies of crime (Chris Hale in Chapter 2); changing networks of crime and social regulation, particularly international policing (Dick Hobbs and Colin Dunnighan in Chapter 3); the growth of CCTV surveillance (Clive Norris and Gary Armstrong in Chapter 4); emerging patterns of private policing (Tim Newburn in Chapter 5); the struggle for and restistance to guns control (Ian Taylor in Chapter 6); patterns of drugs consumption among the young (Howard Parker in Chapter 7); the personal meanings of steroid use (Russell Dobash, Rebecca Dobash and others in Chapter 8); and British penal politics post-Thatcher (Rod Morgan and Pat Carlen in Chapter 9). Each of the essays explores the relationships between a general or specific crime or regulatory problem and recent social change. (Findings from the other projects making up the ESRC Programme, as well as discussion of some of the work reported here, are to be found in the following collections: Ruggiero, South and Taylor (1998), Hope and Sparks (forthcoming), and Pearson and Davies (1998).

Questions of 'law and order' are foremost amongst contemporary issues in creating great anxiety within individuals, households and neighbourhoods. They also prompt fierce public debate within the mass media, in Westminster and in council chambers throughout the land. The dilemmas they provoke are complex. Because they involve fundamental questions about the relationships between social justice, crime, punishment and social regulation, the political and administrative arguments they fuel are never solely about ways and means. At neighbourhood level, for example, they have recently surfaced most starkly in relation to policing priorities. Recurring discussions emphasise the difficulty of taking seriously citizens' reputedly heightened (and socially disabling) fears about criminal risk to persons and property without engaging in a degree of over-policing which, far from assuaging those anxieties, might increase them still further. The balance between adequately protecting the public yet avoiding any police-provoked escalation of public anxiety about the likelihood of individual criminal victimization is a delicate one. So also is the need to protect innocent victims and the need to safeguard the rights of suspects so as to prevent the innocent from being wrongfully convicted.

It is vital that we get these relationships right because getting them wrong could easily result in an almost limitless demand for policing which would be prohibitively expensive to satisfy both in terms of financial cost and the possible erosion of civil liberties and human rights (see Chapter 1). At the deep end of the 'law and order' continuum – in the courts and the prisons – a major concern during the late 1980s was with the question of how best to respond effectively, efficiently and economically to lawbreakers. What policies should be pursued such that there was a likelihood of both further criminal behaviour *and* the spiralling fear of crime being reduced? The early 1990s witnessed the inception of an unashamedly populist penal policy which aimed to calm the public's media-fed fears of and anger about crime by giving more and more offenders a taste of prison. As we approach the end of the century it is unclear to what extent this populist approach, both symbolic and substantive, will be continued (see Chapter 9).

Between these two issues – the day-to-day policing of neighbourhoods and sentencing policy – are a multiplicitity of overlapping 'law and order' anxieties. Questions about: the ecology of crime patterns, long-term crime trends and the extent to which crime, in common with legitimate economic activity, is increasingly organised on global dimensions (see Chapters 2 and 3); worries about changes in the technologies, practices and ideologies of policing and surveillance (Chapters 2, 3, 4 and 5); contemporary fears about the increased use of guns by British criminals on the one hand, and a fierce resentment (by special interest groups) of suggestions that gun ownership be regulated on the other (see Chapter 6); and confusion and fear about the little-understood effects of new youth leisure activities involving alcopops, crack-cocaine and steroids (see Chapters 7 and 8).

Debilitating individual anxieties about the risks of being burgled, robbed, raped or otherwise falling victim to crime, together with public concerns about policing and punishment, are of course not new. On the contrary, they are perennial. But they have become ever more pressing as recorded crime has appeared to rise inexorably, as the social mood of insecurity and uncertainty has deepened, and as the likelihood that households will become the victims of crime, or that one of their number will be criminalised, has increased. Moreover, the social and economic context within which these perennial concerns have been traditionally played out is changing. The dilemmas are subtly altered as old problems appear in new guises.

Criminals and police are engaged in a neck-and-neck arms race to take the lead in communications and surveillance technology (see Chapters 3 and 4), with the consequence that personal security is increasingly sought not through familiar, trusting relationships built up over years, but through the erection of technological, physical and geographical fortresses by, and within, an increasingly deregulated market-place (Chapters 3, 4 and 5). Citizens are encouraged not to rely on the state for their security, but to engage in privatised or do-it-yourself property surveillance (see Chapters 1, 4 and 5). Moreover, the public at large has become much more socially and geographically atomised, privatised and vulnerable to fears of crime and disorder. What was formerly genuine public space has been progressively asset-stripped, sold off or put in the hands of less obviously accountable agencies (see Chapters 5 and 9). More and more public activity now takes place on private land to which the public has only conditional access – that is, access subject to controls organised by vested commercial interests.

Parents are daily assaulted with news items, often dramatically enhanced and made to seem culturally threatening, about designer drugs and new patterns of consumption and leisure among the young (see Chapter 7), though the social implications and consequences of these youth lifestyles are largely unknown. At the same time, adolescents and young adults have become the prime targets of the commercial purveyors of 'style' and, as a result, are continuously and insistently enjoined to shape and clothe their bodies according to some perfectable (and commercially profitable) image of masculinity or femininity. The invitation to 'the body beautiful' (fraudulently) promises psychological confidence while simultaneously fostering deep anxiety in both the young people themselves and those who are either frightened or puzzled by some of their more outlandish reinventions of self (see Chapter 8).

The ease of mobility now enjoyed by the majority of the population has both undermined our sense of place *and* opened up new predatory opportunities for those inclined to take them. And, to cap all other contradictions and ironies, it has become ever more apparent that, while the so-called sovereign state is assuming more and more legal powers to criminalise and punish at a time when its capacity to deliver security and order is rapidly diminishing (see Chapter 9), the operation of global forces, including the growth of international organised crime and policing, is paradoxically making citizens more reliant on what they are able to control at neighbourhood level (see Chapters 1 and 3).

These trends are perplexing and confusing. So, what are the relationships between law, order and crime likely to be in the twenty-first century? At what level of governance should regulation operate? What should be the role of the state? And how should the citizen act responsibly? All these questions are addressed in this volume, and a variety of well-argued and, in some cases, contentious answers are given. The overarching conclusion that we editors draw from the findings presented in the following pages is that the major challenge for the twenty-first century will be to develop a holistic approach to social regulation. This would involve, first of all, adopting an inclusionary policy towards all those who are presently excluded by want of employment, poverty or minority status from getting a decent living without breaking the law (see Chapter 2).

Secondly, holism in social regulation means trying to harmonise the different aims and objectives of the welfare, criminal justice and penal systems so that regulatory and rehabilitative policies in one system (or part of a system) do not subvert similar programmes in another system (or part of a system) (see Chapter 9).

Thirdly, instead of mimicking the contemporary American slogan (we will not call it a 'policy') of 'zero tolerance' towards young people who may not even be breaking the law, but who may merely be adopting deviant leisure-styles or activities found to be threatening largely because of their potential nuisance or style-difference, a holistic, non-exclusionary approach would work for an increase in social tolerance towards youth subcultures through the development of a better informed understanding of the role of different types of drugs in modern leisure activities and of more sophisticated (and less damaging) modes of regulation of dangerous substances than are presently on offer in the United Kingdom (see Chapters 7 and 8). The 'war on drugs' is largely a phoney war in the sense that it is less about some external 'Other' than about 'Us'. It is not a 'Czar' we need but a clear appreciation of the harms involved so that we can sensibly focus on reducing them.

Fourthly, the holistic approach to social regulation involves the development of a more genuinely democratic and less populist approach to questions of policing and punishment. The respondents in the group discussions conducted by Loader, Girling and Sparks (Chapter 1) indicated that they held much more sophisticated views on policing than are usually put forward in the popular press. Hobbs' and Dunnighan's work on the relationships between local and global crime networks (Chapter 3) suggests that it is premature to abandon the focus on the activities of local crime networks, however 'global' their members' contacts and/or the media representation of them.

Fifthly, Ian Taylor's chapter (6) reminds us that it would be richly rewarding in any holistic criminology for researchers to make much more effort to examine the ways in which discourses of patriotism, respectability and masculinity continue to mask what would surely be seen as seriously crimogenic tendencies to violence if they were to surface in the leisure styles and discourses of the young, unmarried, urban poor.

Obviously, and despite the scare-mongers, crime will never be unlimited. Crime is logically limited (as we remind readers in the final chapter) in its very conception. However, if we continue to view crime and justice from an individualised and purely 'risk managerial' and 'market oriented' standpoint it is likely that we will continue to focus on short-term organisational outputs wherein productivity, and thus success, is measured by crime events and criminals put away. There is no self-evident limit to this process as trends in Russia and the United States testify. It would generally be thought odd were a society in which an increasing proportion of the population was in hospital were described as healthy. But many commentators argue that were more citizens behind bars then our society would be more orderly and just. We disagree. An holistic approach to these questions assumes that such an outcome – and it is on outcomes not outputs that we need to focus – would be the antithesis of the good society, the 'public' interest, social justice. What remains to be seen, of course, is whether any government will have the political will and courage to embark on a long-term holistic strategy of crime control in the teeth of virulent opposition from a populist tabloid press much attracted to the short-term sound-bite rhetoric to which, in recent years, politicians from the Left and Right have increasingly succumbed.

REFERENCES

Hope, T. and Sparks, R. (forthcoming) *High Anxiety? Risk, Insecurity and The Politics of Law and Order.*

Pearson, G. and Davies, A. (1998) 'Histories of Crime and Modernity'. *British Journal of Criminology*, Special Issue.

Ruggiero, V., South, N. and Taylor, I. (1998) *The New European Criminology: Crime and Social Order in Europe*. London: Routledge.

1 Landscapes of Protection: the Past, Present and Futures of Policing in an English Town

Ian Loader, Evi Girling and
Richard Sparks

In his latest reflections on our times Zygmunt Bauman (1997) depicts modernity as an epoch in which a good deal of freedom was sacrificed in the name of collectively guaranteed order and security; an era of reliability where people were able (albeit, for many, within severely circumscribed limits) to forge secure identities, plan ahead and hope for the better. According to Bauman, these days have gone. In the post- (or late-) modern age people live under conditions of overwhelming and self-perpetuating uncertainty, such that:

> No jobs are guaranteed, no positions are foolproof, no skills are of lasting utility, experience and know-how turn into liability as soon as they become assets, seductive careers all too often prove to be suicide tracks ... Livelihood, social position, acknowledgement of usefulness and entitlement to self-dignity may all vanish together, overnight and without notice. (ibid. 23)

In short, Bauman suggests, freedom has triumphed over security:

> Individual freedom rules supreme; it is the value by which all other values came to be evaluated, and the benchmark against which all supra-individual rules and resolutions are to be measured. This does not mean, though, that the ideals of beauty, purity and order which sent men and women on their modern voyage of discovery have been forsaken, or lost any of their original lustre. Now, however, they are to be pursued – and fulfilled – through individual spontaneity, will and effort. (ibid. 2–3)

The seductions of free (consumer) choice that so animate Bauman's recent work (1987, chs 10–11; 1988) have of late begun to find echoes within the field of policing. Since the early 1980s, the terminology of the marketplace has increasingly come to infuse the rhetoric and practices of the public police. Under pressure of government exhortation (and legislation) the police have become more 'business-like' and financially accountable. A new managerial ideology has represented the police not as a force but as a service, with the public encouraged to think of themselves as its 'consumers'. Efforts to promote the police and manage their 'product' image have ensued, often handled by specialist departments (Heward, 1994; Schlesinger and Tumber, 1994, ch. 4). So too have a whole panoply of training courses, performance indicators and consumer satisfaction surveys, all geared to creating 'a culture which insists that all officers ... measure up to the requirements of the customer' (Woodcock, 1992, p. 182).

Yet at the same time the police have sought to dampen consumer demand, insisting that the 'insatiable' expectations the public have of them cannot reasonably be met (Audit Commission, 1996; Independent Committee, 1996). In turn, a host of alternative modes of protection have come to the fore. Local authorities have started to 'contract-in' private firms to patrol their estates; some have established their own 'forces' (I'Anson and Wiles, 1995). Anxious and frustrated citizens have on occasions taken matters into their own hands (Johnston, 1996; Girling et al., 1998), while others have turned to the private security industry. Security provision – whether in the form of locks, bars, gates, alarms, surveillance cameras or patrols – appears ever more diverse, fragmented and determined by the ability and willingness of consumers to pay (Johnston, 1992; Jones and Newburn, 1997).

We thus inhabit a moment of flux. For while the centrality once accorded to the public police appears to be waning, and the sovereign state seems no longer able to promise (let alone deliver) security to its citizens (Garland, 1996), the ramifications of this remain unclear. Bauman (1997, pp. 12–13) might well, however, have had policing in mind when he wrote:

> The tendency to collectivize and centralize the 'cleansing' activities aimed at the preservation of purity, while by no means extinct or exhausted, tends in our time to be ever more often replaced with the strategies of deregulation and privatization.

We will not in this chapter attempt to detail these developments or weigh up their likely implications, a task that has, anyway, been undertaken elsewhere (Loader, 1997a; Morgan and Newburn, 1997). Instead, drawing upon our recent research in a medium-sized and somewhat 'typical' English town (Macclesfield, in Cheshire), we offer a sociology of public sensibilities towards these unfolding landscapes of protection.[1] Our purpose is to describe and make sense of how people living in this place talk about the past, present and possible futures of policing (the narratives they construct, the vocabularies they employ, the associations they make), and examine how they embrace, resist and otherwise come to terms with the choices that increasingly confront them. In so doing, we aim to understand how their responses connect with their outlook on various forms of social and cultural change (as this impinges both locally and in more global ways), and to consider what their dispositions might tell us about the prospects for policing at the approach of the millennium. Let us begin in the present.

ON THE CUSP OF CHANGE?: ANXIETIES IN THE POLICING PRESENT

A town of some 49,000 inhabitants, Macclesfield lies between the Cheshire Plain and the Pennine foothills, some 15 miles south of Greater Manchester, the nearest metropolis. Once a working-class mill town dominated by the silk industry, it has in the post-war period undergone considerable economic and social upheaval. The silk industry has all but disappeared, to be superseded by a number of pharmaceutical giants (notably Zeneca and CIBA-Geigy) and a burgeoning service sector and tourist/heritage industry. This restructuring has in turn contributed to an influx of service-class and professional incomers, who have arrived either to work in the town, or to use it as a comfortable 'home' from which to commute to Manchester or elsewhere in Cheshire. Macclesfield is thus in the late-1990s a somewhat prosperous place (it was recently numbered by the Henley Centre for Forecasting among the 30 towns in Britain with the brightest economic prospects), albeit not without its pockets of poverty and deprivation.

Our research[2] suggests that Macclesfield's adult residents (it doesn't so readily apply to the town's teenagers) are generally rather proud of 'their town', believing it to be a homely and for the most part safe place that strives to avoid the worst excesses of contemporary English

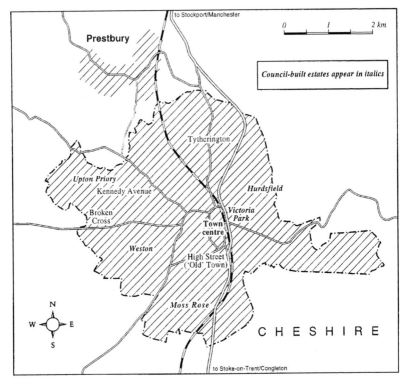

Figure 1.1   Macclesfield and Prestbury

society (drugs, racial tensions and so forth) as they are encountered elsewhere. Notwithstanding worries about burglary and car crime (both believed to be largely the work of 'travelling criminals' from Manchester and Liverpool) and often powerfully voiced concerns about the 'incivilities' committed by local youths (Loader et al., 1998), few among our discussants believed the town to have a significant crime problem. Nor is this view entirely misplaced; in national terms Macclesfield experiences rather low levels of recorded crime (roughly 16 times lower, for instance, than the not so geographically distant Salford in Greater Manchester (Evans et al., 1996)), with Cheshire Police recording 4,150 offences for the town's six beats in 1995. So how, against this backdrop, do the police figure in the 'crime-' and 'place-talk' of Macclesfield residents (cf. Sasson, 1995)? What expectations do people have of the police and how do they assess the 'service' they receive?[3]

Without doubt the pivotal expectation that the town's adult population has of the police is for them to provide a (more) visible presence on the street (the same cannot be said of the young people we spoke to, many of whom thought they saw more than enough of the police already). Time and again in our discussions, high levels of general support for the police (manifest in depictions of them as 'marvellous' or 'helpful and sympathetic' or 'first-class') translated into demands for an identifiable police officer to patrol (more or less permanently) the local streets. This was echoed in a 'Quality of Life' survey conducted by Cheshire County Council (1996) during the time of our research which found that 'putting more police on the beat' was the most common solution to the crime problem proffered by Macclesfield Borough residents; 48 per cent accorded it top priority, 71 per cent made it one of their 'top three'. The same survey found residents of Macclesfield Borough to have the lowest reported levels of 'fear of crime' in Cheshire.

This powerful attachment to the idea of the 'local bobby' was apparent across Macclesfield's diverse neighbourhoods (cutting across lines of both class and gender), and *his* absence (and people generally refer to such a figure as 'he'[4]) constituted the principal source of disquiet and complaint. The following discussion among residents of the 'quiet' Hurdsfield estate illustrates this well:

Don: I think we've got less [*crime and anti-social behaviour*] here than they have on the Moss and Victoria Park, and Upton Priory.
IL: Why do you think that is?
Joy: Good parenting [*all laugh*]
[...]
Don: I'll tell you what it isn't, it's not policing up here, because we never see any.
Joy: No we haven't, have we? I've been looking out for him.
Don: They've been saying we have for two years, and we never see. They say, 'Oh, well, he comes when you're not around'. Well, I think, 'Well, hang on a minute, I'm in and out all hours of the day and night and I've never seen him', and I don't think anybody else has.

Our discussants evinced two main kinds of response to this perceived absence of what Cheshire Police's promotional literature calls a 'benevolent blue presence'. The first largely exempts the police from criticism, preferring instead to direct the blame elsewhere. Here the police are characterised as being deprived by government of the resources needed to maintain an adequate patrol presence, 'let down' by the apparent leniency of the courts, or otherwise burdened by bureaucratic constraints imposed on them from the outside. As a retired businessman from Prestbury put it:

> In all fairness to the police, I think our Home Office has burdened them with far too much paperwork. It seems a terrible shame that a young and active man, who wants to be a policeman, has to spend all his time filling in damn forms.

The resulting climate of constraint is seen not only to limit the number of officers available on the street, but also as inhibiting the police from carrying out their proper task:

Dave: I would guess that the reason most bobbies don't lift somebody now is because if they do they spend their next three hours in the station doing paperwork.

Jim: That's right.

Jean: And then they take them to court and nothing much happens.

Paul: It's then that the prisoner, as he's called, claims that the bobby has hit him, or touched him in any way untoward, and he's then got to spend the next three hours writing out statements. Now I'm not saying that that doesn't go on, I mean there's the Police Complaints Authority, but it's getting to the point where, to be honest, the bobby is actually scared of doing his job.

(Upton Priory residents)

A second strand of thought and feeling is rather less charitable towards the police, believing them to have become a distant bureaucracy, unresponsive to demands that are both sensible and popular. The discrete complaints paraded under this banner concerned such matters as slow response times, a lack of information about reported incidents, and the disproportionate amount of time the police seemingly devote to the regulation of motorists (see further, Girling et al., 1999, ch. 7). Mobilising the vocabulary of consumerism to express his concerns, one Zeneca manager living in Broken Cross encapsulated this mood of disquiet thus:

The police are reacting. They wait for us to ring 999 and ask for the police, and then they go out, reacting. They need to be proactive in terms of looking to prevent the problem before it happens. The only way they'll do that is to combine with Joe Public who comes in in droves and talks to the police. In the same way as people running a business, you listen to your customers. I think the police need to listen to customers to find out what Joe Public wants.

These often powerfully-felt concerns about the lack of visible policing find perhaps their most vehement expression in respect of youths acting suspiciously or creating a nuisance – something that accounted for 16 per cent of the 3,136 calls made to Macclesfield police station in April and May 1995. Here, some of our respondents spoke of the police being called upon unduly to solve problems that were really the responsibility of the community ('the police could manage on the resources they've got if people just got more involved', as one Upton Priory resident put it). Others – such as this young male professional living around Kennedy Avenue – spoke in related terms of people making unreasonable requests of the local police:

> They're not going to start patrolling the streets because somebody of 16 looks like they might have had one cider too many. There's far more important things to deal with in Macclesfield than things like that.

These, however, represented minority outlooks among our respondents, albeit ones that resonate closely with the views of the police officers we spoke to:

PC Smith: We are the answer to everyone's problems as far as they are concerned. Something's happening, call the police. Whether it's our responsibility or not, it doesn't matter, phone the police.

IL: For what reasons do they telephone, because it's the easy solution or . . ?

PC Smith: They won't confront them [*groups of youths*], will they? They don't come out and confront them because they fear they're going to be victimised. They know where they live, they're standing on the corner of the street. They're not going to come out, they're going to call the police [...]

IL:	Is there any way this can be resolved?
PC Smith:	I think each household would like its own personal policeman.
WPC Jones:	Yes, to stand on their front doorstep and keep people away.

The *prevalent* feeling voiced during our discussions is that the police have become increasingly unwilling or unable to take proper action to deal with what amounts to the principal crime-related worry among the town's adult residents (Loader et al., 1998). We repeatedly encountered tales concerning incidents where the police had either failed to respond promptly to calls about teenage incivilities, or had taken what were viewed as insufficient measures upon their eventual arrival. Among some, this apparent inaction aroused the suspicion that the police no longer take seriously people's worries about teenage disorder. As one long-established resident of High Street put it:

> I think the police have sat in their panda cars and divorced themselves from this type of problem. Okay, so it's not petty in our lives and your lives, but it is petty crime, and I think they've been focused on the sort of more typical crime, burglaries, other things like this, because, presumably, they can't do anything to the kids, they can't run them in and stick them in the cells, then they find their hands are tied, they're powerless. [...] I don't think the police look at it as serious, it must be a minimal crime to them, it must be nothing at all, but it really is worrying.

At various public meetings we attended, these anxieties surfaced in often fractious disputes between police representatives and members of the public. In general terms, these disputes revolved around the level and type of patrolling, during which senior officers would often endeavour to 'educate' residents as to the competing demands on police resources and the limits of beat patrols (one police manager was, for instance, at pains to insist that what he called 'modern officers' were quite reasonably unwilling to be either permanently on call, or tied for long periods of their career to one neighbourhood). More specifically, arguments focused upon whether calls concerning 'disorderly youths' were (or ought to be) treated by the police as an 'emergency'. Residents from Upton Priory reflected on one such meeting thus:

Jean: All you get told when you ask about the beat bobby, 'Well do you want us to get less burglaries, less car crimes, or do you want them to always be on your estate and have problems with you.' It's sort of prioritise and all this, we just get nowhere. You saw what happened at that meeting.

Dave: There's cutbacks.

Jean: I know they need more money, they need more police, but surely somewhere they can do something about it. [...] I don't think they realise how worried people are by what's going on. I don't think they realise how it affects people's lives.

Underpinning these various frustrations and complaints are two connected concerns. First, a sense of the police answering to priorities that are either obscure to the public or actively disputed by them; and second, that the police are (especially in the face of chronic if low-level noise, nuisance and disorder) becoming increasingly and improperly remote from everyday life. For many, these developments are encapsulated symbolically in a new telecommunications system (introduced in 1994), which means that people can only contact Macclesfield police station by first ringing police headquarters at Chester. They take on a more concrete form when people realise just how many other people they share 'their bobby' with, as when this officer explains to horrified Weston residents the precise extent of his beat:

PC Harris: If you imagine coming from Bond Street at the traffic lights. I do Bond Street to Park Lane, up Park Lane, the traffic lights at the Flower Pot [*public house*], turn left, down as far as Pennington's Lane. Theoretically then the line straight up to Gawsworth Road, along Gawsworth Road to Broken Cross roundabout, down Chester Road, keep going across Chester Road to the bottom end, until we get to roughly a line level with Bond Street again there, and that's my patch.

Sue: On your own?

PC Harris: On my own.

Sue: It's disgusting.

The crime-talk of Macclesfield residents bespeaks then a powerful attachment, not so much to crime-fighting and its attendant performance indicators, but to the service and guardianship roles traditionally attributed to the English police – in the current jargon of criminal justice to 'problem-oriented' policing (Goldstein, 1990). Their desire is for a reliable and visible patrolling presence on their streets, provided by a known figure who is integrated into the social life of local communities, and thus able to exercise pastoral care over it (and especially its young). Their fear is that this figure – and the kinds of order and security that people associate with him – is becoming an ever more distant prospect and memory.

YEARNING FOR ORDER: NARRATIVES OF A POLICING PAST

That (older) Macclesfield residents yearn for a 'return to' the 'old type' of police officer (the person who 'wandered around the estate, and the kids knew him, and people knew him', as one Weston resident put it) should occasion little surprise. As Pearson (1983) has perhaps most famously demonstrated, invocations of 'golden ages' of tranquillity have long permeated popular discourse about crime (see also Weinberger's (1995) interviews with retired police officers, which resonate with fond reminiscences about the lost world of foot patrols). More broadly, Lash and Urry (1994, pp. 246–8) note how 'an appeal to the past' has become a pervasive feature of life in late-modernity; while Patrick Wright (1985, p. 22) similarly suggests that during periods of rapid social change ('where values are in apparent disorder and where social hierarchy has lost its settled nature') people often find solace in imagined, nostalgic versions of the past.

In making sense of this yearning for order, questions of historical accuracy are not of the upmost importance (Loader, 1997b). For while these 'social memories' (Fentress and Wickham, 1992) ostensibly make reference to 'how things used to be' (and thus raise claims that can in principle be investigated and found more or less wanting), they are mobilised and put to rhetorical use in the present and need to be judged in this light. So what is being communicated when people appeal to – and narrate particular versions of – the past? And how do these 'memories' shape people's understandings of the kinds of policing that ought to be provided in the present?

Two themes are worth highlighting here. First, people seek by means of such stories to communicate the loss of an identifiable authority figure, known by, and belonging to, the community. In our discussions people would frequently refer to the police in terms that denote ownership, and a resort to the past is in part a means of registering such ownership and mourning its subsequent demise. Residents of Prestbury would, for instance, bemoan the recent closure of the police house in 'the village' in precisely these terms, terms which were echoed by those living on the nearby Upton Priory estate: 'They used to live in the community that they policed. That don't happen now. They're divorced from the community they're policing. They're just a figure in a uniform.' Among some – such as these middle-class women living in Broken Cross – the loss of control over the police is couched in terms of a more widespread process of change in the social and moral order of the town:

IL: Has that process of incomers coming to the town had an effect in terms of crime?
Bron: Oh yes.
IL: In what respect?
Bron: I think it does, because you don't know everybody. At one time you tended to know everybody. People went into town a lot more. Lots of people lived in the centre of town, so if you didn't know them you knew somebody's cousin, and you tended to know this. As a result people couldn't get away with it. And of course, if you went home you tended to get what for. If they [*the police*] brought you home you were for it. Nowadays this doesn't happen.
Mary: I suppose we can say the police and their standing in the community ...
Bron: And it was a local police force, which made a difference.
Mary: Of course it did.
Bron: We had our own Chief Constable.
IL: For Macclesfield?
Bron: Yes.
Mary: But I think the way that policing in now being done on this softly, softly approach, whereby they aren't allowed to do what you and I would have expected, a clip round the ear from a police sergeant. [...] Well those days unfortunately have now gone, haven't they.

This brings us to the second theme. What matters for many about this remembered integration of the police into the quotidian life of neighbourhoods was that it meant an authoritative presence was keeping a watchful eye on local teenagers and regulating their activities. Here the subsequent 'withdrawal' of the police is taken to signify, and indeed be causally connected with, a radical loosening of the disciplines that were once thought to bind the young to the moral and legal order of community life. On occasions this view is buttressed with personal recollections about being reprimanded by some feared figure of authority; on others, people make more explicit (and wistful) appeal to the value of combining legal and parental authority:

> *Carol:* The one thing that used to go on, and probably doesn't now, is where the police would sort out problems with younger people by taking their names and reporting back to their parents what's been going on. I don't think that happens any more.
>
> *Gary:* If they've been reported three times they should be ...
>
> *Carol:* I know it was a long time ago, if you did something wrong, the village bobby, if you were caught, you'd get frog marched back home and he'd go and tell your parents what you'd been up to. Then your parents had a chance to deal with it, but they've no chance to deal with it if they don't know what's going on.
>
> *(High Street residents)*

Questions of *ownership* and *integration* thus surface recurrently in people's narratives of how policing 'used to be'; the police being recalled (alongside various mechanisms of informal social control) as part of the 'glue' that held a neighbourhood together and guaranteed its now fondly remembered quality of life. As such, however, the figure of the police officer functions, not merely as a vehicle through which people are able to recall and speak about a more cohesive, orderly past; but also as a powerful 'condensing' symbol of the worrying insecurities that permeate both the present and the future (cf. Turner, 1974). A 'community' no longer watched over by the 'local bobby' is not, it seems, a fit place to grow up in:

> My heart and soul was in the Moss estate. I loved my childhood growing up on the Moss. And when I came back I weren't unhappy about it because I really felt as if I was going home. [...] But now I wouldn't like to think that my grandchildren, great grandchildren, put it that way, would grow up on the Moss estate at the moment.

We are desperately in need of, Renee put her finger on it, really they want a policeman on the beat, don't they?

FREEDOM WITHOUT SECURITY?: ENVISIONING A POLICING FUTURE

In Bauman's view, consumer choice (and this, he argues, is what freedom has largely come to mean in market societies) has provided 'a space for human freedom larger than any other human society, past or present' (1988, p. 57). Not only does consumption offer freedom without the risks of 'elimination' (bankruptcy, job loss and so on) associated with production; it also enables individuals to exercise responsible choice without (for it is part of the function of advertising to prevent this) undermining their self-assurance. As Bauman puts it: 'The world of consumption appears to have cured freedom from ... insecurity. In its consumer version, individual freedom may be exercised without sacrificing that certainty that lies at the bottom of spiritual security' (ibid.).

In the face of the competing demands now made on the police, and their apparent inability to deliver the service that 'consumers' want, it is becoming increasingly easy to imagine a policing future in which individuals and communities 'exit' (to borrow Hirschman's (1970) term) from public provision and use their 'spontaneity, will and effort' (Bauman, 1997, p. 3) to secure the patrolling presence they desire. Some among our discussants felt that things might be headed in precisely this direction, with current difficulties seen as auguring some potentially significant shifts in how policing is delivered:

> Attitudes have changed now. Police today have got so much to do. They've got to like sort out not just theft, but drug problems, violence, domestic violence. They've got such a wide range. Police 20, 30 years ago, they would have to deal with theft, but now they have to cover a whole range. They'll have to change, and perhaps the community will have to change. Perhaps we'll have to do our policing ourselves, in a minor way, we may have to patrol.
>
> (*High Street resident*)

How do Macclesfield residents respond to this possible future? What do they make of the choices that might be available to them in the coming period? Will commercially-provided patrols satisfy their demands for protection?

While our respondents commonly voiced the view that the situation in Macclesfield was 'not that bad' (Women's Institute member, Prestbury) or 'had not reached that stage *yet*' (Kennedy Avenue resident), some did envisage thresholds beyond which such options might become attractive. One man in our Kennedy Avenue focus group believed such a point might already have been reached in the inner-city ('where you are in fear of going out of your house'), while others believed that a continued shortfall in police funding might force them to act. These members of Prestbury neighbourhood watch were confident that, in such circumstances, their village would be able to extract from the market a quality service:

> *Colin:* If they [*the police*] continue to be under-resourced, then
>   I think we're going to be driven to these security firms.
>   I would rather have a security firm than no presence at all.
>   At present we get very little presence where we are.
>
> *Robert:* If I was in Salford I would probably say yes.
>
> *Neil:* You'd get a high class firm.
>
> *Tim:* In Salford, it's mayhem there.
>
> *Neil:* In Salford you buy a low class company. We'd buy a high
>   class company here.

Much of the interest people expressed here surrounded the question of whether the qualities they prized in the police might be obtainable by alternative means. Some displayed enthusiasm in this regard for the provision of more special constables, or for 'cheaper officers' of a 'different grade' (cf. Morgan and Newburn, 1997, pp. 164–73). Others felt that while police officers had obvious advantages in terms of knowledge and experience ('authority is an important difference between being a policeman and being a private security person', as one Prestbury resident put it), these qualities might over time be acquired by others. The following exchange illustrates this well:

> *June:* The uniform makes a difference, doesn't it?
>
> *Terry:* I disagree.
>
> *Geoff:* It commands respect.
>
> *Terry:* I take the point about the village bobby, because then it
>   becomes a part of the community. Now to me, it doesn't
>   matter whether that person originated in the police force

or originated somewhere else, but if they become a community figure with the same responsibilities as the police. They would do, after three or four years as a village whatever, whether you call him the village bobby or the village community officer, whatever. To me ... it doesn't matter whether they come from the official police force or not, but they would do the same job in the spirit of the village bobby.

RS: So you're saying that someone who is privately employed wouldn't have the same authority?

Terry: What I'm saying is, I don't think, pick a firm, Blue Star Security Services, 'we're sending Joe Bloggs down one night, Fred Dee the next'. That's neither use nor ornament. It's got to be somebody who's built up a rapport.

(*Primary school parents, Prestbury*)

This ambivalence bordering on qualified support for non-police patrols was, however, unusual among our discussants. For the most part, members of our focus groups recoiled from the idea that visible patrols might be provided by commercial operators.[5] They do so, firstly, on the grounds that visible protection should be provided by the police and the police alone. One aspect of this amounts to an objection to paying further for what people believe they have already contributed to through general taxation, a sentiment evident in remarks such as: 'we pay enough taxes and where's the bobby on the beat' (Zeneca manager) and 'You're actually encouraging the government to decrease the amount of money that's given to the police' (Zeneca clerical worker).

A cognate theme holds that there are 'matters of principle' (Broken Cross resident) at stake here, with many holding the view that patrolling ought properly to be the '*duty* of the police' (High Street resident). As one High Street resident exclaimed: 'No. You don't want bobbies like that. Why aren't the police allowed to police, that's their job, they should do that.' Some even articulated this point as a more general objection to the commodification of policing:

I'm not so sure that people should be making money out of fear. I think that's the bottom line. To me, that's the ultimate in market force. You've got a situation where people are frightened, and you get some entrepreneur charging a fiver for relieving your fear.

(*Upton Priory resident*)

A second (connected) set of worries concerned the wider (and uncertain) consequences of private patrols. Among some, these concerns revolved principally around the lack of trust they felt in the companies that (might) operate in this market, with discussants echoing a now familiar litany of allegations about low rates of pay, the employment of 'ex-crooks' and 'companies run by roughnecks' (Weston resident). As one security manager working at Zeneca put it: 'I think they just sort of drag whoever they can off the streets and pay them a couple of pounds an hour. If you pay peanuts you end up with monkeys.' Against this backdrop, people would seem to require some reassuring guarantees about quality before taking such a precarious step:

> If it was Marks and Spencers, then I would say yes. If it was a small company it would be definitely no. I think criminals set up protection rackets. I think it's a slippery slope. The price will go up, it's a captive market, and if you don't pay you will be the one that's burgled. You can't guarantee that 100 per cent will pay. How do you know that they aren't a front. What I'm saying is, I would object strongly, because I believe the police are there for that. The only alternative, it would be something of quality, a national company of the standing of Marks and Spencers, or that type of company.
>
> (*Broken Cross resident*)

Intimately bound up with the question of trust is the (more nebulous) feeling that a market in policing would entail some risky and potentially unpleasant consequences. The seemingly fuzzy border between non-police patrolling and 'vigilantism' attracted frequent comment here, as did the possibility of the unscrupulous running 'protection rackets'. People's concern, it seems, is that private policing might unleash social problems more troubling than those it purports to deal with, a feeling expressed in the remarks of two Prestbury residents about private policing 'not sounding right' and 'going against the grain'. It also, relatedly, offends against people's sense of the kind of place – street, neighbourhood, town, nation – they wish to live in; a powerful manifestation of which is the belief that private patrols are somehow 'un-English', an aspect of the 'American way of life' that 'we' ought to resist:

> I would want to know a lot about them before I would consider any action like that. It's like a protection racket in a sense. I don't know

whether it's a good thing at all. It's a bit unhealthy in my view, at least in England. It sounds too American to me.

(Kennedy Avenue resident)

We don't want to become like the 52nd state of America, because it is becoming like that. Each year you seem to get one step closer to America, we seem to be arming ourselves, we seem to be making our homes like fortresses. [...] I can see it eventually where people start carrying guns, and we don't want to become like that, a nation that carries guns.

(High Street resident)

The dominant disposition then among Macclesfield residents is a marked reluctance to embrace a privatised policing future. Despite their worries about crime and (especially) disorder, and their frustrations about the apparent inability of the police to deliver the desired level and kind of service, people recoil from the suggestion that 'exit' is an appropriate option; resist the opportunity to exercise consumer choice in order to secure the protection they would like. Private patrols offer no compelling response to their demands for order.

CONCLUSION

What lessons might we draw from the various sensibilities towards policing documented in the chapter? How might they intersect with current academic and policy debates about the condition and likely futures of English policing at the approach of the millennium? By way of summary and conclusion, let us reflect briefly on these questions.

It is worth noting, first of all, the prevalence of disenchantment and dismay towards the drift of contemporary policing found among people who think of themselves as recipients of police services and who display high levels of *general* support for the police. This has in large measure to do with the great expectations such general (and often sentimental) identification generates; and, more specifically, with an apparent police failure to take seriously people's worries and concerns (not least in respect of teenage 'incivilities') and provide the kind and level of service that they are deemed to warrant. The result, as we have seen, is an often vehemently voiced desire to see a known and visible figure provide a semi-permanent, pastoral watch over the community; a demand that (continued police lip-service to its importance notwithstanding) runs increasingly counter to the direction in which the public police appear to be headed, nationally and globally (Sheptycki, 1995; Francis et al., 1997).

One recent theorisation of late-modern policing has argued, for example, that in 'risk society' the police are not so much oriented towards the (modern) project of tackling crime and securing territorial order, but are preoccupied as 'knowledge workers' generating and disseminating information that assists external institutions – government agencies, insurance companies and the like – in the management of risk (Ericson and Haggerty, 1997). Now is not the occasion for a review of this ambitious and challenging (albeit, we suspect, somewhat over-argued) thesis. What is pertinent to our concerns, however, are the ways in which the developments Ericson and Haggerty highlight *jar* with the kinds of sensibilities towards – and expectations of – policing documented here. Ericson and Haggerty are not primarily concerned with how police practices – and disputes about them – are mediated through national political cultures and local 'structures of feeling' (cf. Loader, 1997b), and they do not consequently foreground these tensions. Yet focusing on them enables us to grasp the legitimation deficits that flow from the police being seen as a distant and introspective bureaucracy obsessed with performance targets, auditing systems and management-speak (complete with its baffling nomenclatures such as 'crime manager') that render policing not only absent from everyday life, but also ever more arcane and mysterious (wasting time on all those 'damn forms'). It's not merely that the police are failing to do what their 'customers' want; but that people are less and less sure what it is they do.

Yet we have seen also that these dissatisfied customers recoil from the prospect of looking elsewhere to secure the patrolling presence they desire. For all the burgeoning of private markets in security hardware and services, and notwithstanding Bauman's (1988) claim that consumption offers freedom cured of insecurity, we find little evidence that the privatisation of the patrol and guardianship functions of the British police exercises much appeal. The dispositions documented in this chapter suggest that policing might even represent a limit case of Bauman's contentions; an example of the risks of consumption exceeding its attendant pleasures, of freedom exercised at security's expense. This in part has to do with the low levels of trust people possess in the firms that (might) provide this service; a product not only of a weak regime of legal regulation, but also, one might suggest, of the aura of murky illicitness that surrounds much of the 'protection' industry. It also flows from the fact that private policing offends against people's sense of the kind of street, or neighbourhood, or town, that they wish to live in. Far from alleviating their anxieties and making them feel secure, people generally resist – even resent – the idea of a market in policing; and take issue, not merely with the 'choices' on offer, but, more profoundly, with being forced to choose at all something they feel the state ought properly to provide, and for which they believe they have already paid with their taxes. People thus have to feel desperately worried about and unprotected from crime, or else – as with some of our Prestbury discussants – possess a robust consumer confidence in their capacity to enlist a 'high class' firm, before entertaining such a prospect. The residents of Macclesfield do not, in the main, feel either that anxious about crime, or that certain of their market position.

This, of course, leaves open the possibility (touched upon by some of our Prestbury respondents) that private policing might appeal as an act of positional consumption (Bourdieu, 1984); something that individuals purchase in order to signify the social distance between them and those forced to depend upon an unresponsive, cash-strapped public service. That policing might in future travel in this direction cannot be ruled out, especially given the trends of which – among others – Ericson and Haggerty (1997) speak. Our research, however, suggests that (notwithstanding their shortcomings) many people continue to evince a powerful (affective) attachment to *the police* as a social institution (indeed, their grumbles are often couched in terms of having been let down by a once reliable and trusted friend). Despite recent attempts to demystify the police and render them another 'mundane institution of government' (Reiner, 1992, p. 270), the police retain traces of a 'sacred' quality within popular sensibilities. People's generally adverse reaction to other modes of patrolling thus flows in part from there being (in contrast to other fields of public provision, such as transport or care in old age) little stigma attached to a reliance upon state policing. Though this seems likely to come under increasing pressure in these individuated, consumer-oriented times (wherein police managers are insisting that 'customers' refrain from making 'unreasonable' demands), the police do not as yet 'receive a low grading in the hierarchy of positional symbols' or 'appear as a liability in the symbolic rivalry serviced by consumption' (Bauman, 1988, p. 70).

As recent debates within policing circles testify, much of this identification is detrimental both to the police and to wider debates about security. It saddles the police with expectations they cannot hope to meet, creates a seemingly 'insatiable' demand for their services, and makes it difficult to generate informed public deliberation about what the police can and cannot contribute to personal and community safety (Independent Committee, 1996; Loader 1997b). It is also, as we have seen, often profoundly nostalgic, imbued with memories of a policing past that people have come to associate with cohesive, disciplined communities, a hierarchical and unquestioned generational order, and a certain – now culturally contested, less hegemonic – kind of paternalistic masculine authority (Weinberger, 1995, p. 206).

Yet this attachment to the police can also be read otherwise, as projecting – in Ricoeur's (1981) terms – alternative, more democratic possibilities. For it signifies rejection of the idea that respect for human safety can be privatized, deregulated, and generally placed upon the shoulders of individuals. It holds an implicit recognition that there is an 'irreducible "public interest" in all security transactions' (Walker, 1996, p. 65). And it communicates support, not only for policing provision committed to the 'traditions' of pastoral care and guardianship, but also to the value of this provision being publicly accountable – a sentiment that manifests itself in people eschewing 'exit' in preference for 'voice' (Hirschman, 1970).

It may be that the era of the police as providers of a universal, routine presence in the quotidian life of communities is drawing to a close, and that as the police become 'disembedded' (Giddens, 1990) from local social relations responsibility for the guardianship of urban space is rendered ever more diffuse and fragmented. It may be that commercial operators come to dominate an increasingly commodified policing scene; or, alternatively, that local authorities assume a prominent role as either purchasers and regulators of (private) policing, or – as is currently the case in a number of English councils – as direct providers of 'community patrols' or Dutch-style 'civic guards' (I'Anson and Wiles, 1995; Hauber et al., 1996). How precisely these landscapes of protection will unfold, it is premature to judge. What can be concluded, however, is that the sensibilities documented here provide reason for insisting on the value of inclusive public deliberation as a means of addressing the legitimation problems that attend the (ongoing) reconfiguration of *the police* (Loader, 1996, p. 7); and on the stubborn relevance to debates about the 'new' forms that *policing* might take in the twenty-first century of some 'old' questions to do with justice and democracy.

NOTES

1. The research was supported by the Economic and Social Research Council under its Crime and Social Order Research Programme (award no. L21025032).

2. Between 1994 and 1996 we conducted in Macclesfield (and the neighbouring affluent 'village-suburb' of Prestbury), a research effort we have chosen to call an 'ethnography of anxiety'. This comprised: an analysis of textual and statistical information on economic, social and demographic change within the town, and of patterns of crime and demands for policing; an analysis of local representations of crime-related matters as contained in the local press and crime prevention literature; a total of 26 focus group discussions with different sections of the local population; a small number of in-depth biographical interviews with local residents; nine individual and six group discussions with criminal justice professionals and other local interest groups and 'opinion-formers' (including police and probation officers, youth workers, magistrates and publicans); and numerous hours devoted to informal conversations, observation and attendance at meetings, including observational research with the police.

    This chapter draws mainly on the following focus group discussions with local adult residents: ten groups of mainly middle-class residents living around Kennedy Avenue (two), High Street (two), Broken Cross (two) and Tytherton, or working at Zeneca (three); one group from each of the town's five council-built housing estates (Moss Rose, Weston, Hurdsfield, Upton Priory and Victoria Park Flats), and five groups with residents of Prestbury (see Figure 1.1). For a fuller account of the project's theoretical orientations, setting, methods and conclusions, see Girling et al., 1998b; 1999).

3. The extracts presented here are taken from discussions in which people were asked (or else ventured their opinion prior to being asked): (i) how they rated the services they received from the local police and what they would say if afforded the chance to meet the divisional commander; and (ii) how they would respond to a leaflet from a company offering to patrol their street in return for a small annual payment from each resident. The names of all discussants have been pseudonymised.

4. This is, of course, partly a (now contested) convention of ordinary language use; but it might also, more critically, be read as revealing an expectation on the part of many people that police officers should be men. As one female resident said of the police response to teenagers congregating in and around High Street: 'sometimes they send women out. It's stupid. What use are they?' This aspect of popular sensibilities towards policing would repay some careful attention.

5. This contrasts markedly with people's dispositions towards another recent crime prevention innovation: CCTV. While a minority among our respondents spoke about surveillance cameras with reference to 'Big Brother' or questioned their likely effectiveness, the dominant mood was enthusiastically supportive, with residents both wanting more

cameras throughout the town, and evincing sometimes hostile dis-
approval towards those who demurred from this view (see Girling et al.,
1999, ch. 8).

REFERENCES

Audit Commission (1996) *Street Wise: Effective Police Patrol* (London:
HMSO).
Bauman, Z. (1987) *Legislators and Interpreters: On Modernity Post-modernity
and Intellectuals* (Cambridge: Polity).
—— (1988) *Freedom* (Milton Keynes: Open University Press).
—— (1997) *Postmodernity and its Discontents* (Oxford: Blackwell).
Bourdieu, P. (1984) *Distinction: A Critique of the Social Judgement of Taste*
(London: Routledge).
Cheshire County Council (1996) *Our Cheshire* (Volume J – Geographical
Variations) (Ellesmere Port: Cheshire County Council Research and
Intelligence Unit).
Ericson, R. and Haggerty, K. (1997) *Policing the Risk Society* (Oxford: Oxford
University Press).
Evans, S., Fraser, P. and Walklate, S. (1996) 'Whom Can You Trust?: The
Politics of "Grassing" on an Inner City Housing Estate', *Sociological
Review*, 44, no. 3, pp. 361–80.
Fentress, J. and Wickham, C. (1992) *Social Memory* (Oxford: Blackwell).
Francis, P., Davies, P. and Jupp, V. (eds) (1997) *Policing Futures: The Police,
Law Enforcement and the Twenty-First Century* (Basingstoke: Macmillan).
Garland, D. (1996) 'The Limits of the Sovereign State: Strategies of Crime
Control in Contemporary Society', *British Journal of Criminology*, 36, no. 4,
pp. 445–71'.
Giddens, A. (1990) *The Consequences of Modernity* (Cambridge: Polity).
Girling, E., Loader, I. and Sparks, R, (1998a) 'A Telling Tale: A Case of
Vigilantism and its Aftermath in an English Town', *British Journal of
Sociology*, 49/3 (in press).
—— (1988b), 'Crime and the Sense of One's Place: Globalization,
Restructuring and Insecurity in an English Town', in V. Ruggiero, N. South
and I. Taylor (eds), *The New European Criminology: Crime and Social Order
in Europe* (London: Routledge).
— (1999) *Crime and Social Change in Middle England* (London: Routledge)
Goldstein, H. (1990) *Problem-Oriented Policing* (New York: McGraw-Hill).
Hauber, A., Hofstra, B., Toornvliet, L. and Zandbergen, A. (1996) 'Some
New Forms of Functional Social Control in the Netherlands and their
Effects', *British Journal of Criminology*, 36, no. 2, pp. 199–219.
Heward, T. (1994) 'Retailing the Police: Corporate Identity and the Met.', in
R. Keat, N. Whitely and N. Abercrombie (eds), *The Authority of the
Consumer* (London: Routledge).
Hirschman, A. (1970) *Exit, Voice and Loyalty: Responses to Decline in Firms,
Organisations and States* (Cambridge, Masss.: Harvard University Press).

I'Anson, J. and Wiles, P. (1995) *The Sedgefield Community Force* (Centre for Criminological and Legal Research: University of Sheffield).

Independent Committee (1996) *The Role and Responsibilities of the Police* (London: Police Foundation/Policy Studies Institute).

Johnston, L. (1992) *The Rebirth of Private Policing* (London: Routledge).

Johnston, L. (1996) 'What is Vigilantism?', *British Journal of Criminology*, 36, no. 2, pp. 220–36.

Jones, T. and Newburn, T. (1997) *Private Security and Public Policing* (Oxford: Oxford University Press).

Lash, S. and Urry, J. (1994) *Economies of Signs and Space* (London: Sage).

Loader, I. (1996) *Youth, Policing and Democracy* (Basingstoke: Macmillan).

—— (1997a) 'Private Security and the Demand for Protection in Contemporary Britain', *Policing and Society*, vol. 7, pp. 143–62.

—— (1997b) 'Policing and the Social: Questions of Symbolic Power', *British Journal of Sociology*, 48, no. 1, pp. 1–18.

——, Girling, E. and Sparks, R. (1998) 'Narratives of Decline: Youth, Dis/order and Community in and English "Middletown"' *British Journal of Criminology*, 38, no. 3, pp. 388–403.

Morgan, R. and Newburn, T. (1997) *The Future of Policing* (Oxford: Oxford University Press).

Pearson, G. (1983) *Hooligan: A History of Respectable Fears* (Basingstoke: Macmillan).

Reiner, R. (1992) *The Politics of the Police* (Brighton: Harvester).

Ricoeur, P. (1981) *Hermeneutics and the Human Sciences* (Cambridge: Cambridge University Press).

Sasson, T. (1995) *Crime Talk: How Citizens Construct a Social Problem* (New York: Aldine de Gruyter).

Schlesinger, P. and H. Tumber (1994) *Reporting Crime: The Media Politics of Criminal Justice* (Oxford: Oxford University Press).

Sheptycki, J. (1995) 'Transnational Policing and the Making of a Postmodern State', *British Journal of Criminology*, 35, no. 4, pp. 613–35.

Turner, V. (1974) *Dramas, Fields and Metaphors: Symbolic Action in Human Society* (Ithca: Cornell University Press).

Walker, N. (1996) 'Defining Core Police Tasks: The Neglect of the Symbolic Dimension?', *Policing and Society*, 6, pp. 53–71.

Weinberger, B. (1995) *The Best Police in the World: An Oral History of English Policing from the 1930s to the 1960s* (Aldershot: Scholar Press).

Woodcock, J. (1992) 'Overturning Police Culture', *Policing*, 7, no. 3, pp. 172–82.

Wright, P. (1985) *On Living in on Old Country: The National Past in Contemporary Britain* (London: Verso).

2 The Labour Market and Post-war Crime Trends in England and Wales

Chris Hale

INTRODUCTION

The discussion below stems from work on an ESRC funded research project which examined trends in crime and punishment in England and Wales. The aim of the project was to use econometric techniques for the analysis of time series data to build statistical models of these trends and to interpret the results of the modelling in the light of broader social, economic and political change. Results capturing both long-run and short-run changes in recorded property crime – burglary, theft and robbery – will be presented and it will be argued that one possible explanation of these may be found in the fundamental shifts which have taken place in the economy, and in particular the changing structure of employment, in the last fifty years.

While the primary focus of the project was post-1945, the research also examined longer term crime trends. It was motivated in part by the need to explain the accelerating trend in crime since the Second World War. For every 100 crimes recorded annually between 1901 and 1905, 538 were recorded in 1946, an increase of over fivefold in four and a half decades. In a comparable period since the war in 1992 when crime had reached its latest peak it had increased a further tenfold from under half a million crimes to over five million. However this doubling of the rate of increase between the two periods hides marked fluctuations in the trend over shorter periods. Before considering models for the post-war period some more detailed consideration will be given to these changes by developing the periodisation of McClintock and Avison (1968).

Developing this work, the trend in crime since the turn of the century may be described by six phases. Prior to the outbreak of the First World War the general level of crime remained fairly constant with minor fluctuations from year to year. This was a the final stage of a downward trend which saw recorded crime per head of population halve between 1857 and 1914 (see Gatrell, 1980).

The trend reversed during the war and the second phase from 1915 to 1930, a period of social turmoil and turbulence saw crime increasing at the rate of approximately 5 per cent a year. During the third phase from 1930 to 1948, a period of deepening economic crisis and political unrest including the Second World War and its immediate aftermath, the growth increased slightly to an average of around 7 per cent a year.

The fourth period from 1949 to 1954 saw the annual amount of crime first decrease then rise and then fall again. Crime levels per head were about 18 per cent lower in 1954 than 1948. The immediate post-war period was one of reconstruction of the economy. Whilst unemployment was low, never rising above the 1946 high of 1.9 per cent, rationing continued and levels of consumption grew only slowly. The major economic crises of the 1920s and 1930s led to the adoption of Keynesianism and greatly increased intervention by the Government in the economy, a process reinforced by the experiences of the command economy during the war. The Beveridge Report (Beveridge, 1942) laid the foundations for a wide-ranging system of social security which became the British welfare state. The state would help promote social progress by acting to improve health, housing and diet, thereby attacking Beveridge's five great evils Want, Disease, Ignorance, Squalor and Idleness. The Labour government of 1945–51 was committed to full employment and improved living conditions for the working class. This 'welfarism' was accepted by the Conservative governments of the 1950s and it became part of the consensus of British political life. As McClintock and Avison (1968, p. 19) note, the expectation at the time was that crime had stabilised and would fall again to its pre-war levels.

However, in the final two periods crime was to rise dramatically – if erratically. In the fifth phase which extends to 1974 crime grew steadily at around 10 per cent per year. This rate of growth, twice that of the 1920s and, furthermore, from a much higher base, during a period which was perceived as heralding the arrival of the affluent society, was one of the warning signs that all was not well with the welfare state. The late fifties was of course the period in which the consumer boom really took off. However, Macmillan's use of the phrase 'you've never had it so good' to describe this era was open to other interpretations. Until the latter part of the sixties unemployment was relatively low, making these years popular with commentators such as Norman Dennis since they apparently prove that unemployment cannot cause crime (see most recently Dennis, 1997, pp. 59–71). 1961 was of course the year when those born in 1946 turned 15 years of age, and the early 1960s saw the steady growth in the population of young males in the most criminally active age groups. The continuing prosperity enjoyed by many through the 1950s and 1960s could not hide the continuing relative decline in the economic position of the UK. The post-war expansion began to falter in the early sixties and, following the balance of payments crisis of 1965–6, the Labour government effectively abandoned the full employment policy and implemented incomes policies to restrain earnings, devalued sterling and encouraged industrial rationalisations. The end of the sixties saw a major upsurge in unofficial strikes and rising unemployment. This industrial unrest intensified during the years 1970–4. In a foretaste of what was to come in the 1980s the Conservative government under Edward Heath was elected in 1970 on a platform which included radical economic reform and a commitment to allow market forces to operate. It was, however, forced by trade union resistance to discard its non-interventionist policies and turn once more to incomes policies and Keynesian demand management measures.

The final period lasts from 1974 until the present and may be characterised as one of increasing levels and fluctuations in unemployment and widening divisions within the working population between those in relatively secure employment and those with unskilled, often part-time, but certainly precarious, jobs. Crime increases in this period have been very large and notwithstanding the drops in recorded levels in the recent years remain at an historically high level. Some indication of the scale of the problem may be gleaned from the fact that the *increases* in recorded levels of crime in 1990 and 1991 were greater than the *total level* of crime in any of the years from 1946 to 1956. While the year on year increases in percentage terms may be relatively stable in this period this should not hide the fact that actual numerical increases were very large. The period began with the world-wide recession triggered by the OPEC oil crises. The Labour government, elected in 1974, by 1975 was arguing that high unemployment was part of the price to be paid for combating high levels of inflation. It began to restrict the money supply and to cut public expenditure in the hope that tight monetary policy linked to increasing unemployment would produce wage constraint. In 1976, after another series of sterling crises and visits from the International Monetary Fund (IMF), major further cuts in public expenditure were announced. Whilst the Labour government presented this abandonment of welfarism and adoption of monetarism as a pragmatic necessity forced upon them by the IMF, the Conservative party embraced them as core parts of their ideology. When they were elected in 1979, on a platform committed to proper monetary discipline and a reduction in government borrowing and expenditure, they faced a massive deepening of the world recession. Additionally they abandoned full employment as a policy objective, prioritising, instead, the need to tackle inflation. Recession and unemployment were the chief anti-inflationary tools. Unemployment in England and Wales leapt from a daily average of 1.4 million in 1979 to 2.3 million in 1981. Industrial production in 1981 had fallen 12 per cent below the 1979 level. Between 1983 and 1986 both employment and unemployment increased. This coincidence can be explained by the growth in the size of the workforce, achieved by women entering the labour market as the economy recovered. Once the economy began to boom between 1986 and 1990 the workforce in employment grew by 2.36 million whilst unemployment fell by 1.7 million (the difference being made up by a net increase in the size of the workforce). Whilst this would be normal in a labour market adjusting to economic growth, it was also a result of government programmes for long-term unemployed which began nationally in 1986. These 'encouraged' people to take jobs they might otherwise not have taken and meant inevitably that the number of less productive, poorly paid, low skilled jobs grew extremely rapidly. Unusually for a period of rapid economic growth, semi-skilled and unskilled work grew almost as fast as skilled work. With the end of the boom of the late eighties, unemployment again began to rise, breaking through the 3 million mark in January 1993. We will return to discuss these labour market trends in more detail below but, for now, we note that this final period from 1974 onwards may be characterised by accelerating crime rates and increased social division.

EXPLAINING POST-WAR CRIME TRENDS

One focus of the research reported here was to model these crime trends and to attempt to explain the different periodisations. Broadly speaking, and space precludes a full theoretical justification for these ideas, explanations for the crime trends can be found under the following headings: labour market conditions, the economic cycle, opportunity, poverty and relative deprivation, family breakdown and demoralisation, demographics, and deterrence. Before a fuller discussion of our methods and results a brief review of some of the key trends in these factors will be presented.

Labour Market Conditions

Unemployment has long been a debated factor in the aetiology of crime. Whilst re-examining the evidence for such a relationship the research attempted to look at broader changes in the labour market which might be related to crime. Along with other developed economies the labour market in the UK has undergone fundamental changes in the last three decades. Amongst other things these have involved:

● *A shift in employment from manufacturing to the service sector*
In the 1960s the manufacturing sector in Britain provided over 8 million jobs. But manufacturing employment began to decline from 1963, making Britain the only major industrial economy to experience such a reversal before the 1973 oil shock. Since then the decline has been continuous, and by 1994 there were only 4.3 million jobs. The loss of jobs on such a scale has had a major impact on the patterns of both work and unemployment (Greenhaigh and Gregory, 1994). While de-industrialisation is not a uniquely British phenomenon, as noted, it began earlier and has been more severe than in other advanced economies. At the beginning of the 1970s one worker in every three was in the manufacturing sector. This proportion has fallen to one worker in every five, and the decline in relative importance shows no signs of reversing.

● *A shift to part-time employment and an accompanying increase in the numbers of temporary and untenured jobs*
Since 1971 part-time jobs have increased by 2.6 million and the proportion of jobs that are part-time has risen from 15 per cent in 1971 to 28 per cent in 1994 (Naylor, 1994). The rate of increase in the proportion of part-time jobs has accelerated since 1990. Women make up 86 per cent of part-time workers and of these women more than half are over 40 years old. In the last ten years the biggest increases in the percentage of jobs that are part-time were in the retail and public sectors. In addition Gregg and Wadsworth (1995) argue that while tenure and security have changed only marginally for the majority of workers,

jobs available to those currently not in work have become increasingly unstable and low paid. The labour market is dominated by part-time and temporary jobs with full-time permanent posts becoming increasingly scarce. Furthermore new jobs increasingly offer far lower wages relative to continuing jobs (Gregg and Wadsworth, 1995, p. 74).

● *A shift in the patterns of employment from men to women*
In 1951 women comprised 31 per cent of the total work-force, a figure little changed since the beginning of the 1930s. This proportion increases slowly but steadily during the following decades to reach 45 per cent in 1987, and by 1994 it was just under 50 per cent. Most of this increase has been driven by married women. In 1941 only 16 per cent of women at work were married; in 1985 the figure was 64 per cent. There has, however, been little increase in women's participation in full-time jobs. All the post-war increase in women's employment may be accounted for by the increase in part-time jobs.

What can be observed is the development of a dual labour market with a primary or core sector and a secondary or peripheral sector. The primary sector consists of skilled workers usually working full-time for large organisations with good rights to benefits. Those in the secondary sector on the other hand are either unemployed or have a high propensity to be unemployed at some time. They have low skills and, when working, low incomes. They are more likely to be employed part-time and have few rights for benefits with regard to sickness, holidays or pensions. The secondary sector is characterised by higher labour turnover among the least skilled. For those at the margins:

> employment in the 1990s has become far more unstable. The penalties attached to job loss, jobless duration, and the reduced wages on return have risen. Hence the secondary labour market has become far riskier. However, this new insecurity has been concentrated on a minority for whom jobs for life will become the stuff of legends. (Gregg and Wadsworth, 1995, p. 89)

When modelling the relationships between variables using time series data it is necessary to distinguish between those factors which explain long-run trends and those which are useful for capturing short-run fluctuations. This issue will be discussed further below, but we note here that while we were unable to find a role for unemployment in explaining long-run crime trends. This is not really surprising when the long-run pattern of unemployment is considered. Over the last century unemployment has fluctuated around a constant mean whereas crime has shown an upward trend. Since 1945 unemployment may appear to have grown but this is not the case over the longer term. Of course arguing that unemployment cannot be a long-run cause of crime *does not mean* that it has no role to play in explaining short-run fluctuations in crime, and indeed we found this to be the case. However, not wishing to abandon labour market conditions as having possible long-run impact on crime, and influenced by the discussion above on the fundamental shifts which have taken place since 1945, we shifted the focus in this paper away from unemployment to consider in addition the structure of employment. In particular we built upon the work of Braithwaite et al. (n.d.), who considered the impact of increasing levels of female *employment* upon the Australian homicide rate, and that of Allen and Steffensmeier (1989) and Carlson and Michalowski (1994), who examine the impact of de-industralisation and the growth of 'hamburger jobs' upon American crime rates.

In order to try and capture these trends we used data on male and female employment as well as unemployment, and looked at the share of the manufacturing sector in the total level of employment. We constructed data series on the numbers of women in employment, the female participation rate in the labour market, and the number and proportion of jobs in the manufacturing sector. These are seen as capturing the fundamental shifts in the labour market commented on above. The data used was for England and Wales rather than, as has been usual previously, for the United Kingdom, or at best Great Britain, as a whole.

The Business Cycle

There is now growing evidence that, whether or not crime and unemployment are linked, crime levels are responsive to the business cycle. Field (1990) found that personal consumption expenditure was the best indicator of the cycle and that short-run changes were negatively associated with short-run fluctuations in crime variables. However, consumption may have a wider role than simply as an indicator of the business cycle. Field's work was carried out before recent methodological work, which allows long-run influences to be modelled separately from short-run movements, was widely used. Using this new methodology Pyle and Deadman (1994) found long-run relationships in the post-war period between property crime (burglary, theft and robbery) and, taking each separately, three economic variables – personal consumption, gross domestic product (GDP) and unemployment. We argued earlier that whereas over the last hundred years crime has shown an upward trend, during the same period unemployment has fluctuated around a constant mean and hence is unlikely to be able to explain the long-run growth in crime. Consumption and GDP, on the other hand, have fluctuated around an increasing trend line and hence may have a long-run role to play.

Opportunity theory emphasises that in order for a crime to take place three things are needed – a motivated offender, a suitable target and a lack of guardianship. Personal consumption expenditure plays a role in measuring the availability of targets. And in the post-war period whilst hopes of eradicating poverty and ending class divisions may have been dashed, 'consumption is the one thing which went right' (Obelkevich, 1994, p. 141). The starting point was the 1950s, which saw the beginning of the long consumer boom which brought one of the biggest improvements in the standard of living in Britain since the Middle Ages. We can identify the beginning of this move to mass consumerism with the lifting of rationing and the end of post-war austerity in the mid-1950s. We do not need to inhabit the wilder shores of postmodernism to accept that the rising affluence and the increased consumerism which has accompanied it has had a major impact in undermining 'traditional' societies. It is possible to develop at more length a thesis which ties the development of distinctive youth cultures and increasing individualisation at least in part to the massive explosion in consumption since the 1950s. Nor should it be forgotten that along with these trends, unemployment and the changes in the job market discussed above have impacted particularly hard on the young – in the depths of the recession of the early 1990s, for example. Finally, and more mundanely, along with increased availability of such consumer durables as radios, televisions, videos and telephones there has been a pronounced move to miniaturisation of products. In terms of opportunity theory not only are there more targets, there is less guardianship.

In our empirical work we used data on personal consumption, gross domestic product and unemployment as possible indicators of short-run changes in the business cycle with the expectation that, for the reasons indicated, personal consumption might have a longer term impact upon crime levels. In fact we found that consumption has both a long-run and a short-run dynamic impact upon property crime levels. A fuller discussion of these results may be found in Hale (1997a) and Hale and Caddy (1995). As noted above, here the focus is on the possible long-run relationship between labour market changes and crime trends.

Poverty and Relative Deprivation

Along with unemployment, poverty plays an important theoretical role in explanations of crime. This may be seen either through absolute levels of poverty or more usually through notions of relative deprivation. As noted above, the increase in crime which began in the mid-1950s came as blow to reformers who believed that post-war reforms would lead to the end of poverty as a widespread problem. However, Abel-Smith and Townsend (1965) showed that in fact the reforms had not had the desired impact, and that in the 1960s by comparison with 1953 the numbers who were poor had greatly increased. The numbers who were claiming either National Assistance or, after 1966, Supplementary Benefits increased from 1.3 million in 1950 to 2.7 million in 1970. This figure held steady with minor fluctuations throughout the 1970s. In the 1980s the comprehensive Rowntree Report (1995) shows that the distribution of income rapidly became more unequal. Their research found that since 1979 the lowest income groups had not benefited from economic growth and that since 1977 the proportion of the population with less than half the average income had more than trebled. There was a rapid growth in the 1980s in the numbers living in low income families with children. In order to try and capture the changing nature of poverty we have used two different measures. One, the Gini coefficient, is a single figure used to capture the level of income inequality in the population as a whole. The second measures the ratio of the share of incomes going to the highest 10 per cent of income earners with that going to the lowest 10 per cent. Unfortunately we were only able to find data from 1961 onwards in Goodman and Webb (1994), and so we estimated our models twice, once over the larger data set from the late forties onwards and then including the poverty measures from 1962 only.

Family Breakdown and Demoralisation

Families or their breakdown are another source of theories on the causes of crime. As we noted in the previous paragraph there has been an increase in the numbers living in low income families with children.

More generally the 'demise' of the nuclear family has been blamed for moral decay and increased delinquency. Certainly there have been significant changes in the post-war period. As Utting (1995) notes:

- Marriage rates have reached their lowest point since records began.
- Cohabitation has increased in a quarter of a century from the experience of 6 per cent of brides before their wedding day to 60 per cent.
- Nearly one in three births (31 per cent) occur outside marriage compared with one in sixteen (6 per cent) 30 years ago.
- There has been a sixfold increase in the annual divorce rate since 1961. One in five families with dependent children (20 per cent) are headed by a lone parent compared with one in 12 (8 per cent) in 1971. The proportion of families headed by single mothers who have never married has grown from 1 per cent to 7 per cent.

We were unable to construct data series which captured all these trends in the composition of the family. However, data on the numbers of divorces and marriages and on births inside and outside marriage were used in an attempt to capture some of the changes in family structure which commentators have considered important (see e.g. Dennis, 1993; Morgan, 1995).

Demographics

Empirical evidence suggests that the individuals most active in criminal pursuits are young males between the ages of 15 and 25. In 1994, for example, just over two out of every five known offenders were under the age of 21, and a quarter were under 18 (Home Office, 1995). The peak age of known offending for males was 18 and for females 14 in 1994. Prior to 1972 the peak age for both males and females was 14. For males this rose to 15 in 1972 following the raising of the school-leaving age from 15 to 16, and increased to 18 in 1988. In 1994 81 per cent of known offenders were male, almost unchanged from 84 per cent in 1984 (Home Office, 1995). Consequently it is important in any study of crime trends to control for the changing numbers in the cohort of men in these age groups.

Deterrence

Finally, any model of crime trends must include variables which might be considered to capture the deterrence effects of the criminal justice system. Advocates of a tougher approach to crime place great emphasis on the efficacy of increasing the costs of offending. In addition they point to the incapacitation effect of imprisonment. More sophisticated analysts point to the importance of distinguishing between the certainty and severity of punishment. If the probability of detection and arrest is low then increasing the harshness of punishment is unlikely to have a major impact upon the levels of crime. The level of attrition within the criminal justice system is high. Evidence from the British Crime Surveys suggests that the percentage of offences which are recorded by the police may be as low as 27 per cent of the total of offences actually committed (Home Office, 1995). Of the total number of offences only 4.9 per cent are cleared up, and in only 2 per cent of cases is the end result a conviction. Figures like these suggest that increasing either the numbers imprisoned or the average sentence length is unlikely to have a major impact upon the level of crime. Nevertheless, we did use available data to test whether there was any deterrence or incapacitation effect from changes in the operation of the criminal justice system. The variables used were (i) numbers of police, (ii) crimes cleared up by the police by offence, (iii) numbers found guilty or cautioned by offence, (iv) for each offence the proportion of those found guilty receiving a custodial sentence, and (v) for each offence the average sentence length.

A fuller discussion of the variables used and their sources may be found in Appendix 1, at the end of this chapter.

RESULTS

In this section we present, in a non-technical manner, the results of our analyses of the determinants of recorded property crime – burglary, theft and robbery. The interested reader will find more details of the statistical methods used in modelling the data in Appendix 2. We begin by discussing results related to the long-run impact of changing labour market conditions upon levels of recorded property crime. In particular we will concentrate on those models which used the female employment participation rate and the share of the manufacturing sector in total employment.

Time series statistical modelling requires variables used to be stationary, which, roughly speaking, means they should have a mean and variance which do not change over time. Variables which are not stationary can usually be made so by differencing the data one or more times. The first step in any analysis is therefore to determine the degree of differencing required to ensure stationarity of the variables to be used. In our case we follow Hale (1997a), to which reference should be made for the detailed results, in arguing that our independent variables – recorded burglary, theft and robbery – all need differencing once for stationarity. This result should not surprise us since we have already noted the upward trends in the post-war recorded crime. Similar results were shown to hold for the set of explanatory variables considered: all require first differencing before they are suitable for use in our models. Hence our final dynamic models will have as their dependent variables the year on year changes in recorded crime and, with one possible exception discussed in the next paragraph, all explanatory variables will be of a similar first differenced form.

The exception arises if we are able to establish that there exists a long-run equilibrium relationship between the levels of the crime variables and the levels of some of the explanatory variables. If any such equilibrium relationships exist then the variables are said to be cointegrated and lagged values of the levels should be included in the short-run dynamic model. The lagged levels will incorporate information about the long-run equilibrium relationship into the short-run dynamic model. If no equilibrium relationship exists then as indicated above only first differenced data should be used. As we have already noted there is already substantial work which shows that burglary and theft are cointegrated with personal consumption and GDP (Hale, 1997a,b; Hale and Caddy, 1995; Osborn, 1995; Pyle and Deadman, 1994), but the evidence for the existence of any such equilibrium relationship for robbery is less clear. For a discussion and interpretation of the relationship between crime and consumption see, *inter alia*, Field (1990), Hale (1997a,b) and Pyle and Deadman (1994).

The primary focus of the work presented here was the relationship of crime to trends in the labour market. The question of whether or not recorded property crime has a long-run equilibrium relationship with unemployment is still debated, but the analysis carried out here could find no evidence to support the hypothesis of cointegration (for similar negative results for a wider range of crimes see Hale and Sabbagh, 1991). As noted earlier, over the last century unemployment has been relatively stable, fluctuating around a constant mean, while crime has shown a distinctive upward trend. In the shorter post-war period unemployment has displayed an upward trend, but even over this more limited time there is no evidence of an equilibrium relationship with crime. Hence in seeking to explain long-run trends in property crime in terms of changes in the labour market it is necessary to look beyond unemployment.

We have argued that there have been fundamental shifts in the pattern of employment in the post-war period, sectoral shifts from manufacturing to service, gender shifts from males to females and tenure shifts from full-time to part-time jobs. The obvious next step therefore was to consider whether there was any evidence of a long-run relationship between these changes and trends in crime. The results for manufacturing employment and female participation rates are presented in Table 2.1.

These show that both have equilibrium cointegrating relationships with burglary and theft. Neither however is cointegrated with robbery – a result which is in line with our other investigations which have been unable to establish any long-run equilibrium relationships for recorded robbery (Hale, 1997a; Hale and Caddy, 1995; Hale and Sabbagh, 1991). Similar conclusions for each of the property crimes were reached from alternative models which, instead of rates, used the total number of females in employment and the total number of jobs in the manufacturing sector. Given the lack of any long-run connection between robbery and the labour market, variables for the rest of this paper discussion will be restricted to results for burglary and

Table 2.1   Testing the long-run relationship of crime with labour market variables

Statistic	Burglary[a]		Theft		Robbery	
	Jobs in Manu-facturing	Women in Labour Force	Jobs in Manu-facturing	Women in Labour Force	Jobs in Manu-facturing	Women in Labour Force
ADF	–4.18*	–4.299*	–3.951*	–5.151*	–1.109	–0.829
(augmentation)	(2)	(1)	(1)	(1)	(1)	(1)
R^2	0.957	0.955	0.966	0.976	0.912	0.877

[a] The regression for burglary also included a dummy variable to allow for the change in definition in 1969.
* Significant at the 5% significance level indicating acceptance of the alternative hypothesis that the variables are cointegrated.
The approximate critical values for burglary are (MacKinnon, 1991) –4.63 (1%) and –3.94 (5%); or (Charezma and Deadman, 1997) –4.63 (1%) and –3.71 (5%).
The approximate critical values for theft and robbery are (MacKinnon, 1991) –4.15 (1%) and –3.37 (5%) or (Charezma and Deadman, 1997) –5.35 (1%) and –3.84 (5%).

theft. Further, we will present results based only on the cointegrating relationship between the crime variables and manufacturing employment. The results for female participation rates at present appear to be less robust than for manufacturing, but some brief comments are necessary as the theoretical implications of the results are of interest. Braithwaite et al. (n.d.) discuss their Australian findings relating homicide rates to male unemployment and female *employment* both via criminal opportunity and routine activities theories, but also by focusing on the role of women within a patriarchal society and the crisis in the traditional male role as breadwinner and provider which the employment trends reported here have undermined. The resonance with the descriptions of aimless young males in, for example, Bea Campbell's *Goliath* (Campbell, 1993) are clear. To summarise the results of the first stage of our investigation, we have shown that there is a long-run equilibrium relationship between trends in recorded burglary and theft and trends in the structure of employment. The long-run growth in the levels of these crimes has, in the post-war period been tied to the shifts in patterns of employment from the manufacturing to the service sector, from males to females and from full-time 'jobs for life' to increasingly precarious and often part-time employment. We noted earlier that crime began to increase in the late 1950s, the period when these labour market trends first became apparent. In the period since 1974 during which these employment shifts became even more pronounced the growth in crime has accelerated.

Establishing the existence of long-run patterns is only half the story. We now need to consider the factors which explain year on year fluctuations in crime levels around their trend. The final dynamic model for burglary, incorporating both long- and short-run effects, is presented in Table 2.2. The model is well-specified and passes the usual specification test for serial correlation, functional form, normality and heteroscedasticity. The long-run relationship between burglary and the manufacturing employment rate is captured by including in the statistical *levels* of burglary and manufacturing employment lagged one period.[1]

The estimated coefficients on both lagged levels are of the correct *a priori* sign and statistically significant, confirming that there is indeed, as discussed above, a long-run equilibrium relationship between burglary and the decline of manufacturing employment. The other variables which appear in Table 2.2 are measured in first differences[2] and explain short-run changes in recorded burglary around its long-term

Table 2.2   Final dynamic model for burglary: 1950 to 1993; dependent
variable: changes in recorded burglary

Explanatory Variable	Coefficient	Standard Error	t-ratio
Burglary (–1)	–0.176	0.059	–2.986
Manufacturing (–1)	–1176.3	268.9	–4.374
ΔConsumption	–7.311	1.348	–5.424
ΔMale unemployment	0.082	0.034	2.407
ΔConviction Rate	–1125.0	409.5	2.745
ΔAverage sentence	–3.975	2.361	–1.684
Constant	491.3	107.2	4.583

$R^2 = 0.820$, F Statistic $F(6,37) = 28.155$ (p = 0.000)
Lagrange Multiplier Test for serial correlation, $\chi^2(1) = 0.348$ (p = 0.556)
Test for Heteroscedasticity $\chi^2(1) = 0.045$ (p = 0.832)

trend. A positive coefficient indicates that increases (decreases) in the corresponding variable are associated with increases (decreases) in burglary whereas a negative sign points to increases (decreases) leading to decreases (increases). The estimated dynamic short-run effects are all in the directions anticipated theoretically. Changes in consumption in this model may be interpreted, as in Field (1990), as capturing a business cycle effect – as the economy improves, consumption levels increase, and other things being equal, in the short-run burglary levels will decline. Conversely if personal consumption falls the model predicts that burglary levels will rise. Changes in male unemployment also figure over and above changes in consumption with burglary increasing in line with increases in the numbers of unemployed males. Field (1990) found no role for unemployment once changes in personal consumption had been taken into account. We differ in this respect from his conclusions in finding an independent role for unemployment in determining changes in burglary levels. However it must be stressed once again that in the models used here unemployment has only a short-run role in helping to explain movements around the long-run trend of burglary, it does not explain the trend itself. None of the measures for family breakdown were significant nor were various measures tried to capture the changing size of the population of young males. Furthermore over the period from 1950 to 1993 the estimated models found no evidence that changes in the numbers of Police, changes in the numbers found guilty or cautioned or changes in the use of custodial sentences had any impact in changing burglary levels. Of the deterrence variables used, only the conviction rate is clearly

Table 2.3   Dynamic model for burglary including measures of income inequality: 1962 to 1991; dependent variable: changes in recorded burglary

Explanatory Variable	Coefficient	Standard Error	t-ratio
Burglary (–1)	–0.430	0.122	–3.528
Manufacturing (–1)	–1924.9	445.0	–4.325
ΔConsumption	–7.015	1.700	–4.128
ΔTotal unemployment	0.100	0.035	2.856
ΔConviction Rate	–1114.3	484.6	–2.299
ΔIncome Ratio	85.986	45.19	1.902
Burglary dummy	41.875	19.481	2.150
Constant	806.5	178.9	4.511

$R^2 = 0.877$, F Statistic $F(7,22) = 22.447$ (p = 0.000)
Lagrange Multiplier Test for serial correlation, $\chi^2(1) = 0.050$ (p = 0.823)
Test for Heteroscedasticity $\chi^2(1) = 0.032$ (p = 0.858)

significant while the average sentence length can at best be considered weakly significant.[3] However if we look at the estimated model in Table 2.3, which is the result of modelling changes in recorded burglary over the more limited period 1961 to 1992, to allow the inclusion of measures of income inequality, we see that the average sentence variable has disappeared completely and that the only deterrence variable which is now statistically significant is the clear-up rate. The results here do not provide great support for those who advocate sending more convicted offenders to prison for longer periods.

The results in Table 2.3 indicate the impact of changing inequality upon burglary. Of the two measures considered the Gini coefficient was not found to be statistically significant, but that based upon the ratio of the income of the top 10 per cent to that of the bottom 10 per cent of earners was found to be important. The estimated model shows that as income inequality increases recorded burglary will rise. Other differences between the models in the two tables are that for the shorter, more recent period, it is total unemployment, rather than male unemployment, which is statistically significant, and a dummy variable which captures the changes in the definition of burglary which took place between 1968 and 1989 is required. Finally it should be emphasised that all other variables, for example the numbers of young males in the population, which were discussed as possible explanatory factors have been tested and found to be statistically insignificant.

Table 2.4 Final dynamic model for theft: 1950 to 1993; dependent variable changes in recorded theft

Explanatory Variable	Coefficient	Standard Error	t-ratio
Theft (−1)	−0.229	0.071	−3.217
Manufacturing (−1)	−249.3	700.5	−3.211
ΔTheft (−1)	0.444	0.134	3.316
ΔConsumption	−12.96	2.474	−5.237
ΔConsumption(−1)	13.385	3.398	3.940
ΔMale unemployment	0.207	0.082	−2.511
ΔPolice numbers	−10.711	5.744	−1.865
Constant	980.9	294.68	3.329

$R^2 = 0.760$, F Statistic $F(7,35) = 16.557$ (p = 0.000)
Lagrange Multiplier Test for serial correlation, $\chi^2(1) = 1.746$ (p = 0.186)
Test for Heteroscedasticity $\chi^2(1) = 0.285$ (p = 0.594)

The results of the modelling exercise of the short behaviour of recorded theft are reported in Table 2.4.

Again the estimated model has sound statistical properties passing all the usual specification tests at the 5 per cent level although now to ensure serially independent residuals the lagged change in recorded theft is required. As in the burglary model, the first two lagged terms measure the long-run relationship between levels of recorded theft and the decline of manufacturing jobs. Changes in current and lagged consumption are significant and again the important unemployment variable is the change in total unemployment rather than just male unemployment. The only deterrence variable which is significant is the numbers of police. Again any variable which does not appear in Table 2.4 will have been included but discarded as statistically insignificant. Unlike burglary this also applies for measures of poverty and hence for theft we have no equivalent table to Table 2.3.

Finally, we return to the issue of the periodisation of crime and explore whether or not there was evidence for any change in the underlying structure of the statistical model explaining crime in 1974 after the first major post-war recession in 1973 exacerbated by the OPEC oil price rise and embargo of the same year. While space and a sense of self-preservation caution against entering the debate as to whether the changes which have taken place in the organisation of the economy and society mean that we have entered a distinct post-modern age, we can agree with Harvey that the period since has been

Table 2.5   Testing for structural change in models in 1974

Burglary	Predictive Failure Test, $\chi^2(20) = 41.2482$ (p = 0.003)
	Chow F test, $F(7,30) = 2.717$ (p = 0.026)
Theft	Predictive Failure Test $\chi^2(20) = 154.524$ (p = 0.000)
	Chow F test, F (8,28) = 3.367 (p = 0.008)

For details of the tests see for example Charezma and Deadman (1997, pp. 30–1).

Both tests test the null hypothesis that the parameters underlying the estimated model are constant over the whole sample period 1950–93 against the alternative hypothesis that the underlying parameters change between the two periods.

a troubled one of 'economic restructuring and social and political readjustment' (Harvey, 1989, p. 145). Table 2.5 presents results from testing that there was a structural break in the underlying explanatory model for both burglary and theft in 1973/4.

The results in both cases support the contention that there has been a shift in the determinants of property crime between the two periods. This result should not surprise us since the assumption of constant parameters in time series models in socio-historical studies has been the subject of criticism from Griffen and Isaac (Isaac and Griffin, 1989; Griffin, 1992; Griffin and Isaac, 1992). Their basic complaint is that by assuming parameter constancy over long historical periods researchers are denying the possibility of both sudden and gradual social change.

> critical contingencies of social change, understood as the sudden or gradual temporal conditioning of historical-structural relationships are generally ignored in quantitative explorations of historical processes.   (Isaac and Griffin, 1989, p. 873)

In the context of the work considered here, for example, they would ask whether it is sensible to assume that the explanations for crime levels in the early 1950s would be the same as similar changes during the 1980s. Clearly our results suggest that their reservations would be well founded and that the changing dynamics of crime in the post-war period is an area which needs more detailed investigation. For now we simply note that while the underlying determinants of crime have changed in the post-war period the impact of changes in the labour market has been an increasingly dominant feature. These changes began in the late 1950s and accelerated after 1974 in parallel with our periodisation of crime changes.

CONCLUSIONS

In this chapter we have examined a statistical time series model of the determinants of property crime since the end of the the Second World War. We have argued that while unemployment cannot be cited as a long-run determinant of crime levels that the structure of employment, the shift from stable to precarious employment, from the profile of the typical worker being male, skilled, in full-time work in the manufacturing sector, to being female, unskilled in part-time work in the service sector, has had a major impact upon crime levels.

If changing patterns of employment are important factors in statistical models explaining long-term trends in crime, short-run fluctuations were related to changes in economic activity, as the economy improved, other things being equal, crime would fall. The indicators of economic activity which best captured these aspects were personal consumption and unemployment. We found no evidence to support the incapacitation argument. Neither the likelihood of receiving a custodial sentence nor, when measures of inequality were considered, the average length of sentence were significant in our models. There were some aspects of the criminal justice system which had an impact. Increasing the conviction rate would be predicted to reduce burglary, and increasing the numbers of police would lead to a decline in theft levels.

The major finding of the results reported here is that the state of the economy and particularly trends in the labour market are primary factors in explaining post-war crime trends. The challenge for the next century is how we might begin to deal with these changes in ways which are inclusive rather than exclusive, is how we find ways which tackle the issues presented by the economic and social upheaval of the last thirty years, not by attempting to turn back the clock to some (non-existent) golden age of the patriarchal family, but by seeking to provide real equality of opportunities for both women and men.

Appendix 1: *Definitions of Variables and Sources of Data*

1. *Crime variables*
    (i)   Offences of theft and handling of stolen goods recorded in England
          and Wales.
          Up to and including 1969: categories 38 to 49 inclusive and category
          54.
          1970 and after: categories 39 to 49 inclusive and category 54.
    (ii) Offences of burglary recorded in England and Wales.
          Up to and including 1969: categories 28 to 32 inclusive.
          1970 and after: categories 28 to 31 inclusive.
    (iii) Offences of robbery recorded in England and Wales.
          Category 34.
Source: Criminal Statistics, England, and Wales (various).

2. *Conviction rates*
    For each offence defined as the number of convictions divided by the
    number of recorded offences. The number of convictions is the number of
    persons found guilty in all courts. After 1970 this includes the number of
    offenders who were cautioned for an offence.
Source: Criminal Statistics, England, and Wales (various).

3. *Imprisonment rates*
    For each offence defined as the proportion of those found guilty or cau-
    tioned receiving a custodial sentence.
Source: Criminal Statistics, England, and Wales (various).

4. *Sentence length*
    For each offence defined as the average sentence length in months.
Source: Criminal Statistics, England, and Wales (various).

5. *Police officers*
    Defined as the number of officers (men and women) in England and
    Wales on actual strength at 31 December each year. It excludes special
    constables and seconded officers.
Source: Annual Abstract of Statistics (various).

6. *Numbers of males aged 15–19 years, 20–4 years, 25–9 years*
    For England and Wales, mid-year estimate.
*Sources: Annual Abstract of Statistics (various), OPCS Population Trends
(various) and OPCS Monitor (various).*

7. *Numbers of marriages and divorces in England and Wales*
Source: Annual Abstract of Statistics (various).

8. *Numbers of births inside and outside marriage*
Source: Annual Abstract of Statistics (various).

9. *Gini coefficient*
   Measure of income inequality.
Source: Goodman and Webb (1994).

10. *Income ratio*
    Ratio of income share of top 10 per cent of earners to income share of
    bottom 10 per cent of earners.
Source: Goodman and Webb (1994).

11. *Gross Domestic Product*
    The average measure of Gross Domestic Product at factor cost in 1985
    prices for the UK.
Source: Economic Trends.

12. *Personal consumption*
    Consumers' expenditure in 1985 prices for the UK.
Source: Economic Trends.

13. *Unemployment*
    Numbers of people registered as unemployed in England and Wales by
    gender, excluding adult students.
*Source: 1951–1968 British Labour Statistics Historical Abstracts; 1969–1976
British Labour Statistics Year Book (various); 1976–1993 Regional Trends.*

14. *Employment*
    Numbers of people in employment in England and Wales by gender.
*Source: 1951–1968 British Labour Statistics Historical Abstracts; 1969–1976
British Labour Statistics Year Book (various); 1976–1993 Regional Trends.*

15. *Total numbers in employment in manufacturing sector*
Source: Annual Abstract of Statistics (various).

Appendix 2: *Methods: Integration, Cointegration and Error Correction Models*

The approach to modelling the long-run crime data adopted here is based
upon developments of the methodology proposed by Engle and Granger
(1987). This has been used in earlier work analysing British crime data. For
example Hale (1989) utilises it to examine imprisonment rates in England and
Wales while Hale and Sabbagh (1991), Pyle and Deadman (1994) and Osborn
(1995) have employed it to consider the relationship between post-war crime
trends and the economy. The discussion here draws heavily upon that in Hale
(1996).

The Engle–Granger approach begins by recognising that for the standard
results of multiple regression analysis to be valid the variables used must
be stationary, which (roughly) means their properties should be constant
over time. In particular they should not exhibit any tendency to drift

upwards or downwards (constant mean) and should have constant variance. Variables which are not stationary should be differenced until they are. Variables which need differencing once for stationarity are referred to as being integrated of order one I(1), twice as I(2) and so on. In this schema stationary variables are I(0). The first step in any analysis is therefore to test all the data for levels of integration in order to identify the appropriate difference operator to apply to each series to achieve stationarity. It is the appropriately differenced data which should be used in modelling relationships.

There is, however, a further stage to be considered. Much economic theory is in terms of long-run equilibrium relationships between variables. Differencing data has the effect of purging it of long-run information (the trend) and hence ignoring these possible long-run relationships. Excluding this information when such relationships exist does not seem sensible. The way to get this back in is to consider the possibility of using error correction models (ECM) which incorporate both long- and short-run aspects of the data. Usually combinations of non-stationary variables will also be non-stationary. However, it is possible that there exists a linear combination of non-stationary variables which is itself stationary. If such a linear combination of variables exists the variables have a long-run equilibrium relationship and are said to be cointegrated.[4] The short-run dynamic model involving the differenced data must then be expanded to included lagged levels of these cointegrated variables. It is these lagged levels which capture the long-run equilibrium relationship. Conversely, if the variables are not cointegrated, that is, if any linear combination of them is also non-stationary, then we are only able to model the short-run dynamic relationship between them using only differenced data and excluding the lagged levels. This procedure will be explored in more detail below.

In summary, conventional regression analysis faces two threats from non-stationary variables. The first arises because regressing two unrelated I(1) variables against each other results in more high values of t and F statistics than would be predicted by a statistical theory based upon stationary variables. Consequently the use of standard distributions when the variables are unrelated and non-stationary will lead to too frequent rejection of the null hypothesis that there is no relationship between the variables. It is to avoid such spurious regressions that Granger and Newbold (1974) propose that in such cases the regressions be conducted in terms of first differences rather than levels of the variables. Cointegration analysis, on the other hand, avoids such problems by using the correct rather than incorrect statistical distributions.

The second problem arises with non-stationary variables that are truly related. As noted above using a model in first differences in this situation results in a misspecified regression equation since the long-run relationship has been ignored. The error correction term connecting the cointegrated variables is missing from the estimated equation. (For an interesting and amusing discussion of these issues see Murray, 1994.)

More formally let us consider the simplest bivariate case of a possible relationship between two variables X and Y. Suppose X and Y are both I(1) and that there exists a long-run equilibrium relationship between them which may be expressed as

$$Y = a + bX \tag{1}$$

then short-run deviations

$$Y_t - a - bX_t = u_t \tag{2}$$

should not show any tendency to increase over time. That is to say, they should be stationary.

Looked at in another way, what we have is two variables which are I(1) but a linear combination of which, $Y_t - a - bX_t$, is stationary or I(0). In this case as we have seen Y and X are said to be cointegrated.

To determine whether the relationship in (1) actually holds we fit the model and test the regression residuals, the estimates of u_t for stationarity. If the Y and X are cointegrated then Engle and Granger (1987) show that the error correction model of the form

$$\Delta Y_t = q_0 + q_1 \Delta X_t + q_2(Y_{t-1} - a - bX_{t-1}) + e_t \tag{3}$$

is the appropriate form for modelling the short-run dynamic behaviour. The term in brackets $(Y_{t-1} - a - bX_{t-1})$ is the error correction term which, if q_2 is negative corrects short-run deviations from the equilibrium level implied by (1), hence the name error correction. If the variables are not cointegrated then

$$\Delta Y_t = q_0 + q_1 \Delta X_t + e_t \tag{4}$$

is the appropriate form to consider.

Clearly an important first step in any regression analysis using time series data is to establish the level of integration of the variables to be used. Once this has been done it is possible to move to the second stage and look for possible cointegrating relationships between any set of I(1) variables in order to establish whether our modelling strategy should be based upon a generalisation of equation (3) or whether (4) is correct specification. It is, however, important to emphasise that tests for cointegration are critically dependent upon the first stage being correct, that is to say that the variables included in the cointegrating regression are indeed all I(1). It is argued in Hale (1997a) that recorded levels of burglary, theft and robbery are I(1) and not, as claimed by Pyle and Deadman, I(2). In the results presented in this paper we follow Hale (1997a) and assume that the recorded crime variables are indeed I(1).

If cointegrating relationships between variables are found then the next stage is to estimate the dynamic model (4). The problem which immediately arises is how to estimate the error correction term $(Y_{t-1} - a - bX_{t-1})$. Engle and Granger (1987) suggest a two-stage procedure using the lagged residuals from Ordinary Least Squares (OLS) estimation of the long-run regression (5):

$$Y_t = a + bX_t + u_t \tag{5}$$

as estimates of the error correction term in (3). Since all the terms in (3) are by definition stationary this may be done by OLS; Engle and Granger show that the resulting parameter estimates are not only consistent but also asymptotically efficient. This two-stage procedure has, however, been criticised on the grounds of the small sample bias present in the OLS estimation of the cointegrating equation. Bannerjee et al. (1993) propose overcoming this bias by estimating the long-run and short-run parameters in a single step. If we rewrite (3) by multiplying out the brackets we obtain

$$\Delta Y_t = q_0 - q_2 a + q_1 \Delta X_t + q_2 Y_{t-1} - q_2 b X_{t-1} + e_t \tag{6a}$$

or in unrestricted form

$$\Delta Y_t = d_0 + d_1 \Delta X_t + d_2 Y_{t-1} + d_3 X_{t-1} + e_t \tag{6b}$$

Although Y_{t-1} and X_{t-1} are I(1) variables, OLS can still be applied since there is a linear combination which is I(0). There is evidence from small sample simulation studies that the small sample properties of estimates of (6) are superior to those from the Engle–Granger two-step procedure. For further discussion of the asymptotic properties of the estimates, reference should be made to Sims, Stock and Watson (1990). They show that the individual OLS parameter estimates for the d's in (6b) have asymptotic normal distributions and hence the standard procedures can be applied. It is this latter, Sims, Stock and Watson, procedure which is used in producing the results discussed here.

NOTES

1. These variables are the first two rows in the 'Explanatory Variable' column in Table 2.2 indicated by 'Burglary(–1)' and 'Manufacturing(–1)', where the (–1) is to indicate that they have been lagged one period.
2. The symbol Δ indicates that a variable has been differenced. Hence $\Delta Y_t = Y_t - Y_{t-1}$ and is the change in the variable Y between period $t-1$ and period t. Second differencing is indicated by Δ^2, where $\Delta^2 Y_t = \Delta Y_t - \Delta Y_{t-1} = (Y_t - Y_{t-1}) - (Y_{t-1} - Y_{t-2}) = Y_t - 2Y_{t-1} + Y_{t-2}$ third differencing by Δ^3 and so on.
3. If a one-tailed test is used the estimated t statistic just fails to reach the 10 per cent significance level.
4. Formally variables are said to be cointegrated if they are all I(d), d > 0 and there exists some linear combination of them which is I(b) where b < d, that is, the combination needs differencing fewer times than the

original variables for stationarity. In practical terms the case of interest is where d = 1 and b = 0, the original variables need differencing once and the combination is stationary.

REFERENCES

Abel-Smith, B. and Townsend, P. (1965) *The Poor and the Poorest*. London: Bell and Son.

Allen, E. A. and Steffensmeier, D. J. (1989) 'Youth, Underemployment, and Property Crime: Differential Effects of Job Availability and Job Quality on Juvenile and Young Adult Arrest Rates'. *American Sociological Review*, 54, 107–23.

Bannerjee, A., Dolado, J., Galbraith, J. W. and Hendry, D. F. (1993) *Co-integration, Error-Correction, and the Econometric Analysis of Non-Stationary Data*. Oxford: Oxford University Press.

Beveridge, W. (1942) *Social Insurance and Allied Services*. London: HMSO.

Braithwaite, J., Chapman, B. and Kapuscinski, C. (n.d.) *Unemployment and Crime: Resolving the Paradox*. American Bar Foundation Working Paper no. 9201.

Campbell, B. (1993) *Goliath: Britain's Dangerous Places*. London: Methuen.

Carlson, S. M. and Michalowski, R. J. (1994) 'Structural Change in the Economy, Economic Marginality and Crime'. Paper presented to the American Society of Criminology Conference, Miami, November, 1994.

Charezma, W. W. and Deadman, D. F. (1997) *New Directions in Econometric Practice*. Aldershot: Edward Elgar.

Davidson, R. and MacKinnon J. G. (1992) *Estimation and Inference in Econometrics*. Oxford: Oxford University Press.

Dennis, N. (1993) *Rising Crime and the Dismembered Family*. Institute of Economic Affairs Health and Welfare Unit Choice in Welfare no. 18. London: Institute of Economic Affairs.

Dennis, N. (1997) *The Invention of Permanent Poverty*. Institute of Economic Affairs Health and Welfare Unit Choice in Welfare no. 34. London: Institute of Economic Affairs.

Engle R. F. and Granger, C. W. J. (1987) 'Co-Integration and Error Correction: Representation, Estimation and Testing'. *Econometrica*, 55, 251–76.

Field, S. (1990) *Trends in Crime and their Interpretation: A Study of Recorded Crime in Post-war England and Wales*. Home Office Research Study 119. London: HMSO.

Gatrell, V. A. C. (1980) 'The Decline of Theft and Violence in Victorian and Edwardian England'. In Gatrell, V. A. C., Lenman, B. and Parker, G. (eds), *Crime and the Law: The Social History of Crime in Western Europe since 1500*. London: Europa.

Goodman, A. and Webb, S. (1994) *For Richer for Poorer: The Changing Distribution of Income in the United Kingdom 1961–91*. London: Institute of Fiscal Studies.

Granger, C. W. J. and Newbold, P. (1974) 'Spurious Regressions in Econometrics'. *Journal of Econometrics*, 2, 111–20.

Greenhaigh, C. and Gregory, M. (1994) 'Why Manufacturing Still Matters'. *Employment Policy Institute Economic Report*, 8, no. 5.

Gregg, P. and Wadsworth, J. (1995) 'A Short History of Labour Turnover, Job Tenure, and Job Security, 1975–1993'. *Oxford Review of Economic Policy*, 11, 73–90.

Griffin, L. J. (1992) 'Temporality, Events and Explanation in Historical Sociology: an Introduction'. *Sociological Methods and Research*, 20, 403–27.

Griffin, L. J. and Isaac, L. W. (1992) 'Recursive Regression and the Historical Use of "Time" in Time-series Analysis of Historical Process'. *Historical Methods*, 25, 166–79.

Hale, C. (1989) 'Unemployment, Imprisonment and the Stability of Punishment Hypothesis: Some Results using Co-integration and Error Correction Models'. *Journal of Quantitative Criminology*, 5, 169–91.

Hale, C. (1997a) 'Crime and the Business Cycle in Post War Britain Revisited'. *The Structural and Cultural Determinants of Crime and Punishment*, Working Paper no. 3, University of Kent, Canterbury.

Hale, C. (1997b) 'Crime and Consumption'. *The Structural and Cultural Determinants of Crime and Punishment*, Working Paper no. 5.

Hale, C. and Caddy, M. (1995) 'Long Run Crime Trends in England and Wales: 1857–1993'. Paper presented to the 1995 Annual Conference of the American Criminological Society. *The Structural and Cultural Determinants of Crime and Punishment*, Working Paper no. 2.

Hale, C. and Sabbagh D. (1991) 'Testing the Relationship between Unemployment and Crime: A Methodological Comment and Empirical Analysis using Time Series Data from England and Wales'. *Journal of Research in Crime and Delinquency*, 28, 400–17.

Harvey, D. (1989) *The Condition of Postmodernity*. Oxford: Blackwell.

Home Office (1995) *Information on the Criminal Justice System in England and Wales Digest 3*, eds Barclay, G. C. with Tavares, C. and Prout, A. London: Home Office Research and Statistics Department.

Isaac, L. W. and Griffin, L. J. (1989) 'Ahistoricism in Time Series Analyses of Historical Process: Critique, Redirection and Illustrations from US Labor History'. *American Sociological Review*, 54, 873–90.

McClintock, F. H. and Avison, N. H. (1968) *Crime in England and Wales*. London: Heinemann.

Morgan, P. (1995) *Farewell to the Family: Public Policy and Family Breakdown in Britain and the USA*. Institute of Economic Affairs Health and Welfare Unit Choice in Welfare no. 21. London: Institute of Economic Affairs.

Murray, M. P. (1994) 'A Drunk and Her Dog: An Illustration of Co-integration and Error Correction'. *The American Statistician*, 48, 37–9.

Naylor, K. (1994) 'Part-time Working in Great Britain – An Historical Analysis'. *Employment Gazette*, Dec. 1994, 473–84.

Obelkevich, J. (1994) 'Consumption'. In Obelkevich, J. and Catterall, P. (eds), *Understanding Post-War British Society*. London: Routledge.

Osborn, D. R. (1995) *Crime and the UK Economy*. European University Institute Robert Shuman Centre Working Paper no. 95/19.

Pyle, D. J. and Deadman, D. F. (1994) 'Crime and the Business Cycle in Post-War Britain'. *British Journal of Criminology*, 34, 339–57.

Rowntree Report (1995) *Inquiry into Income and Wealth*. York: Joseph Rowntree Foundation.

Sims, C. A., Stock, J. H. and Watson, M. W. (1990) 'Inference in Linear Time Series with some Unit Roots'. *Econometrica*, 55, 1035–56.

Utting, D. (1995) *Family and Parenthood: Supporting Families, Preventing Breakdown*. York: Joseph Rowntree Foundation.

3 Serious Crime Networks: the Police Response to a Local Problem
Dick Hobbs and Colin Dunnighan

THE PROBLEM

Recent years have seen the development of new forms of organised and serious criminal activity that are widely perceived as a major threat to society. Leaving aside the difficulties in defining what constitutes serious criminal activity (for an attempt, see von Hirsch and Jareborg, 1991), it can reasonably be claimed that it is typically drug related and is no longer the preserve of certain criminal families in 'East End' London engaged in 'wheeling and dealing' and imposing their will within strictly defined geographical areas. This view was echoed by many of those with whom we spoke during a three-year period in which we gained access to a number of serious crime networks. Using a variety of ethnographic techniques, we carried out observations (both covert and overt) and interviewed criminals, their associates, friends and relations. We also consulted and interviewed law enforcement officers from a number of UK and foreign agencies involved in tackling serious and organised crime (for a fuller account, see Hobbs and Dunnighan, 1997).

Our informants generally accepted that whilst the threat of serious organised crime was not as great in the UK as in some countries, where it had undermined political and economic stability, the last decade had, however, seen a new order of crime emerge. As one active, late middle-aged, professional criminal told us:

Today ... [it is] totally different. Once ... [crime families such as the Krays] earned a little bit of respect. I remember the time when if you wanted to slap someone on somebody else's turf, you had to go and see the man and ask if you could fucking do it. You couldn't just go and grab hold of him and give him a bat. You had to go and see the man whose pitch he lived on to see if it was alright to go and give him a slap, burn his house down, break his legs or whatever. But today ... it's totally different. The Frankie Frazers wouldn't last two minutes the way things are now.

We argue that the traditional neighbourhood crime firm has not totally disappeared, but that socio-economic forces beyond the remit of any law enforcement agency have conjured various mutations of this traditional form. There are, however, bigger local money makers than the traditional family firms. The major impact on the local order is still made by the traditional neighbourhood firms rather than the serious crime entrepreneur. The former provide a degree of spatial governance that is congruent with the immobility of the working-class population, the continuity of neighbourhood boundaries and the relevance of familial ties. The emergent culture of serious crime has followed the same trajectory as that of communities based upon traditional industries (Soja, 1989). Below we will consider two such variations of the traditional neighbourhood firm.

UPTON

Upton is a locality of immobile population grounded in traditional notions of the family and neighbourhood, both of which have managed to remain relatively intact. In Upton, an active but stationary population has preserved a cultural inheritance that enabled its principal crime groups to reflect the city's traditional profile (family based and territorially orientated) in a way that has become a persistent feature of the local landscape across generations. The style of organised crime in Upton is firmly entrenched in the locations, working practices, occupational cultures and oppositional strategies of the industrial working class. It represents an ideal synergy with the past. This graphic reaffirmation of local heritage is a way of maintaining the internal order and identity of traditional cultures. They play a role in retaining coherent leisure market potential by 'lifting out' (Giddens, 1991, p. 18) symbolic impressions of traditional leisure strategies and rearticulating them in the locale and space of pragmatic consciousness (see Davis, 1990, ch. 5; Horne and Hall, 1995; Hobbs, 1988). In Upton it is relatively easy to map the origins, nature and operations of the city's organised crime groups.

DOWNTON

In Downton, by contrast, attempts at mapping organised crime have proved futile for nearly a quarter of a century. The territory that once defined and shaped organised crime groups has disintegrated. Serious crime has become removed from the terrain that spawned elementary forms of criminal organisation (King, 1991, p. 6). The transformation of the traditional family firm into either individualistic mutations, or actively disorganised deviant scavengers, reflects the dramatic economic changes that this region has sustained since the 1960s. Stripped of the traditional industrial contours that once structured community life (local labour market, neighbourhood ecology, extended family networks and leisure time), Downton's working class population has fragmented against the backdrop of a redundant industrial landscape. The community's material base has fractured and new, blurred socio-economic coalitions have formed. Immigration to Downton has also introduced patterns of crime markedly different from the white, indigenous (and dominant) variety.

In particular, the delineation of Downton's traditional neighbourhoods and housing settlements has inspired a blurred and confused set of boundary distinctions that has succeeded in distributing the local serious crime community and its progeny over a wide, amorphous territory. The transitory nature of most of these arrangements (depending on their degree of embeddedness) and their fluctuating engagements with legitimate opportunities (Smith, 1980), in no way diminish their potency. In the section that follows we trace this shift in emphasis from traditional neighbourhood organised crime to contemporary entrepreneurial activity via the career of one family whose neighbourhood hegemony in the immediate post-war period was based on violence.

ESSEX MEN

The fragmentation of both traditional working-class neighbourhoods and local labour markets (Pakulski and Walters, 1996), has made it difficult for family-based units to establish the kind of parochial dominance previously enjoyed by the feudal warlords of the 1950s and 1960s (Pearson, 1973). Traditional forms of organised crime that were reliant upon this industrial milieu and upon traditional family structures either dissolved or fragmented. The Nob family – a family which illustrates a particular mode of family-based criminal organisation which we generally characterise as 'Essex Men' – has succeeded in adapting from the traditional to the post-industrial environment.

The culture of contemporary organised crime occupies a central position within the virtual communities of consumption that are no longer determined by territorially-driven notions of a local hegemonic order. The new arenas occupied by the 'Essex Men' are entrepreneurially orientated: within them are a plethora of money-making opportunities. Unlike the traditional neighbourhood 'firm', abiding by formal relations inherited and adapted from the indigenous socio-economic sphere (Block, 1983, ch. 2), the contemporary serious crime community is the 'arch enemy of uniformity' (Bauman, 1992, p. 52). Though steeped in traditional notions of criminality and established according to the precedents of indigenous markets, these new networks of criminal entrepreneurs are not restrained by the parameters of specific neighbourhoods. Like their predecessors they do not inhabit a 'culturally constituted world' (McCracken, 1988). Material success depends on the ability to perform successfully within the constraints of the structural dynamics of a local class milieu that has not disappeared, but realigned according to the dictates of global markets. The dialectic between the local and the global (Giddens, 1990, p. 64; 1991, p. 22) epitomises and underlines markets where complex affinities between global and local spaces are negotiated, creating an enacted environment consisting of indigenous renditions of global markets (Robins, 1991). This environment is where

> the business of crime is planned, contacts are made, some crimes are carried out, the fruits of crime are often enjoyed, and the methodologies for the integration of organised criminals into civil society are established.   (Block, 1991, p. 15)

The culture of contemporary organised criminality is now expressed through local trading networks (Dorn et al., 1992, pp. 3–59; cf. Piore and Sabel, 1984), and the continual realignment of local precedents in the context of global markets assures a measure of commercial viability (Giddens, 1991, pp. 21–2; cf. Hobbs, 1995, ch. 5). Traditional neighbourhood hegemony based on violence, has given way to interlocking, ever mutating, networks that utilise cultural inheritance, legend and myth to populate trade routes forged both by forbidden leisure and the suburban colonisation of post-industrial urban and rural landscapes. For instance, when our 'Essex Men' originally shifted east they brought with them their communal reputation from their now defunct homeland *and* they imported relevant knowledge in the form of business contacts. The exploitation of these contacts enabled the family to expand, organise cannabis smuggling, and invest in a number of small businesses. The latter included a fitness centre, a pub and a restaurant run by a family with whom they had briefly collaborated in the 1970s.

Violence did not completely disappear from their lives. The eldest son served a sentence of two years' imprisonment for an assault in the late 1980s, when a market trader who owed the family money made violent threats and was subsequently stabbed and beaten. Violence is a tried and tested strategy that has no substitute as a regulating device within the new market-place: it also serves as a reassuring touchstone with the past. Yet most of the old strategies, practices and allegiances receive little more than a passing nod. Territoriality and its associated tribal tensions have become increasingly irrelevant and business coalitions now thrive where gangsters once feared to tread. Two south London associates of the family were arrested in 1990 for dealing in amphetamines. The Nobs, who rarely operate as a coherent group, are one of many outlets for a counterfeit currency network with premises in south and central London. After the arrest of the two south London men it becomes possible to link the Nobs to ecstasy importation. They apparently use premises in industrial estates some distance from the homeland's pubs and lock-up garages. Moreover, when the family are not importing and wholesaling their own goods, the senior family member will wholesale on his own behalf.

The destruction of this neighbourhood and the opening up of trade routes into suburban and rural terrains is the focus of this network. The breakdown of the old territory has been accompanied by the breakdown of the traditional organised crime group, and the new territories are rapidly occupied by their remnants who thrive by no longer restricting themselves to one 'turf'. Their activities often involve the crossing of both national and international borders – with a significant number basing themselves in countries outside the jurisdiction (and view) of UK law enforcement agencies.

NETWORKED CRIME

This organisational flexibility of crime was reflected in the material that we collected on a network of car thieves. This complex network involves the theft, ringing and sale of four-wheel-drive vehicles. It stretches the length and breadth of the UK and into southern Ireland. It features numerous self-contained sub-networks with dedicated functions the members of which have no knowledge of any aspect of the network beyond their own enacted environment. Like the other networks featured in our research they are non-hierarchical and not controlled by any one person. Several legitimate businesses are involved, and one key member of the network is a business partner of an international drug dealer. The self-contained cells of this network constitute localised criminal activity that overlaps with the activities of other cells, and only manifests itself as an international serious crime network when subjected to the gaze of the police or, indeed, academics. This was also the case of our burglary network which revolved around the highly localised activities of one man, whose dependant network was multinational, but not transnational. The hubs of this network involved the trade in stolen antiques and depended on the existence of international borders and their assocated controls to inflate the value of the commodities traded in.

Of course most of the activities of those involved in serious crime are hidden from the day-to-day operations of local police. For instance the Chinese network that we uncovered, which initially appeared to conform to a classic model of organised crime, extorts money from businesses within the Chinese community, predominantly restaurants and takeaways. Although a formal hierarchy that stretches across the globe does exist, the proceeds of crime do not filter through to the top of the system. The everyday activities of the network are overwhelmingly local and insular, and the extortion is regarded as a way of life seldom generating violence. This network also intrudes on the gaming industry and is linked to illegal gambling and to organised walk-outs and the picketing of licensed casinos. We also believe it may be extending its activities into extortion from non-Chinese businesses. This global network manifests itself as a distinctly local, essentially covert, phenomenon. It is seldom visible to the local police who, in the main, concern themselves with the detection of comparatively low-level (but numerous) crimes such as burglary, car theft and the main-tenance of order on Friday and Saturday nights when the pubs and clubs are emptying. As an assistant chief constable of a provincial police force told us:

What many Divisional Commanders are interested in is seeing an improvement in the clear-up rate in their area. They're not interested in the money-launderer or the international drug trafficker who's making millions, even though that trafficker is responsible for flooding their area with drugs which, as you know, impacts on crime rates because people commit offences to feed their [drug] habit ... [However] ... if we ignore the wider picture and simply concentrate on local issues we could soon end up with a very major organised crime problem.

In addition to these variations in serious crime networks, an added problem for law enforcement agencies is that there is growing evidence that whilst many of those involved in organised and serious crime have completed a standard criminal apprenticeship before graduating to activities of greater seriousness (see the cases of 'Bill and Ben' in Hobbs and Dunnighan, 1997), increasing numbers appear to have taken the fast-track route and entered at 'management' level. There is the case of 'Jake', for example, who had grown wealthy running a small chain of garages. His was a reputable company and 'Jake' had no involvement with the police other than when he sold the local Superintendent a new car every two years. At the age of 44, however, on the promise of a quick return, he 'invested' £5,000 with a young motor mechanic who was selling cannabis on a small scale to friends. Within twelve months 'Jake' was himself a serious player, distributing cannabis through a quickly established network from which he realised more income in one year than he had done in the previous five through his legitimate business activities. One consequence of the 'management-level entry' trend is that law enforcement agencies no longer have access to the vast amounts of intelligence data invariably gathered during a traditional criminal career and which can be used to assist in matters such as the identification of associates, addresses and vehicles.

THE RESPONSE

Unlike other countries, the UK has no legislation directed specifically at 'organised crime'. In response to the House of Commons Home Affairs Committee recommendation that 'should the apparent growth in organised crime not be contained then ... consideration should be given to establishing an offence of "'membership of a criminal organisation"' (Home Affairs Committee, 1995, para. 172), the government has indicated that although they will keep the situation under review, they are satisfied that, for the present, the law of conspiracy is adequate for dealing with organised crime in the UK (Home Affairs Committee, 1996, para. 39).

Although the reasons are complex, and not solely related to the issue of serious and organised crime, UK law enforcement agencies have responded to the problem by moving away from traditional reactive methods of policing and adopting proactive intelligence-driven strategies with a concomitant increase in the use of sophisticated covert techniques (involving both technical and physical surveillance), paid informers, undercover police officers and 'sting' operations (Dunnighan and Norris, 1996; Maguire, 1998). Accompanying this approach has been the expansion, increasing centralisation and internationalisation of intelligence gathering and the growth of specialist units dedicated to tackling serious and organised crime (see Fijnaut, 1993; Nadelmann, 1993). The National Criminal Intelligence Service (NCIS), formed in 1992, amalgamated and brought under one control various regional and national intelligence units and now maintains national indices in relation to categories of criminal activity such as counterfeit currency, drug trafficking, money-laundering, football hooliganism, organised crime, paedophilia, kidnapping and extortion.

With an annual budget of £31.8 million and employing 562 staff (drawn from the police service, HM Customs and Excise, the civil service and other law enforcement and intelligence agencies), NCIS provides strategic threat analyses to HM Government, law enforcement and other relevant agencies on changing trends and patterns in organised and serious criminal activities. However, its primary role is the gathering of intelligence on serious and organised crime and criminals nationally. During 1996/7 some 156 people satisfied their criteria for selection as a 'core nominal' in that they were regarded as a major criminal of international, national or regional significance believed to be involved, at the highest level, in the commission of serious and organised crimes. Raw data on the 'core nominals' (and some 2,200 potential 'core nominals') are collated, processed, analysed and evaluated before being offered to law enforcement agencies (NCIS, 1997a).

As part of its national intelligence gathering role, NCIS also maintains the National Informants Database (NID) to which, from April 1997, all regional crime squads and the majority of the police forces of England and Wales subscribe. By the use of a secure system, details of registered police informants nation-wide are stored on the database (true identities are never entered) which, based on their geographical distribution and competency, enables, under strictly controlled criteria, the tasking of informants to gather intelligence on those involved in the commission of serious criminal offences. In the first six months of operation, details of over 33,000 informants were entered on the NID. In an effort to facilitate the gathering of intelligence on those criminals based outside of the UK, but operating within it, NCIS has posted seven officers to work in other European Union countries and one in the USA. These Crime Liaison Officers (CLOs) deal with enquiries from UK police forces and cooperate with local agencies in the exchange of information and intelligence. Currently based in Germany, Italy and the US, recent calls have been made by the Director General of NCIS for CLOs also to be posted in Cyprus, Hong Kong, the Caribbean Islands, Canada and Australia (NCIS, 1997b). In addition, NCIS manages fifteen drug liaison officers (DLOs) in various European countries who are supported by teams of desk officers based in London.

NCIS also acts as the contact point between UK police forces and foreign police agencies through the organisations EUROPOL and INTERPOL. In December 1996 Britain became the first member state of the European Union to ratify the Europol Convention, giving EUROPOL, a police intelligence agency based in The Hague, legal status. With an annual budget of around £5 million and staffed by liaison officers from member states, it does not have an operational capacity and is primarily concerned with facilitating information exchange between law enforcement agencies of member states and the analysis of information. During 1996 there were 700 transactions from the UK via EUROPOL (Gibbon, 1997). As provided for in the Security Services Act 1996, NCIS is also the coordinating authority for Security Service activities in support of law enforcement agencies in the prevention and detection of serious and organised crime, with a small number of MI5 personnel seconded to NCIS in an intelligence gathering role. Additionally, during 1997, MI6 diverted some of its resources to combating drug trafficking overseas (*The Times*, 31 October 1997).

The National Crime Squad (NCS) took over from the existing regional crime squads in England and Wales in April 1998. With a headquarters in London, this new squad, which will have its own Chief Constable, is seen by its supporters as providing a potentially sharper and more coordinated response by the police service to national and international crime carried out by 'serious professional criminals working together in shifting alliances' (*The Guardian*, 3 July 1996). Indeed, in recent years, the majority of RCS work have been directed at national and international criminality.

Research carried out by the Home Office suggests that around 10 per cent of all recorded crime is committed by those who live outside the force area in which the offence is committed, with most offenders travelling between neighbouring forces (Porter, 1996). However, as the research report points out, cross-border crime is, by its very nature, difficult to detect and it is likely, therefore, that this figure considerably underestimates the extent of the problem. Indeed senior police officers expressed their concerns to us that the NCS would no longer be able to tackle the problem of criminals crossing force boundaries – the role for which RCSs were created in the 1960s. The problem is regarded as essentially structural. If the NCS focuses on crime from an overwhelmingly national perspective, it is feared that a void will be created in which cross-border criminals will be allowed to operate virtually unhindered. Such concerns have been recognised by the Association of Chief Police Officers. The ACPO has issued guidance on the resources available to tackle such criminal activity and is encouraging the formation of Regional Tasking and Coordinating Groups to maintain an overview of cross-border crime within their region and the operational activity which is being undertaken to address it (ACPO, 1997, p. 21).

However, management and intelligence systems are currently often incompatible between forces. This makes it difficult to identify cross-border crime patterns and impedes the sharing of intelligence. Though the introduction of software programs, such as WATSON, 'The Analyst's Notebook' or HOLMES, and the development of the National Comparative Case Analysis Database facility of the Police National Computer, have led to an increasing use of technology as an aid to intelligence gathering and the tackling of serious and organised crime, many police force computerised intelligence databases are incompatible with one another. British Telecom, however, announced at the 1997 ACPO conference that it was planning to allocate some £500,000 towards the development of a new computer network aimed at encouraging more effective use of intelligence. Their network would, they argued, allow data held by individual forces to be entered and collated within a single system, allowing officers from any force to access it.

As further evidence of the centralisation of resources to tackle serious and organised crime, a National Crime Faculty (NCF) has been established. Based at the Police Staff College, Bramshill, it operates a help desk for the use of any police officer investigating serious offences. The Faculty also acts as host for courses for European senior detectives during which information is exchanged and networks devel-

oped. Whilst officers from the bureau will not take over the investigations of crime, they will analyse the data relating to each case, identifying possible links with other offences and providing leads to possible
suspects. As we have argued elsewhere (Dunnighan and Hobbs, 1996),
it is evident that no single agency is currently capable of handling the
problem alone. This is particularly so when complex illegal financial
transactions are involved. Money laundering (see Chaikin, 1991), for
example, is nearly always international in nature and consequently
difficult to tackle. In the UK it usually involves money coming into
London from another country, being processed through financial institutions, and going abroad again. In an effort to combat the problem,
the Bank of England, the Financial Fraud Information Network, the
Securities and Investment Board, the Insolvency Service and the
Serious Fraud Office (SFO) all now participate in operational groups,
such as the Joint Action Group on Organised Crime, which is chaired
by the Metropolitan Police. The Department of Trade and Industry
also plays an increasingly important role in carrying out investigations
under powers conferred by the Companies Act 1985. Legislation is
also in place which puts a legal obligation on banks to inform NCIS
about suspicious financial transactions (see Levi, 1991; Gold and Levi,
1994).

In 1996 there were nearly 16,000 referrals to NCIS and there is
concern that there are insufficient resources available effectively to
follow up each one. Even when followed up, it is often difficult, if not
impossible, to trace a money trail back to the original or predicate
offence without accessing the relevant accounts (for a discussion of
the necessity of tackling money-laundering on an international basis,
see Nilson, 1991; and Snider, 1995). The problem is that whereas in
the UK where the Criminal Justice and Public Order Act 1994 allows
the SFO to use its powers to assist overseas jurisdictions making
enquiries in the UK, in many other countries it has to be proved that
suspect money is the proceeds of crime before a court order can be
gained to access an account.

Apart from cooperation between agencies in dealing with money-
laundering, there are many other other joint operations targeted at
serious and organised crime – particularly between HM Customs and
the regional crime squads in tackling the drug market. Agencies com-
plain, however, that their efforts are restricted by a lack of coordina-
tion and resources. In an attempt to deal with this, the new Labour
Administration kept a promise made by Tony Blair prior to the 1997
General Election to follow the lead of the USA and set up an

'overlord' to coordinate the war against drugs. In January 1998 Keith Hellawell, Chief Constable of West Yorkshire, took up that position with the remit of managing the entire anti-drugs programme from education and support services to HM Customs and Excise, prisons and the police. Answerable to the Prime Minister, Hellawell will have the power to call in any of these agencies and ministries with the aim of coordinating attacks on both supply and demand.

THE PROBLEM WITH THE RESPONSE

The last two decades have, then, seen the development of national and international squads and agencies. We contend, however, that this approach has been too simplistic. It fails to tackle what is happening at a local level. For crime is always local, albeit interconnected with other crimes in other localities, or facilitated by a range of regional, national and international 'hubs'. The notion of territoriality is vital to understanding the police response to serious and organised crime. We maintain, consequentially, that consideration of the increasingly complex relationship between territory and serious crime networks is vital in considering the appropriateness of these policing developments. Our findings regarding both traditional neighbourhood organised crime groups, and non-traditional contemporary serious crime networks, indicate that organised crime, like legitimate commercial interests, involves constant mediations and renegotiations. The scope and extent of this activity depends upon the degree of connectivity between groups and individuals. It is this connectedness rather than corporate identity that forms the structural connotation inherent in 'organised crime'. This is particularly the case within non-traditional serious crime networks. Here the entire range of traditional and contemporaneous collaborations, legitimate and illegitimate enterprises and a series of commercial arrangements that cross continents are featured. We investigated, for instance, a network that involved sovereigns and half sovereigns minted in Turin and Beirut, imported into Britain and sold as high premium Victorian coins. The enabling network involved legitimate jewellery shops, and mobile traders working the national antique market circuit. The network also featured a prominent traditional neighbourhood crime group which included prominent players in the drug trade.

Despite its international hubs and terminals, contemporary organised criminality is expressed through local trading networks (Dorn et al., 1992, pp. 3–59; cf. Piore and Sabel, 1984; Hobbs, 1997). Their commercial viability is assured by the continual realignment of local precedents in the context of global markets (Giddens, 1991, pp. 21–2: cf. Hobbs, 1995) and, as Potter explains, these networks are 'flexible, adaptive networks that readily expand and contract to deal with the uncertainties of the criminal enterprise' (1994, p. 2).

What constitutes effective intelligence regarding these networks parallels the true nature of the collaborations themselves, that is, that they are overwhelmingly local. And, as a consequence of the net-worked nature of these activities, effective police intelligence systems must avoid the traditional hierarchies of the police and antiquated notions of organised crime. For instance, we have elsewhere been critical of the very concept of 'transnationality', particularly in rela-tion to organised crime (Hobbs, 1998). There is an extraordinary lack of data concerning actual, as opposed to assumed, organised crime, and when we move to a discussion of the international implications of organised crime, the evidence becomes secondary to statements sup-portive of transnational police responses (House of Lords, 1995). For example, Sheptycki's recent work on policing emphasises the develop-ment of global police systems (1995, 1998) and the evolution of police work as knowledge work (cf. Erikson, 1994). But knowledge of what? The legitimising logic driving these changes in the policing of organ-ised crime is located in a perception of a changing world, where criminal collaborations flourish across international boundaries (NCIS, 1993), and this perception is shared by commentators across Europe and beyond (Borricand, 1997). To a certain extent these perceptions can be attributed to the destruction of national bound-aries (Hobsbawm, 1994, pp. 558–85), the subsequent redundancy of cold-war narratives (see Labrousse and Wallon, 1993; Williams, 1993; Calvi, 1993), and the substitution of 'crime war' scenarios amongst the ever shifting budgetary conflagrations of the developed nations (Naylor, 1995). The result is a form of 'alien conspiracy' theory ideally shaped to fit the fortress mentalities of late twentieth-century Western states.

The persistence of 'alien conspiracy' theories has not been limited to academic debate (cf. Cressey, 1972). Threat assessments contrived by NCIS have concentrated upon a range of exotic criminal organisa-tions (NCIS, 1993 and 1997a), and the identification of aliens as the principal organised crime threat to British society, is a device that con-veniently excuses British society from taking responsibility for its own maladies. It conforms to a mythological version of globalisation

(Ferguson, 1992), an overriding of the particular that constitutes a reworking of 'mass society' rhetorics.

Identifying aliens as the principal organised crime threat to the state, however, constitutes rather more than the mere scapegoating of minorities. When political arenas suddenly expand, as happened in the aftermath of the Second World War, organised crime is usually brought, via devices controlled by the state, to the forefront of public consciousness. What became known as the Kefauver Commission condensed what were essentially localised community-based crimes into 'organised crime'. Mundane violence and corruption were replaced with a national conspiracy (Block, 1983, p. 123). Despite the failure of the Committee to provide sufficient evidence for the existence of a nation-wide hierarchical ethnic conspiracy (Moore, 1974), the model that subsequently developed reinforced the public's growing belief that, 'forces outside of mainstream American culture are at work which seek to pervert an otherwise morally sound, industrious, and democratic people' (Potter, 1994, p. 10).

Many of the shifts in policing strategies described in this paper display characteristics of the American post-war experience. 'Suitable enemies' (Christie, 1986) do seem to emerge at times of insecurity, and by presenting policing as a highly rational, organised activity based upon scientific precepts (Beck, 1992), fear can be allayed and a sense of solidarity built upon expert systems of scientific control allowed to emerge. The more that criminality can be associated with recent change, the destruction of national boundaries, and shifts in population, the more that variations in the enacted environment of both organised crime, and attempts to police it, are ignored. Law enforcement agencies need to confirm their assumptions and seek out criminal hierarchies that mirror the organisational hierarchies of policing (Reuter, 1986). As Chambliss points out: 'the law enforcement system maximises its visible effectiveness by creating and supporting a shadow government that manages the rackets' (1978, p. 92). Many of the early outpourings from NCIS echoed this experience, albeit shrouded in classic British understatement.

National and international police systems, driven by the possibilities created by technological advances, utilise versions of globalisation to justify the flow of resources to ever expanding policing agencies. However, in the light of our findings, our reading of globalisation reflects that of Robertson (1992, 1995): globalisation has intensified the distinctiveness and viability of locality as a context for a distinct social order. It is central to our findings that the new criminal market, in common with its legitimate counterpart, is structured within networks of small flexible firms that, in classic post-fordist style, feature short-term contracts and lack of tenure (Hall and Jaques, 1990). These networks are essentially locally constituted, and it is possible to draw close parallels between local patterns of immigration and emigration, local employment and subsequent work and leisure cultures with variations in serious crime networks.

CONCLUSIONS

All of the networks mentioned above have some kind of international connection, and provide evidence of the impact of foreign cultures on indigenous markets, or new trading arrangements that do not ignore, but utilise, national boundaries. The nature of these criminal activities is also an enabling device for passage from one sphere to another. It represents a transition of cross-cultural interests that is an expedient dynamic for the criminal careers of contemporary serious criminals whose career trajectories are no longer limited to specific, often stereotyped urban 'underworld' geographic locations (Hobbs, 1997). Rather they are committed to a reorientation of their practices to the temporality of the commercial overworld. Contrary to the manufactured outpourings of the media and the control agencies (NCIS, 1993; Sterling, 1994; Williams, 1993; Williams and Savona, 1995), organised crime is not practised nationally, globally or transnationally. These are abstract fields devoid of relations (Strathern, 1995, p. 179).

As we continue to realign the resources of police and security agencies in the after-shock of the curtailment of the cold war (Godson and Olson, 1993; Naylor, 1995), such global rhetorics should be treated carefully: 'For the moment we are not only without an adequate cartography of global capitalism, we lack political maps of our own backyards' (Cooke, 1988, p. 489). As indicated by Robertson (1992, 1995), the 'glocal' – the intensification of locality within the context of globalisation – constitutes a distinct social order. Ever mutating networks of serious crime are part of that order. They are 'local at all points', constituting 'continuous paths that lead from the local to the global, from the circumstantial to the universal, from the contingent to the necessary' (Latour, 1993, p. 117).

If, as our research overwhelmingly suggests, organised/serious crime manifests itself as a series of ever changing local networks that interlock with other networks and locales, the trend towards the centralisation of intelligence should be regarded with some concern. We are not suggesting that the technological and organisational genies be forced back into the bottle. Rather, that both the nature of serious/organised crime and the status of local intelligence, which is after all the source of all national and international data bases, be acknowledged. This could be achieved by the negotiation of flexible regional objectives which could be used to establish interlocking intelligence networks. This acknowledgement of the importance of locality may have some impact on the dissemination of intelligence, the drift of resources to the south of the country, and, ultimately, the maintenance of some semblance of local accountability within a nationally organised police system.

REFERENCES

Association of Chief Police Officers ACPO (1997) *Cross Border Crime*, London: ACPO Crime Committee.

Bauman, Z. (1992) *Intimations of Modernity*, London: Routledge.

Beck, U. (1992) *Risk Society*, London: Sage.

Block, A. (1983) *East Side–West Side: Organizing Crime in New York, 1930–1950*, Newark, NJ: Transaction.

Block, A. (1991) *Masters of Paradise*, New Brunswick, NJ: Transaction.

Borricand, J. (ed.) (1977) *Criminalité organisé et ordre dans la société*, Marseille: Presses Universitaires d'Aix-Marseille.

Calvi, F. (1993) *Het Europa Van de Peetvaders, De Mafia Verovert een Continent*, Leuven: Kritak Balans.

Chaikin D. A. (1991) 'Money Laundering: An Investigatory Perspective', *Criminal Law Review*, 467–8.

Chambliss, W. J. (1978) *On the Take*, Bloomington: Indiana University Press.

Christie, N. (1986) 'Suitable Enemies', in H. Bianchi and R. Swaaningen (eds), *Abolitionism – Towards a Non-Repressive Approach to Crime*, Amsterdam: Free University Press.

Cooke, P. (1988) 'Modernity, Postmodernity and the City', in *Theory Culture and Society*, 5, no. 2–3.

Cressey, D. (1972) *Criminal Organisation*, London: Heinemann.

Davis, M. (1990) *City of Quartz*, London: Verso.

Dorn, N. et al. (1992) *Traffickers*, London: Routledge.

Dunnighan, C. and Hobbs, D. (1996) *A Confidential Report on the NCIS Organised Crime Notification Survey*, London: PRG Home Office.

Dunnighan, C. and Norris, C. (1996) 'A Risky Business: Recruitment and Running of Informers by English Police Officers', *Police Studies*, 19, no. 2, pp. 1–25.

Erikson, R. (1994) 'The Division of Expert Knowledge in Policing and Security', *British Journal of Sociology*, 45, no. 2, pp. 147–76.

Ferguson, M. (1992) 'The Mythology about Globalisation', *European Journal of Communication*, 7.

Fijnaut, C. (1993). *The Internationalization of Police Co-operation in Western Europe*, Deventer: Kluwer.

Gibbon, S. (1977) 'Euro Feds', *Police Review*, 3 Jan.

Giddens, A. (1990) *The Consequences of Modernity*, Cambridge: Polity.

Giddens, A. (1991) *Modernity and Self-Identity*, Cambridge: Polity.

Godson, R. and Olson, W. (1993) *International Organised Crime: Emerging Threat to U.S. Security*, Washington: National Strategy Information Center.

Gold, M. and Levi, M. (1994) *Money-laundering in the UK: An Appraisal of Suspicion-Based Reporting*, London: The Police Foundation.

Hall, S. and Jaques, M. (eds) (1990) *New Times: The Changing Face of Politics in the 1990s*, London: Lawrence and Wishart.

Hobbs, D. (1988) *Doing the Business: Entrepreneurship, Detectives and the Working Class in the East End of London*, Oxford: Clarendon Press.

Hobbs, D. (1995) *Bad Business*, Oxford: Oxford University Press.

Hobbs, D. (1997) 'Professional Crime: Change Continuity and the Enduring Myth of the Underworld', *Sociology*, 31, no. 1, pp. 57–72.

Hobbs, D. (1998) 'Going Down the Glocal', *Howard Journal*, Special edition on organised crime.

Hobbs, D. and Dunnighan, C. (1997) *Serious Crime Networks*, Final Report to the Economic and Social Research Council.

Hobsbawm, E. (1994) The *Age of Extremes*, Harmondsworth: Penguin.

Home Affairs Committee (1995) *Third Report from the Home Affairs Committee Session 1994–95: Organised Crime*, London: HMSO.

Home Affairs Committee (1996) *Government Reply to the Third Report from the Home Affairs Committee Session 1994–95: Organised Crime*, London: HMSO.

Horne, R. and Hall, S. (1995) 'Anelpis: A Preliminary Expedition into a World without Hope or Potential', *Parallex.*, 1, pp. 81–92.

House of Lords (1995) Select Committee on the European Communities; EUROPOL (HL Paper 51) London: HMSO.

King, A. D. (1991) 'Introduction', in A. D. King (ed.), *Culture, Globalisation and the World System*, London: Macmillan.

Labrousse, A. and Wallon, A. (eds) (1993) *La Planete des Drogues*, Paris: Seuil.

Latour, B. (1993) *We Have Never Been Modern*, London: Harvester Wheatsheaf.

Levi, M. (1991) *Customer Confidentiality, Money-Laundering, and Police–Bank Relationships*, London: Police Foundation.

Maguire, M. (1998) 'Covert and Deceptive Policing in England and Wales: Issues in Regulation and Practice', *European Journal of Crime, Law and Criminal Justice*.

McCracken, G. (1988) *Culture and Consumption*, Bloomington: Indiana University Press.

Moore, W. H. (1974) *Kefauver and the Politics of Crime*, Columbus, Miss.: University of Missouri Press.

Nadelmann, E. (1993) *Cops Across Borders; The Internationalization of US Law Enforcement* University Park, Pa: Pennsylvania State University Press.

Naylor, R. T. (1995) 'From Cold War to Crime War' *Transnational Organised Crime*, Vol. 1. No 4. pp. 37–56.

NCIS (National Criminal intelligence Service) (1993) *An Outline Assessment of the Threat and Impact by Organised/Enterprise Crime Upon United Kingdom Interests*, London: NCIS.

NCIS (1997a) *Annual Report*, London: Home Office.

NCIS (1997b) *Press Release* 8/97, June 12.

Nilson, H. G. (1991) 'The Council of Europe Laundering Convention: A Recent Example of a Developing International Criminal Law', *Criminal Law Forum*, 2, 419.

Pakulski, J. and Walters, M. (1996) *The Death of Class*, London: Sage.

Pearson, J. (1973) *The Profession of Violence*, London: Granada.

Piore, M. & Sabel, C. (1984) *The Second Industrial Divide*, New York: Basic Books.

Porter, M. (1996) *Tackling Cross Border Crime*, Crime Detection and Prevention Series Paper 79, London: Home Office, Police Research Group.

Potter, G. W. (1994) *Criminal Organisations*, Illinois: Waveland Press.

Reuter, P. (1984) *Disorganised Crime*, Cambridge, Mass.: MIT Press

Reuter, P. (1986) *Methodological and Institutional Problems in Organised Crime Research*, paper prepared for the conference on Critical Issues in Organised Crime Control, Washington, DC: Rand Corporation.

Robertson, R. (1992) 'Globality and Modernity', *Theory Culture and Society*, 9, no. 2.

Robertson, R. (1995) 'Glocalisation: Time–Space and Homogeneity–Heterogeneity', in Featherstone, M., Lash, S. and Robertson, R. (eds), *Global Modernities*, London: Sage.

Robins, K. (1991) 'Tradition and Translation: National Culture in its Global Context', in Corner, J. and Harvey, S. (eds), *Enterprise and Heritage*, London: Routledge.

Sheptycki, J. (1995) 'Transnational Policing and the Making of a Postmodern State', *British Journal of Criminology*, 35, no. 4, 613–35.

Sheptycki, J. (1998) 'The Global Cops Cometh', *British Journal of Sociology*, March.

Smith, D. C. (1980) 'Paragons, Pariahs, and Pirates: A Spectrum based Theory of Enterprise', *Crime and Delinquency*, 26, 358–86.

Snider, W. J. (1995) 'Development in Criminal Law and Criminal Justice. International Co-operation in the Forfeiture of Illegal Drug Proceeds', *Criminal Law Forum*, 6, 337.

Soja, E. W. (1989) *Postmodern Geographies*, London: Verso.

Sterling, C. (1994) *Crime Without Frontiers*, London: Little Brown.

Strathern, M. (1995) 'Afterword: Relocations', in Strathern, M., *Shifting Contexts: Transformations in Anthropological Knowledge*, London: Routledge.

von Hirsch, A. and Jareborg, N. (1991) 'Gauging Criminal Harms: A Living Standard Analysis', *Oxford Journal of Legal Studies*, 11, 1.

Williams, P. (1993) 'Transnational Criminal Organisations and National Security', *Survival*, 36, 96–113.
Williams, P. and Savona, E. (eds) (1995) 'The United Nations and Transnational Organised Crime', in *Transnational Organised Crime*, 1, no. 3.

4 CCTV and the Rise of Mass Surveillance Society

Clive Norris and Gary Armstrong

How, in a society of strangers, is trust possible? This is the question posed in S. Nock's book *The Costs of Privacy* (1993). The twentieth century has undergone a major transformation which, though it has increased personal autonomy, has, at the same time, broken down traditional community ties and informal modes of surveillance. Increases in social and geographical mobility, urbanisation, the rapid rise of mass transportation systems and the changing family and household structure have given rise to a society of strangers. However, as individuals are freed from the constraints of familial obligations and surveillance and disembedded from traditional community networks, it becomes more difficult for them (and others) to know what kind of persons they really are; or even if they really are who they say they are! For Nock, the cost of autonomy and privacy lies not so much in the growth of surveillance but in a change in its form: from the local and intimate, based on personal knowledge and mutuality of associations, towards the impersonal, the standardised and the bureaucratic.

In situating the social meanings of CCTV, Fyfe et al. (1998) have argued that another consequence of the rise of the 'stranger society' is the 'fear of difference'. Historically, this fear has been double-edged. For while fear may be considered undesirable, the urban form gave rise to an arena in which difference could be both managed and celebrated. Following Simmel (1971) Fyfe and Bannister (1998) contend that previously the appeal of the city lay in its provision of public space in which individuals were no longer constrained by tradition and familial ties. In the anonymity of the city they could expand their horizons through their encounters with others from different classes, cultures and backgrounds. Urban spaces could certainly excite fear, but it was a fear tinged with the frisson of discovery. If crime should occur, order on the streets was maintained not by the police but via the routine surveillance and stategic intervention of the inhabitants and proprietors of the street. However, the process of city planning with its emphasis on zoning into segregated residential, retail and business areas, and the privatisation and commodification of space epitomised by the development of the Mall, have seen the decay of traditional forms. As urban space has become subservient to the interests of business and defined by an 'ecology of fear', difference is no longer to be celebrated but a threat to be managed, segregated and excluded (Davis, 1990 and 1992).

It is the growth of the 'stranger society' that, we argue, provides one of the key historical trends underlying the push for more surveillance throughout the world. In Britain it is also necessary to move beyond the limited concerns of crime and disorder and consider the particular configuration of social trends which has given rise to British citizens becoming the most surveilled population in the world. This article describes and analyses the rise of CCTV in relation to changes in the technological, legal, political and economic context and examines the evidence as to whether indeed it does 'work' in the deterrence and detection of criminals. In conclusion it raises questions about the appropriate regulation of CCTV in a democratic society.

A BRIEF HISTORY OF CRIME CONTROL AND THE PHOTOGRAPH

The use of photography for the purposes of crime control is nearly as old as the camera itself. By the 1840s, less than a decade after the photograph became a practical reality, the 'potential for a new juridical photographic realism was widely recognised' (Sekula, 1992, p. 344). By 1854, for instance, the governor of Bristol Gaol, James Gardner, was photographing prisoners in order to identify habitual criminals, and recommended the practice be introduced 'upon a broad and national scale' (Gardner, 1854).

It was not just in the field of the Administration of Justice that photography was making its impact; the emergent discipline of criminology, with its Lombrosian concern for identifying the characteristic which 'marked off criminals as in some way different from the law abiding' (Garland 1994, p. 40), also found in the photograph an ideal tool for the recording and documentation of the criminal type. In 1883, Galton published the results of 15 years' study in his *Inquiries into Human Faculty* which, through statistically based photographic syntheses, produced composite portraits of the diseased, the healthy and the criminal (Sekula, 1992, p. 367).

These early uses of photography were concerned with two distinct problems of classification: the individual and the statistical. Individual classification was about producing a photographic record so that 'habitual criminals' could be identified by the courts in order 'to eliminate from the community a class which professedly lives by the plunder of others' (Cartwright, 1865, p. 118). This would either be through transportation or imprisonment. However, with the demise of the transportation system, and a juridical and financial limit to how long recidivist criminals could be incarcerated, the photographic record became an important element in enabling the police to monitor, and keep under surveillance, offenders within the community (Crofton, 1863; Sekula, 1992, p. 344).

Statistical classification involved documenting the physical characteristics of habitual criminals for the purposes of establishing the hereditary basis of criminality. This theoretical endeavour was seen to have practical significance. Francis Galton, who had pioneered the use of photography for the identification of the hereditary criminal, was also the founder of the eugenics movement; and in 1914 the British Eugenics Society was arguing that 'our object is to prevent these innate qualities from reappearing in future generations' by preventing 'those who have committed many crimes from becoming parents' through the prolonged incarceration and 'segregation of these criminals during their period of fertility' (Darwin, 1914, pp. 8–10).

Throughout the eighteenth and nineteenth centuries surveillance had become the primary means of controlling and disciplining institutionalised populations (Foucault, 1977). But this architecture of surveillatory power, typified by Bentham's panoptic design of the new model prison, relied on the direct, unmediated, human monitoring of the overseers. While the camera could take single 'snapshots' of subjects, these had to be captured on to a chemically coated film and then processed and developed. The power of the camera to offer a deterrent to criminal activity was therefore severely limited, and it could not be used for routine monitoring. In fact, it was not until the invention of the television, which became commercially viable in the 1930s, that the surveillance of remote sites by cameras became possible. Even then, camera surveillance was limited, since the film still had to be developed before it could be viewed – an expensive and time consuming process.

It was not until the 1960s, with the advent of videotape and the video cassette recorder (VCR), that camera images could be captured on film without the need for chemical processing, thereby allowing a cheap and simple method of recording and the prospect of instant play-back. Thus, around 130 years after the birth of photography, the camera's true panoptic potential was realised. Cameras could now be linked to centralised control rooms where the images could be remotely monitored by a single person and a permanent record kept of everything seen. As Virilio (1994, p. 44) points out, this marked a significant extension of panoptic principles. Human visual capability has difficulty competing with the high surveillance capabilities of the camera: the camera does not blink, sleep or get bored; and, unlike images captured on videotape, the results of human visual surveillance systems cannot be rewound or replayed in a court of law. The significance of these technological developments was not lost on those who wished to control crime and, in 1967, Photoscan launched CCTV into the retail sector primarily as a means of deterring and apprehending shoplifters.

For the next twenty years CCTV was mainly used in the private retail sector and the surveillance camera became a routine feature of the corner shop, supermarket and department store (Beck and Willis, 1995). Thus, while shoppers were increasingly under the ever-present gaze of the camera, this was so only within the private space of the commercial store. The blanket surveillance of citizens in fully public spaces was not yet on the agenda. The 1970s and early 1980s saw the gradual extension of CCTV from private to fully public space.

The first permanent and systematic use of CCTV outside the private retail sector came in 1975. In an effort to combat robbery and assaults on staff, London Transport introduced CCTV cameras in the semi-public space of the stations on the Northern Line of the London Underground system. Over the next decade, other small-scale systems were introduced on the eastern end of the Central Line and at Oxford Circus (Webb and Laycock, 1992).

On the roads, it was congestion rather than crime that gave the initial impetus to the deployment of cameras and, by 1974, in an attempt to speed the flow of traffic on London's streets, 145 cameras were being deployed to monitor the major arterial roads of the capital under its Central Integrated Traffic Control system (Mainwaring-White, 1983, p. 91).

The police were not slow to realise that a system introduced for one purpose could be used for another and that CCTV could be used to monitor public order incidents and demonstrations (BSSRS, 1985, pp. 41–2). The Lynx system of eight cameras was permanently installed to provide surveillance of the major rallying points for public protest in Central London demonstrations. Pickets during the miners strike of 1984–5 (Coulter et al., 1985) and football supporters (Armstrong and Guilianotti, 1998) have, among others, also been subject to camera surveillance. The Football Trust provided grants both to football clubs (so they could establish CCTV systems in their grounds) and to the police (for a mobile surveillance facility, 'the Hoolivan', which could be deployed outside the grounds) (Davies, 1996, p. 186). Overall, however, the extension into public space was limited to the monitoring of traffic flow and specific events thought likely to cause disorder; and, by implication, to people deemed to be marginal – the demonstrator, the picket and the football hooligan.

It was in 1985 that the permanent surveillance of public space, and all those who ventured into it, became a reality. The occasion? The opening of a CCTV system covering the promenade of the rather genteel English seaside town of Bournemouth. But there was no rush to follow Bournmouth's lead. By the end of the decade, there were, as far as we have been able to ascertain, still only four other public systems covering city-centre streets – in King's Lynn, Coventry, Wolverhampton and Plymouth (see also Bulos and Sarno, 1994). Thus, in 1990, 16 years after its introduction on the London Underground, and five years after the Bournemouth system was launched, CCTV continued to occupy only a marginal position in the history of detection and crime prevention. Yet, within eight years, CCTV was to become *the* crime prevention initiative of the century.

In 1998, all the major cities in the UK with a population over 500,000 boast city-centre CCTV schemes. There are in excess of 500 police and local authority schemes operating in high streets and smaller towns. What has been happening in city centres has also been mirrored on the roads and railways. There are now some 450 surveillance and enforcement cameras operating on the roads in London and on all the major motorways. Each year the systems already in place are being extended.

The railways have also seen a dramatic increase in camera surveillance. The London Underground, for example, now has over 5,000 cameras monitoring its stations and platforms. Railtrack has recently installed 1,800 cameras to watch over the 16 major stations in London (*CCTV Today*, Nov. 1997).

The public sector has not escaped. Schools (Home Office, 1996), housing estates and residential areas (*CCTV Today*, May 1996) and hospitals (*The Guardian*, 12 Feb. 1995) are increasingly coming under the camera's gaze. In this context it is not surprising that the total annual expenditure on CCTV products in 1995 was estimated to be around £300 million pounds, and there are now probably in excess of 100,000 security cameras operating in public and semi-public spaces in Britain. CCTV has moved from the private domain of the shop, through the semi-public domain of the underground system and football stadium, to the fully public domain of city streets. The trajectory which started in Bristol Gaol in 1854 with the photographing of the individual known offender has reached a point, 154 years later, where there is routine photographic surveillance of the mass of the population (regardless of status or criminal history) as they go about their daily business. This shift of focus, while technologically dependent, was not technologically determined. It was occasioned by changes in law, politics and economics. It is to these legal, political and economic changes that we now turn.

THE WIDER CONTEXT OF THE RISE OF MASS SURVEILLANCE

Penology and the Law

Feeley and Simon (1994, p. 173) have argued that during the 1990s we are witnessing a paradigm shift in the discourse of criminal justice policy, one that moves away from an Old Penology (concerned with the identification of the individual criminal for the purpose of ascribing guilt and blame, and the imposition of punishment and treatment) to a New Penology ('concerned with techniques for identifying, classifying and managing groups assorted by levels of dangerousness' based not on individualised suspicion, but on the probability that an individual may be an offender). In the context of this new penology, justice is becoming 'actuarial', and its interventions are based on risk-assessment, rather than on the identification of specific criminal behaviours. Consequently, we are witnessing an increase in the legal sanction of actuarial penal strategies such as preventative detention, offender profiling and mass surveillance (Feeley and Simon, 1994, pp. 180–5).

Historically, British legal discourse attempted to limit police surveillance, both technological and personal, on the basis of 'reasonable' (and individualised) suspicion. Thus, the rules governing stop and search, originally codified under the Police and Criminal Evidence Act (1984), required suspicion to be individualised. However, under the 1994 Criminal Justice and Public Order Act (CJPOA), the police have the power to stop any vehicle within a specified locality where an officer of the rank of Superintendent believes that incidents 'involving serious violence may take place in a locality in his area' (CJPOA, 1994, IV, 60, 1). The power to stop and search, then, no longer requires individualised suspicion and may be based on mere presence in an area. The legal safeguard which prevented police stop and search operations (a form of surveillance in their own right) being based, for example, merely on subcultural affiliation or the colour of a person's skin, has been removed.

The law has made specific classes of people subject to mass and routine surveillance in more subtle ways. The 1985 Sporting Events Act in effect gave the police the general right to stop and search coaches, minibuses and fans going to football matches. While maintaining the illusion of reasonable suspicion, the legislation is so permissively framed that the police would almost always be justified in stopping a vehicle and searching it and its occupants, since an officer merely has to have reasonable grounds for believing that alcohol is somewhere on the coach or in the possession of one of its occupants or that an act of drunkenness is being or has been permitted (English and Card, 1991, p. 507).

Finally, in serious cases (especially murder and rape) where conventional policing has revealed few leads as to the identity of the culprit, the police are increasingly resorting to the blanket DNA testing of entire communities. Testing is voluntary, but failure to provide a sample is viewed as indicative both of possible involvement and of grounds for further investigation (*Hull Daily Mail*, 13 Oct. 1996).

The rise of mass CCTV surveillance can be seen as part of a broader transformation, to a new form of penology based on 'actuarial justice', which in practice has repeatedly led to the legalised substitution of generalised suspicion in place of individualised suspicion in police investigations. However, in Britain the proliferation of cameras in public space has not been facilitated by the passing of new legislation but by the absence of legislation to regulate or check their installation. Thus, there is no legal regulation of the taking of photographs in public space or of those who wish to set up systems for the purpose of taking photographs. By contrast, in several other European countries video surveillance is regulated by statute (Maguire, 1998). Furthermore, in British law there is no general right to privacy. Those seeking to challenge the right of a local authority or of the police to photograph them would therefore not be able to do so on the grounds of invasion of privacy. Instead, complaints would have to refer to trespass and nuisance, defamation, breach of confidence or breach of copyright. According to Sharpe (1989, ch. 5) none of these would succeed in relation to a CCTV system operating in public space. The Data Protection Act may afford some limitations on the use and exchange of information about individuals whose identities are known and recorded, but there are wide-ranging exemptions for law enforcement agencies (Liberty, 1997).

The Political Context

The subtle shifts in legal discourse noted above have been mirrored by more obvious ones within the body politic. While the technology of mass video surveillance became available from the early 1970s, the political climate of the time proved to be an impediment to its swift introduction and wide implementation. The 1970s and early 1980s saw an increasingly fierce political confrontation between elements of the local state (particularly Labour-controlled local authorities) and the police regarding police accountability (Bundred, 1982; Simey, 1982). It was argued that the growing technological sophistication of policing was especially deployed against trade unionists, peace campaigners and animal rights activists, and that there was little or no democratic control over these practices (Bunyan, 1977; Bowden, 1978; Hain, 1979; Aubrey, 1981; Mainwaring-White, 1983). Many saw the inner-city riots of the early eighties as being a response to the hostile, aggressive and essentially racist policing of ethnic minorities (Scraton, 1982). These arguments, while not necessarily wholly endorsed, undoubtedly found some resonance with a population who had routinely been exposed (as part of the Ordinary Level examinations syllabus) to the dystopian vision of the total surveillance society in George Orwell's *1984*.

For those not convinced by the radical rhetoric of the drift towards totalitarianism there was, however, a more pragmatic reason for the slow uptake of CCTV – cost. In the early eighties the government was determined to reduce public expenditure. Forced to cut back on their most basic services, local authorities could not justify spending several hundred thousands pounds of capital expenditure and tens of thousands of pounds in annual running costs on installing CCTV systems – even if they had wanted to. However, at the same time as many local authorities were either ideologically or financially opposed to the introduction of CCTV, the Conservative government was dismayed by its inability to stem the seemingly unstoppable rise of recorded crime. They had increased police pay, increased staffing levels and, between 1982 and 1991, increased capital and revenue spending by 43 per cent (Audit Commission, 1993). Despite this, between 1979 and 1992 recorded crime doubled from just under three million offences per annum to over six million. In 1991 and 1992 there were two more massive rises – of 17 and 16 per cent.

In the wake of the huge rise in recorded crime, the Audit Commission, which had been set up by a previous Conservative administration to promote the responsible use of resources within government departments (HMSO, 1982), in 1982 turned its attention to the efficiency of the Criminal Investigations Departments.

The ensuing report was scathing about the inability of the police to stem rising crime rates or catch those responsible. It stated that

> given current trends in crime figures and clear-ups, by 2002 the number of recorded crimes will have exceeded 9 million and the overall clear-up rate could drop to 18 per cent. Society is thus in danger of losing the 'battle against crime'. (Audit Commission, 1993, pp. 8–9)

The Commission called for a massive expansion of proactive, intelligence-led policing, and singled out CCTV as having a major role to play in crime prevention. In October 1994, Michael Howard, the then Home Secretary, announced that two million pounds would be provided to fund CCTV by means of competitive tender (*The Guardian*, 19 Oct. 1994, p. 4).

The Home Office received 480 bids and, despite increasing the amount disbursed to £5 million, could only fund 106 of the applications (*CCTV Today*, Nov 1995, p. 5). In response to this demand, two further competitions were staged in 1995/6 and 1996/7 with £15 million allocated to each.

The competitive nature of the funding was important in a number of ways. First, the government would only grant money to fund the capital costs of the schemes on condition that partnership funding (preferably from business) was also found. Thus, for an outlay of £37 million, around £100 million of investment in CCTV was generated, though the government took no responsibility for meeting the running costs associated with the schemes. These had to be met locally – predominately by local councils. Those who were unsuccessful in their bids for funds did not suddenly relinquish their aspirations for CCTV systems. Instead, they sought other ways to fund them – by increased car-parking charges, European regeneration money, or the introduction of a special 'earmarked' tax.

CCTV was attractive to the government for reasons other than those related to crime control. It dovetailed neatly with their ideological demands for privatisation of the public sector. The private sector would be fully involved in building, equipping and maintaining the systems. Moreover, given that local councils were rate-capped and therefore unable to pay for increased expenditure through increased taxation, this silver bullet could be financed with almost no implication for the public sector borrowing requirement.

There is one final element in the story: there was by 1994 almost no political resistance to CCTV. The tragic murder of the toddler Jamie Bulger in February 1993 had served to crystallise fears about public safety. It had also dramatically launched CCTV into the public debate surrounding the control of crime. Even though CCTV had not saved the little boy from his fate, it had contributed to the identification of the killers (Smith, 1995). In the wake of the killing the public mood (as evidenced by the newspapers of the time), made those who tried to raise objections to CCTV appear either callous or too concerned with the rights of criminals. Furthermore, the Labour Party (under New Labour leader Tony Blair) was no longer in ideological battle with the police over accountability, and its shadow Home Secretary was determined that Labour could not be accused of being soft on crime or anti-police (Reiner, 1992, pp. 261–6). CCTV was eagerly embraced by the Labour leadership and even the civil liberty pressure group, Liberty, was not opposed to the introduction of mass surveillance, arguing only for statutory regulation of the CCTV industry.

The Economic Context

So far we have focused on CCTV in the context of the legal and political response to crime and its control. This is only part of the story. The recessions of the early eighties and nineties not only resulted in lengthening dole queues, they also put tremendous pressure on high street retailers who witnessed a dramatic fall in consumer spending at the same time as they were being squeezed by the emergence of out-of-town shopping centres. These cathedrals of consumerism, with their ease of parking, cheaper goods, and gleaming, purpose-built environments, were diverting consumers away from the high street. The major national chains relocated into the out-of-town sites, leaving empty premises in their wake. Smaller retailers who relied on their magnet effect then found their margins squeezed to the point of bankruptcy as they experienced the full impact of a 40 per cent decline in high street spending (Cahill, 1994, ch. 5; Reeve, 1998).

The economic decline also exacerbated feelings that town centres, as opposed to shopping malls, were dirty, threatening places. The favoured solution was to fund any new-style safe-shopping strategies, including CCTV, to attract the consumer back from the out-of-town mall (Beck and Willis, 1995; Reeve, 1998). Retailers committed to high street operations were also acutely aware that, unless the 'environmental competitiveness of the out of town retail centres and in-town malls' could be challenged, their 'continued investment in such locations would no longer be profitable' (Reeve, 1996, p. 9).

The concept of Town Centre Management (TCM) was developed by Peter Spindal of Marks and Spencer. The stated aim is 'to give coherence to the principle of managing any urban centre with a retail focus as a single entity' (Reeve, 1996, p. 7). In essence, the principle of town-centre management is to coordinate the activities of various parties with an interest in the city centre (both public and private sector) in order to promote competitive advantage. A recent study of town-centre managers by Reeve (1996) revealed that a substantial number wanted to divert certain people and activities from the city centre. Thus, a quarter wanted to discourage political gatherings, half wanted to discourage youths from 'hanging out', and half wanted to prohibit begging in the streets (1996, 22). The number of towns operating town-centre management schemes has risen from less than six in 1986 to over a hundred in 1995 (Reeve, 1996, p. 13).

The TCM movement has provided yet another impetus for CCTV, as well as creating a platform for joint, public–private funding of schemes which prioritise commercial concerns in the management of city-centre space. And it was the argument that CCTV would promote the 'feel-good factor' and revitalise the high street and city centre that provided the sales pitch to attract business funding. Thus, the Glasgow Development Corporation (GDA) stressed the financial benefits under the slogan 'CCTV doesn't just make sense – it makes business sense'. The GDA backed up this claim by calculating that CCTV would encourage 22,500 more visits to the city a year, create 1,500 jobs and produce an extra £40 million of income to city-centre business. Similar claims were made elsewhere (Fyfe and Bannister, 1996).

MASS SURVEILLANCE AND CRIME CONTROL

> CCTV is a wonderful technological supplement to the police....
> CCTV spots crimes, identifies law breakers and helps convict the
> guilty ... CCTV is a real asset to Communities: a great deterrent to
> crime and a huge reassurance to the public. (*CCTV Today*, May
> 1995)

Despite Michael Howard's enthusiasm, the government-funded
expansion of CCTV into town centres preceded any systematic evaluation of its effectiveness in reducing crime in such locations. What evidence did exist, prior to 1994, came from small-scale evaluations of
systems in: car parks (Poyner, 1991); buses (Poyner, 1988); housing
estates (Musheno et al., 1978); football stadia (Hancox and Morgan,
1975), and the London Underground (Burrows, 1979). The results of
these independent and competently conducted evaluations were 'fairly
contradictory regarding the effectiveness of CCTV as a crime prevention method' (Short and Ditton, 1995, p. 2), with some initiatives
showing no effect (Musheno et al., 1978), others suggesting high levels
of displacement of crime to other areas (rather than an overall reduction) (Burrows, 1979), and yet others showing clear reductions
(Poyner, 1988 and 1991).

The evidence used by politicians and those wanting to garner
support for the introduction of CCTV was not that of the professional
and independent evaluator. Instead, and according to Pawson and
Tilley (1994), they relied on 'post hoc shoestring efforts by the
untrained and self interested practitioner'. One set of figures to be
consistently quoted in support of CCTV came from Airdrie after
Chief Inspector Graham Pearson told a London Press conference that
total crime had been reduced by 74 per cent (*The Guardian*, 16 April
1993, p. 6) and later claimed that detection rates had almost trebled
(*The Independent*, 6 July 1994, p. 19). These figures were then given
extensive media coverage and were cited by the Home Secretary (*The
Guardian*, 19 Oct. 1994, p. 4), the Audit Commission (1993) and local
councils as providing sufficient justification for the introduction of
CCTV. However, the independent evaluation of Airdrie when it was
published two years later told a different story. While CCTV had
indeed reduced crime it was only by 21 per cent (a third of the amount
claimed by the Chief Inspector), and, rather than a tripling, the clear-
up rate had increased by only one-sixth (Short and Ditton, 1996).
Even so, in crime prevention terms, these figures are impressive,

especially as there was no evidence of displacement. The findings of other properly conducted independent evaluations of major town-centre schemes are more equivocal.

The Home Office evaluation of the Newcastle system provides the clearest support for the Aidrie findings, confirming police claims of a 19 per cent fall in crime, although the 'number of public disorder offences remained unchanged' and 'the effect of the cameras on some offences began to fade after a period of time' (Brown, 1995, p. 26). In Brighton, Squires and Measor (1997) found only a 10 per cent reduction over all and, despite claims that CCTV was helping to 'make the county one of the safest in Britain' (*CCTV Today*, Sept. 1995), violent crime actually increased by one per cent and there was some evidence that it was being displaced to the surrounding area (Squires and Measor, 1996 and 1997). In Doncaster, the overall effect of introducing CCTV was a reduction in recorded crime of six per cent, though, again, there was strong evidence of displacement – with outlying townships experiencing a 31 per cent increase in recorded crime after the cameras were introduced into the town centre (Skinns, 1997, pp. 30–5).

The Home Office evaluation of Birmingham's City Centre System found there was a 'failure of the camera system to reduce directly overall crime levels'. Indeed, robberies and theft from the person actually increased as did theft from vehicles, and there was strong evidence of displacement to the surrounding areas (Brown, 1995, pp. 34–43). Finally, in Sutton (Bulos and Grant, 1996), there was no evidence that CCTV led to a reduction in crime rates for, while there was a 13 per cent reduction in recorded crime in the areas under surveillance, crime reduced by 29 per cent in the borough as a whole. CCTV did little to reduce assaults and there was strong evidence of displacement of theft (not including shoplifting) from the streets under surveillance to inside commercial premises (Bulos et al., 1995; Sarno, 1996).

On the strength of the best available evidence, the jury is still out as to the effectiveness of CCTV. In some areas, it has led to reductions in recorded crime of about one-fifth; in others success has been far more modest and may have fuelled displacement of crime to areas without benefit of CCTV.

However, as we have argued elsewhere, (Norris and Armstrong, 1997a; 1997b) merely to focus on CCTV's impact on crime, as these evaluations have, is to focus on the outcome of mass surveillance rather than the processes through which it is achieved. CCTV enables far more than criminal surveillance. It is about the power to keep watch over a variety of situations, whether they be criminal or not. Our research involving nearly six hundred hours' observation of three CCTV control rooms showed that the gaze of the camera does not fall equally on all users of the street. In the busy high street or town centre CCTV operators are overwhelmed by images from dozens of screens displaying hundreds of people. One response to this sensory overload is for operators to single out those who, they believe, are most likely to have criminal intent. As there are usually few objective criteria on which the inference of criminal intent can be made, a limited set of 'visual clues' such as age, race, gender, clothing and deportment are relied upon to assess both moral character and behavioural intent.

The result of these common-sense working rules is the massive over-representation of male, teenage youth, and a significant over-representation of black people as targets for extended surveillance. This over-attention is not necessarily based on overt behaviour or per-sonalised knowledge: two-thirds of teenagers and three-quarters of black people observed during the period of our research were recorded as being surveilled for 'no obvious reason'. Nor could the surveillance later be justified in terms of outcome: arrest was almost solely confined to white males in their twenties.

Furthermore the research found little evidence to suggest that CCTV was having a major impact on detection rates or crime reduction through the apprehension of prolific offenders. In 592 hours of observation, involving nearly 900 occurrences of targeted surveillance, only 12 incidents led to an arrest predominately for order-related offences and crimes such as assault that arose from them.

However, these negative findings are unlikely to have a significant impact on reducing demand for more systems, primarily because negative findings are crowded out by the industry- and practitioner-led claims of 'success' which dominate the newspapers and trade magazines. Moreover, if there is further evidence of displacement, areas without CCTV will be put under increasing pressure to intro-duce their own systems. Already when serious crime occurs in an area not under camera surveillance, the absence of cameras is seen as partially responsible. For example, the *Guardian* story on the murder of a Woolworth's shop assistant ran under the headline 'Killer raided stores without security cameras': and quoted a Detective Superintendent describing Woolworth's as 'easy pickings' as they had no security cameras in their stores (*The Guardian*, 5 Nov., 1994).

Secondly, for many towns and cities there is also an element of 'keeping up with the Joneses' or, more acccurately, 'keeping up with the Airdries'. This is not just a matter of unjustified civic rivalry. As cities are increasingly competing to attract and keep inward investment from ever more mobile multinational corporations, CCTV is seen as part of a package of measures to attract and keep business and, therefore, jobs in the town.

Thirdly, and regardless of its effects on the overall crime rate, CCTV can be a very useful tool in investigating statistically rare but serious criminal offences such as acts of terrorism, murder and rape. If all the video footage from public and private systems is painstakingly examined, evidence of suspects or their vehicles may be revealed (Norris et al., 1998a). Moreover, even when CCTV is shown to have a limited impact on crime, it provides a very useful tool for the police to manage the problem of informational uncertainty and for allocating resources to incidents.

Finally, the appeal and importance of CCTV perhaps lies less in its immediate role in crime prevention and detection, than in its integration with the computerised information, intelligence and enforcement systems, through the use of the new digital technologies.

THE DIGITAL PHOTOGRAPH AND CRIME CONTROL IN THE TWENTY-FIRST CENTURY

One of the key limitations of mass surveillance systems has been their inability to link a picture of a person to a named individual. Programmes such as *Crime Watch*, *Crime Stoppers* and *Most Wanted*, with their appeals for viewers to ring in with the names of those captured on camera, are a testimony not so much to the power of CCTV as to its limitation in identifying suspects. At present the vast majority of people watched by the cameras remain anonymous. Norris and Armstrong (1997a, p. 12) found that only 3 per cent of targeted surveillances by CCTV operators were based on personalised suspicion.

The advent of digital photography is rapidly threatening to undermine this cloak of anonymity. The importance of digitalised images is that they facilitate the identification of people and vehicles *en masse*, as they move through public space. A number of related technological developments promote this possibility: the introduction of high speed/high volume digital transmission systems such as fibre-optic cables; the rapid development of image manipulation and pattern recognition software; and the development of a new generation of sophisticated database products which can not only link all existing databases, regardless of the platform they were created on, but also hold pictorial as well as textual information. While these technological developments have not been driven by crime control concerns (Norris et al., 1998a), they are rapidly being exploited by control agencies to extend and enhance the surveillance capacities of their CCTV systems.

In 1996, Dectel, a Scottish-based software company, unveiled their Crime Net facial recognition system. At present, the system is being used to compare digitalised photographs of unidentified Building Society robbers against a database of known offenders. The system is as yet only semi-automatic. Each face is coded manually according to the distinctive spatial relationships between key points such as the corner of the mouth and the bridge of the nose. This gives each face a unique identifying code. As new faces are added to the database for identification, they are measured, and automatically compared with the other images. The system has been piloted by the Metropolitan Police's Flying Squad, and Dectel aims to market the system for use by retailers to identify shoplifters and in town-centre surveillance systems (*CCTV Today*, Sept. 1996, 10–11). A more advanced system was lauched in 1997 by Software & Systems International (SSI). They described the system (*Mandrake*), as 'the ultimate in non-invasive, user friendly security'. The product information leaflet goes on to explain that 'Mandrake can be used as a recognition tool by comparing a "face in a crowd" via CCTV for instance with an existing database of known identities' (SSI, 1997, p. 1). This represents a major advance in facial recognition software and, since it exploits neural network technology which enables it to take into account 'variations of head orientation, lighting conditions, skin colour, spectacles, make-up and earrings, facial expressions, facial hair, and ageing' (SSI, 1997, p. 1), overcomes many of the limitations described previously by Norris et al. (1998a). The system was tested at Watford Football Club to see if it could automatically identify known trouble makers in the crowd and, as these trials were successful, the system is expected to become fully operational by 1998 (*Computer Weekly* 24 July 1997).

While the newest systems represent a major extension of the power of the camera, they are still limited in that they rely on pre-existing databases of photographs such as the National Criminal Intelligence Service's database of suspected football hooligans (*The Guardian*,

10 Feb. 1996). In the case of vehicles, the problem of identification is made much easier through the storing of licence plates and vehicle ownership details with the Driver and Vehicle Licensing Authority computer at Swansea, and this can be routinely accessed through the Police National Computer.

The capacity to use CCTV for the purposes of automatically identifying and logging all vehicles in an area was first used in the City of London which, in 1996, enhanced the 'Ring of Steel', set up after the IRA Bishopsgate Bombing with an automated licence plate recognition system. The system creates a computerised database of the licence plates of all cars entering and exiting the area. This can then be automatically run against any number of other databases, for instance, an index of stolen cars or the vehicles associated with known suspects. At present, the system logs and checks over 100,000 vehicles each day and these systems are set to multiply. The Metropolitan Police are planning to introduce Automatic Licence Plate recognition throughout the capital (*Independent*, 22 July 1997); Customs and Excise are investing in technology to log the licence plates of every vehicle entering the UK; and the DVLA is planning to set up a nation-wide system of cameras to identify untaxed cars on the roads, and the data from that system will also be shared with the police (*Sunday Telegraph*, 15 Sept. 1996, p. 9).

While all vehicle registrations are held by the DVLA and link licence plates to named individuals, there is no national archive of faces. At present, therefore, systems such as Mandrake can only be used to locate already-known offenders within a crowd but not to identify an as yet unknown suspect. But change is imminent: the new driver's licence with photo is almost certainly going to be held in digital form (Davies, 1996, p. 196); and the Passport agency has just announced that they are now storing passport photographs digitally on computer (*Computer Weekly*, 3 July 1997).

The latest systems not only enable automatic identification and tracking, but automated surveillance and enforcement as well. The real-time analysis of digital photographs as they enter a computer system allows automated recognition of vehicles breaking the speed limit, jumping a red light, or performing illegal U-turns. Individuals who are barred from locations such as football grounds and city-centre shops can automatically be identified and police or security guards dispatched to remove them; and the algorithms fused to match faces and identify license plates can be programmed to identify suspicious behaviour – such as a sudden congregation or dispersal of people.

DISCUSSION

The combination of digital photography, image recognition and matching software brings with it the very real prospect of a mass surveillance society – a society in which movements and interactions in public spaces are regularly monitored, recorded and logged. Maybe, therefore, public and civic life can no longer be viewed as carrying with it an expectation of anonymity. Every journey, meeting and encounter may now be officially recorded stored and matched to other centrally held records – social security, health, and criminal records, to name but a few.

We have discussed elsewhere the implications of these developments for widening the net of social control, reducing the discretionary and human element of policing, and the increased social exclusion, of undesirable 'flawed consumers' from public and semi-public space (Norris, 1995; Norris et al. 1998; and Norris and Armstrong, 1997). In this concluding discussion we develop our argument as to why the rise of mass surveillance urgently requires that proper systems of legal control and democratic accountability be put in place.

The rise of mass surveillance has resulted in many more people than the individually known offender being dossiered. Each of us becomes potential dossier-fodder as we acquire a 'digital persona' in camera-surveilled public space. Poster has argued that this 'digital persona' leads a life of its own beyond the control and, at times, even the knowledge, of the real self (Poster, 1990, pp. 97–8). Moreover, these personae have more than just an electronic existence: they have concrete material effects. This was revealed dramatically in the case of two Welsh football fans when they were erroneously entered on to the National Football Intelligence Unit's database of suspected hooligans. As a result, when the two were travelling to an overseas match in Belgian, they were identified by the Belgium police and subsequently arrested and deported. Their (erroneous) electronic classification as 'suspects' had had greater authority and impact than their otherwise-known biographies as 'respectables'. After a six-year campaign, the brothers found their indentities had been logged on various databases throughout Europe. They managed to have their names removed from the Belgian records, though it is as yet unclear how many other databases still list them (*Statewatch*: March/April 1993; July/Aug. 1996).

In the context of CCTV, database and image recognition technologies, it is not just the potential for error and the difficulty of redress which signal the need for proper oversight and accountability. If we are all to become 'data subjects' for the purposes of law enforcement we need mechanisms that ensure that systems are used fairly and equitably and in accordance with democratic principles. In the absence of democratic oversight and accountability of CCTV, we are in effect hostages to our faith that those operating and running such systems will do so in an enlightened way. Unfortunately the history of the twentieth century is replete with examples of how, in the absence of proper accountability, the surveillance capacity of the liberal state has been used for profoundly undemocratic ends: the anti-communist witch-hunts of Senator McCarthy and James Edgar Hoover in the USA, and the targeting of activists from the Campaign for Nuclear Disarmament by the security services in Britain are but two examples.

The practice of CCTV surveillance is socially differentiated along the lines of age, race, gender and class (Norris and Armstrong, 1997a; Norris et al., 1998). It is the product of discretionary decisions taken by operators, systems managers and designers as to where to place the cameras and who and what to monitor. With the development of licence plate and facial recognition technology, the ability to collate, store and analyse the behaviour of named individuals as they move through public space will become increasingly possible, and it will be driven by the move towards intelligence-based proactive policing strategies (Audit Commission, 1993). The choice of who will become the object for such intensive targeting and surveillance will also rest on a discretionary judgement.

Lustgarten has persuasively argued that the high levels of discretion which necessarily and inevitably exist within law enforcement agencies require a proper system of democratic accountability and control. Discretion brings with it the very real prospect of both over-enforcement and under-enforcement, and although each individual decision may be lawful, the cumulative effect may produce a socially biased and discriminatory form of policing (Lustgarten, 1986, esp. ch. 10). Drawing on a Rawlsian notion of justice, Lustgarten argues that:

> no structure of power [can] be regarded as just unless rational persons would agree that, within its contours, they would be willingly subject to those whose material interests were radically different from their own. Hence no relationship of power would be justified unless the person in the superior position would agree to exchanging roles with those occupying the subordinate position. ...

A rational person will consent to such an allocation of power provided it is subject to limits and controls restricting its use solely to the purposes for which it is granted ... which ensures that everyone, regardless of social or economic condition, ethnic origin or political belief, be treated equally.   (Lustgarten, 1986, pp. 62–3).

At present we have no such guarantees and, as Kitchen and Green of the Local Government Information Unit (LGIU) have observed, the cameras used so effectively in Tiananmen Square, as part of the brutal repression of the pro-democracy movement in China, were sold to the Chinese government by Seimens Plessey as an advanced traffic control system. Technology may be politically neutral, but the uses to which it is put are not. To impede the translation of a mere modern traffic control system into an advanced 'dissent capture technology' it is imperative to ensure that the regulation of all new technology adheres to the principle of democratic accountability (LGIU, 1997).

REFERENCES

Armstrong, G. and Giulianotti, R. (1998) 'From Another Angle: Police Surveillance and Football Supporters', in C. Norris, J. Moran and G. Armstrong (eds), *Surveillance*, Closed Circuit Television and Social Control. Aldershot: Ashgate.

Aubrey, C. (1981) *Who's Watching You?* Harmondsworth: Penguin.

Audit Commission (1993) *Helping with Enquiries: Tackling Crime Effectively.* London: HMSO.

Beck, A. and Willis, A. (1995) *Crime and Security: Managing the Risk to Safe Shopping.* Perpetuity Press: Leicester

Bowden, T. (1978) *Beyond the Limits of Law.* London: Quartet Books.

Brown, B. (1995) *Closed Circuit Television in Town Centres: Three Case Studies.* Crime Prevention and Detection Series Paper 73. Home Office: London

British Telecom (1995) *CCTV Transmission Guide, Remote Video Applications.* London: British Telecommunications.

BSSRS (British Society for Social Responsibility in Science, Technology of Policital Control Group) (1985) *TechnoCop: New Police Technologies,* London: Fress Association Books

Bulos, M., Chaker, W. Farish, M., Mahalingham V., and Sarno, C. (1995) *Towards a Safer Sutton? Impact of Closed Circuit Television on Sutton Town Centre.* London: London Borough of Sutton.

Bulos, M. and Grant, D. (eds) (1996) *Towards a Safer Sutton? CCTV One Year On.* London: London Borough of Sutton.

Bulos, M. and Sarno, C. (1994) *Closed Circuit Television and Local Authority Initiatives: the First National Survey.* London: School of Land Management and Urban Policy, South Bank University.

Bulos, M. and Sarno, C. (1996) *Codes of Practice and Public Closed Circuit Televison Systems*. London: Local Government Information Unit.

Bundred, S. (1982) 'Accountability and the Metropolitan Police, A Suitable Case for Treatment', in D. Cowell, T. Jones and J. Young (eds), *Policing the Riots*. London: Junction Books.

Bunyan, T. (1977) *The Political Police in Britain*. Harmondsworth: Penguin Books.

Burrows, J. (1979) 'The Impact of Closed Circuit Television on Crime in the London Underground', in P. Mayhew, R. Clarke, J. Burrows, M. Hough, and S. Winchester, *Crime in Public View*. Home Office Research Study, no. 49, London: HMSO.

Cahill, M. (1994) *The New Social Policy*. Oxford: Blackwell.

Cartwright, C. (1865) *Criminal Management*. London: National Association for the Promotion of Social Science.

Coulter, J., Miller, S. and Walker, M. (1985) *State of Siege*. London: Canary Press.

Crofton, W. (1863) *A Few Observations on a Pamphlet Recently Published by The Rev. John Burt on the Irish Convict System*. Bristol: Arrowsmith.

Darwin, L. (1914) *The Habitual Criminal*, Presidential Address to the Eugenics Education Society. London: Eugenics Education Society.

Davies, S. (1996) *Big Brother: Britain's Web of Surveillance and the New Technological Order*. Pan Books: London

Davis, M. (1990) *City of Quartz: Excavating The Future In Los Angeles*. Verso: London.

Davis, M. (1992) 'Beyond Blade Runner: Urban Control. The Ecology of Fear', *Open Magazine*, pamphlet no. 23.

English, J. and Card, R. (1991) *Butterworths Police Law*. London: Butterworths.

Feeley, M. and Simon, J. (1994) 'Actuarial Justice, the Emerging New Criminal Law', in D. Nelken (ed.), *The Futures of Criminology*. London: Sage.

Foucault, M. (1977) *Discipline and Punish: The Birth of the Prison*. New York: Vintage.

Fyfe, N. R. and Bannister, J. (1996) 'City Watching: Closed Circuit Television Surveillance in Public Spaces', *Area*, 28, no. 1, pp. 37–46.

Fyfe, N. R., Bannister, J. and Kearns, A. (1998) 'Closed Circuit Television and the City', in C. Norris, J. Moran and G. Armstrong (eds), *CCTV, Surveillance and Social Control*. Aldershot: Ashgate.

Gardner, J. (1854) *Photography as an Aid to the Adminstration of Criminal Justice*, held in the Pamphlet Collection of the London School of Economics Library.

Garland, D. (1994) 'Of Crime and Criminals: The Development of Criminology in Britain', in M. Maguire, R. Morgan and R. Reiner (eds) *The Oxford Handbook of Criminology*, 1st edn. Oxford: Clarendon Press.

Graham, S., Brooks, J. and Heery, D. (1996) 'Towns on the Television: Closed circuit TV in British Towns and Cities', *Local Government Studies*, 22, no. 3, pp. 3–27.

Hain, P. (ed.) (1979) *Policing the Police*, 2 vols. London: John Calder.

Hancox, P. and Morgan, J. (1975) 'The Use of CCTV for Police Control at Football Matches', in *Police Research Bulletin*, vol. 25, pp. 41–4.

HMSO (1982) *Efficiency and Effectiveness in the Civil Service*, Cmnd. 8616. London: HMSO.

Home Office (1996) *Closed Circuit Television Challenge Competition 1996/7 Successful Bids*. London: Home Office.

Justice (1997) *Digital Images as Evidence* – Submission to the House of Lords Select Committee on Science and Technology, September 1997. London: Justice.

LGIU (Local Government Information Unit) (1997) *Digital Images as Evidence* – Submission of the Local Government Information Unit to the House of Lords Select Committee on Science and Technology, September 1997. London: LGIU.

Liberty (1997) *Digital Images as Evidence* – Submission of Liberty to the House of Lords Select Committee on Science and Technology, September 1997. London: Liberty.

Lustgarten, L. (1986) *The Governance of the Police*. London: Sweet and Maxwell.

Maguire, M. (1998) 'Restraining Big Brother? The Regulation of Surveillance in England and Wales', in C. Norris, J. Moran and G. Armstrong (eds), *CCTV, Surveillance and Social Control*. Aldershot: Ashgate.

Mainwaring-White, S. (1983) *The Policing Revolution: Police Technology, Democracy and Liberty in Britain*. Brighton: Harvester.

Memex (1996) *Inside Information* (product information). Memex, 2 Redword Court, Peel Park, East Kilbride, G74 5PF, UK.

Musheno, M., Levine, J. and Palumbo, D. (1978) 'Television Surveillance and Crime Prevention: Evaluation an Attempt to Create Defensible Space in Public Housing', *Social Science Quarterly*, 58, no. 4, pp. 647–56.

Nock, S. (1993) *The Costs of Privacy,* Aldine De Gruyter: New York.

Norris, C. (1995) 'Algorithmic Surveillance', *Criminal Justice Matters*, 20, Summer, pp. 7–8.

Norris, C. and Armstrong, G. (1997a) *Categories of Control: The Social Construction of Suspicion and Intervention in CCTV Systems*, mimeo, Centre for Criminology and Criminal Justice, University of Hull.

Norris, C. and Armstrong, G. (1997b) *The Unforgiving Eye: CCTV Surveillance in Public Space*, mimeo, Centre for Criminology and Criminal Justice, University of Hull.

Norris, C., Moran, J. and Armstrong, G. (eds) (1998a) *CCTV, Surveillance and Social Control*. Aldershot: Ashgate.

Norris, C., Moran, J. and Armstrong, G. (1998b) 'Algorithmic Surveillance: The Future of Automated Visual Surveillance', in C. Norris, J. Moran, and G. Armstrong (eds), *CCTV, Surveillance and Social Control*. Aldershot: Ashgate.

Pawson, R. and Tilley, N. (1994) 'What Works in Evaluation Research?', *British Journal of Criminology*, 34, no. 3, pp. 291–306.

Poster, M. (1990) *The Mode of Information*. Cambridge: Polity Press.

Poyner, B. (1988) 'Video Cameras and Bus Vandalism', *Journal of Security and Administration*, 11, pp. 44–51.

Poyner, B. (1991) 'Situational Crime Prevention in Two Parking Facilities', in R. Clarke, (ed.), *Situational Crime Prevention: Successful Case Studies*, Harrow and Heston: New York.

Reeve, A. (1996) 'The Private Realm of the Managed Town Centre', *Urban Design International*, 1, no. 1, pp. 61–80.

Reeve, A. (1998) 'The Panopticisation of Shopping: CCTV and Leisure Consumption', in C. Norris, J. Moran and G. Armstrong (eds), *CCTV, Surveillance and Social Control*. Aldershot: Ashgate.

Reiner, R. (1992) *The Politics of the Police*. London: Harvester Wheatsheaf.

Sarno, C. (1996) 'The Impact of Closed Circuit Television on Crime in Sutton Town Centre', in M. Bulos and D. Grant (eds), *Towards a Safer Sutton? CCTV One Year On*. London: London Borough of Sutton.

Scraton, P. (1982) *The State of the Police*. London: Pluto Press.

Sekula, A. (1992) 'The Body and the Archive', in R. Bolton (ed.), *The Contest of Meaning: Critical Histories of Photography*. Cambridge, Mass: MIT Press.

Sharpe, S. (1989) *Electronically Recorded Evidence: A Guide to the Use of Tape and Video Recordings in Criminal Proceedings*. London: Fourmat Publishing.

Short, E. and Ditton, J. (1995) 'Does CCTV Affect Crime?', *CCTV Today*, 2, no. 2, pp. 10–12.

Short, E. and Ditton, J. (1996) *Does Closed Circuit Television Prevent Crime? An Evaluation of the use of CCTV Surveillance Cameras in Airdrie Town Centre*. Edinburgh: Scottish Office Central Research Unit.

Simey, M. (1982) 'Police Authorities and Accountability: the Merseyside Experience', in D. Cowell, T. Jones and J. Young (eds), *Policing the Riots*. London: Junction Books.

Simmel, G. (1971) 'The Metropolis and Mental Life', in P. Kasinitz (ed.), *Metropolis: Centre and Symbol of Our Times*. London: Macmillan, pp. 30–45.

Skinns, D. (1997) *Annual Report of the Safety in Doncaster Evaluation Project*. Oct. 1995–Sept. 1996. Doncaster: Safety in Doncaster.

Smith, D. (1995) *The Sleep of Reason: the James Bulger Case*. London: Arrow Books.

Squires, P. and Measor, L. (1996) *Closed Circuit TV Surveillance and Crime Prevention in Brighton: Half Yearly Report*. Brighton: University of Brighton.

Squires, P. and Measor, L. (1997) *Closed Circuit TV Surveillance and Crime Prevention in Brighton: Follow up analysis* (no pagination). Brighton: University of Brighton.

SSI (1997) *Mandrake: Face-Recognition. The Ultimate in Non-invasive, User Friendly Security*. Product Information, Software Systems International, 3 Bristol Way, Slough SL1 3QE.

Virilio, P. (1994) *The Vision Machine*. Indiana: BFI Publishing, Indiana University Press.

Webb, B. and Laycock, G. (1992) *Reducing Crime on the London Underground: An Evaluation of Three Pilot Projects*. Crime Prevention Unit Paper no. 32. London: Home Office.

5 Policing Public and Private Space in Late Modern Britain

Trevor Jones and Tim Newburn

There is a growing body of work, generally described as 'environmental criminology', which examines the way in which spatial factors impact on the activities of individuals and organisations, and how this relates to crime, criminality and disorder (see Bottoms and Wiles, 1997). Much of this work has focused criminological attention on the ways in which the urban environment, and in particular urban space, affects the way that people interact with each other and their situation. Our focus here is on one specific element within this body of work: that criminology which examines how far and in what ways different spatial forms impact on policing (Evans et al., 1992). In particular we look at changes in spatial forms and developments in policing in late modern Britain. We begin by looking at contemporary developments in British policing, in particular the growing fragmentation and complexity of 'policing' agencies which have been noted by a number of authors (see, for example, Johnston, 1992; Jones and Newburn, 1998). The second section considers previous attempts to link developments in policing directly to the changing nature of urban space, and in particular the 'mass private property' thesis of Shearing and Stenning (1981). Drawing on a recent study of private policing (Jones and Newburn, 1998) we then examine how far this thesis fits with the British evidence. We conclude with a brief discussion of the implications of these developments for the future of policing in Britain.

POLICING IN LATE MODERN BRITAIN

The growing complexity of policing forms has been a central theme of much recent writing about the police. Reiner (1992) has argued that in a number of senses policing in end-of-the-century Britain displays the characteristics of fragmentation and pluralism which have become

99

associated with the alleged transition from 'modernity' to a new social order. Johnston's work (1992, 1996) has emphasised 'sectoral blurring' and complexity of policing forms in Britain, with policing services delivered by a range of agencies, which cannot simply be divided into the categories of public and private. This work builds upon the explosion of criminological interest in the police in Britain which has developed over recent decades (see Reiner, 1995). Until relatively recently, the bulk of this attention was focused almost exclusively on public constabularies and rarely strayed to the 'private sector', or to other forms of public law enforcement. However, beginning with the work of South (1988) and continued by Johnston (1992), there has been a growing focus on policing in a broader sense. It is possible to identify three general aspects to the growing complexity of policing forms in Britain. First, the growing pressure of managerialism within the police organisation, summarised by Johnston (1996) as the appearance of a 'privatisation mentality'. Secondly, and the most commented-upon aspect, the significant growth of the private security industry. Thirdly, the growing interest in the policing functions carried out by bodies other than public constabularies and the private security industry.

The Privatisation Mentality

Recent years have seen a rash of reforms of policing in Britain, many of which form part of a long process of official concern about the effectiveness of the police, dating back to the early 1980s. In 1983 the Home Office circular 114/83, *Manpower, Effectiveness and Efficiency in the Police Service* signalled the extension of the British government's Financial Management Initiative to the police service. This sought to promote better value for money across a range of government departments and public services. During the 1980s the Home Office issued a series of circulars (105 and 106/88, and 81/89) which took the financial management of the police several steps further. The growing emphasis on performance review, efficiency and value for money was also promoted by the Audit Commission. From the mid-1980s onwards the Audit Commission published a series of papers which applied private sector business management principles to policing. The basic aim was to encourage the police to link resources to outputs, to measure performance more effectively, and to consider what their core functions and central organisational objectives are. In particular, the Commission recommended the flattening of police organisational structures, the devolution of responsibility and financial delegation, and the general application of performance measurement and targets. The 'market-isation' of the police service came to a head with the government's proposals for reform in the early 1990s. The Sheehy Inquiry and the White Paper on *Police Reform* presented the most radical blueprint yet for the reorganisation of the police in Britain along market lines (for details see Jones and Newburn, 1997). Although some of the more radical proposals were in the event dropped, significant elements of the reform package survived to become part of the Police and Magistrates' Courts Act 1994. This applied a purchaser–provider split to policing, made police authorities responsible for the publication of local 'business plans' for policing; introduced a system of key national objectives with attendant performance indicators; and included various other measures with the aim of enhancing the managerial efficiency of the police service. For the first time police forces were allowed to contract with local authorities to provide extra policing services, further establishing the principle of private purchasing of public policing.

The Growth of Private Policing

It is generally accepted that private security is a growth industry across most industrialised nations. Many of the available data concern North America, where interest in private policing has a long history (Shearing and Stenning, 1981). Comparable data for Britain have been harder to come by, though a range of estimates of the size of the industry have been made (McClintock and Wiles, 1972; Randall and Hamilton, 1972; Bunyan, 1977; George and Button, 1994). Such estimates suggest that although its private security industry has grown less extensively than in North America, there has also been significant growth in Britain.

The best available estimates for change in employment over time are derived from Census estimates of employment in the 'security and related' occupational categories.[1] They suggest that there has been a sustained growth in employment in security occupations over the last 40 years or so. The main period of expansion appears to have occurred during the 1960s and 1970s, with the rate of growth having slowed down in later years. The figures suggest that since 1951 there has been a very large increase (approximately 240 per cent) in the numbers of people employed in security and related occupations (see Table 5.1).

We should note that these figures do not include employment in what may well have been the major growth area, namely, the manufacture, installation and maintenance of electronic security equipment.

Table 5.1   Employment in the public police and private security
(Great Britain, 1951–91)

Year	Security occupations	Police officers
1951	46,950	75,650
1961	99,820	100,130
1971	129,670	118,770
1981	136,240	129,910
1991	158,920	148,930

Source: Census of Population (occupational estimates).

None the less, the available data are a useful source, for much of the current debate is based on the assumption of a dramatic expansion in employment, particularly in what has been termed 'manned guarding'. We can compare these trends with figures charting the growth in employment of police officers. The rate of growth since 1971 in numbers of police officers is quite similar to that of 'private security personnel' as measured by Census estimates. Taking comparisons back to 1951, these estimates suggest that police officer numbers have increased by almost 100 per cent, significantly less than the growth in security occupations (which doubled in size between 1951 and 1961). This indicates that employment in security and related occupations probably overtook that of police officers during the 1960s, since when both have shown similar rates of expansion.

The private security sector has not been expanding in size alone. A number of commentators have noted that it has also been growing in 'pervasiveness'. By this they usually mean that the functional remit of private security has grown, with the industry increasingly impinging on areas previously seen as the preserve of the public police. For example, much attention has been focused on the alleged growth of private security patrols on housing estates (McManus, 1996), the privatisation of functions such as prisoner and court escort services and the enforcement of local parking regulations (Jones and Newburn, 1998).

Other Forms of Policing

There is a range of organisations – outside of public constabularies – which have, as a central or defining purpose, formal 'policing' functions in terms of crime investigation, law enforcement, order maintenance, or crime prevention. In Britain there have been several studies of the law enforcement activities of public bodies other than Home Department police forces (*inter alia* Loveland, 1989; Hutter, 1988; Miller and Luke, 1977), bodies characterised by Johnston (1992) as 'hybrid' policing agencies, being neither Home Department police forces nor those individuals and organisations which make up what is generally referred to as the private security industry. Although the policing literature has paid little attention to these bodies, recent work has shown the central role they play in local regulation and law enforcement. Although such bodies are often included in discussions about the contemporary fragmentation of policing agencies, in fact their growth should probably be analysed independently of the rise of private policing. It appears to us that such agencies are largely related to the growth of the welfare state and the associated regulatory functions of national and local government since the beginning of the twentieth century. These policing bodies are an important element in pluralist contemporary policing.

SPATIAL EXPLANATIONS OF CONTEMPORARY TRENDS IN POLICING

The Nature of Urban Space

The term 'space' is used here in a broad sense. It includes the physical environment and the way it is configured (for example, the built environment of the city), and also the interactional and experiential space which, although it has some physical attributes, is also a product of social convention. As Reiss argues: 'the definition of space, and others in relation to it, is a social construction of one's reality as one moves about in everyday life' (Reiss, 1988). Other more abstract notions of space include Hannah Arendt's 'public realm' (Arendt, 1963), which is defined as a distinctive field of action which emerges where people deliberate and act collectively. This notion of 'public space' has no specific location (in geographical terms), and is structured by institutions, political parties and movements rather than by physical boundaries. Finally, there is now a 'cyberspace' of technological information exchange, which itself has major implications for policing (see Wall, 1997).

There is a large and growing literature about the development of space in the modern city (see Taylor et al., 1996). Some of the most influential writings about the growth of modern cities combine both the experiential and physical aspects of space. In this sense, 'public space' has been presented as a realm of 'heterogeneous sociability' (Kasinitz, 1995). It is argued that social life in the modern city is increasingly polarised between the important public realm (the state, the market and bureaucratic organisations) and a private realm of intimacy and emotionality. Perhaps the main focus of much of this work has been on the implications of the built environment and the design and uses of physical space within the urban environment (Jacobs, 1961). Feminist writers have distinguished another conception of space, in which the public realm of the state, market and other life is contrasted with the more hidden 'domestic' sphere of family. The conceptual starting point in feminist discourse is to define what is to count as 'the private' (the family), and the 'public' realm is a residual category outside of this. This view of 'private space' has important implications for the way in which the 'family' is policed (Stanko, 1988).

While we may define different kinds of space as 'public' or 'private', it is important to note that the 'spaces' are rarely homogenous. Within different kinds of urban space there may, and probably will, exist a host of relatively 'public' and relatively 'private' spaces, delineated both by social convention and by physical controls. In an approach which parallels some recent work on public and private sectors, Hunter's (1995) analysis of on urban space includes an intermediate spatial arena between 'public' and 'private'. He distinguishes between three different kinds of 'order': the public, the parochial and the private, each with its particular institutional and spatial domain. This approach questions the usefulness of a stark division between public and private sectors, concluding that it is necessary to allow for an intermediate sphere of parochial order. The private order focuses around the institution of the family and informal 'primary groups' based on sentiment, social support and esteem. The parochial order arises from the interlocking of these networks and local institutions – such as local stores, schools, churches, community associations and so on – which service the 'sustenance' needs of the local residential community. Finally, the public social order is found mainly in the bureaucratic agencies of the state. The 'public order' is ultimately structured by the state, which claims a monopoly over the legitimate use of force. It is argued that a weakening of the parochial institutions through which much informal social control has been exercised, linked in particular to a reduction in commitment to the geographical locality, has led to control being increasingly based at the public level. Although crime and the fear of crime has led to overwhelming demands on the police and criminal justice system, arguably the private and parochial orders provide for much more effective social control. Kasinitz (1995) argues that the structure of 'public life' is in decline in many urban areas. The salience of poverty and homelessness in many large cities has caused the private lives of the destitute to emerge into public places. Crime and social disorder have discouraged people from using public spaces and participating in public life (Skogan, 1990). Some political and design measures which are intended to reduce crime may actually diminish further the likelihood of meaningful participation in public life by most people (Coleman, 1985). Writers concerned to link developments in policing with changes in the nature of urban space have also turned their attention to an apparent shrinkage in the form of the public domain, with an increasing focus upon the 'privatisation of public space'.

The Privatisation of Public Space

We will focus upon two aspects of the privatisation of public space. The first concerns the 'mass private property thesis' of Shearing and Stenning (1981, 1983, 1987) which directly links changes in policing to developments in urban space. Indeed, Shearing and Stenning explain the growth of 'private policing' in North America primarily in terms of the growth of 'mass private property'. They argue that the growth of private security, both in extent and pervasiveness, is due to the increasing amount of 'public' space that is actually privately owned. In sum, they argue that the natural domain of the public police is shrinking whilst that of private security is growing. This, according to Shearing and Stenning, is a more fundamental cause of what is happening in policing than direct privatisation, or financial constraints on public police expenditure.

By 'mass private property' Shearing and Stenning are generally referring to large shopping malls; privately-owned 'gated' communities and large, enclosed residential blocks, private parks and other open spaces; and large recreational and educational complexes. Although these large spaces are privately owned, they are more or less routinely open or accessible to significant numbers of people. Thus, more and more 'public life' is now taking place on 'private property', and policed by the corporate agents of the property owners. Thus, it is argued, more people are dwelling in large private blocks, gated communities or privately-owned condominiums, rather than in houses on traditional public street patterns. Furthermore, people spend more time shopping in privately-owned malls rather than on traditional 'public' high streets, and spend leisure time in large private complexes rather than in publicly-owned parks and open spaces. 'The modern development of mass private property controlled by vast corporate conglomerates, and so frequently consisting of essentially "public places", is the critical change that has paved the way for the modern growth and influence of private security' (Shearing and Stenning, 1981, p. 240). Shearing and Stenning have argued that, as a consequence, a 'new feudalism' is emerging, in which private corporations have the legal space and economic incentives to do their own policing. In this view, mass private property has given large corporations a sphere of independence and authority which can rival that of the state. What we are witnessing, therefore, is not so much the emergence of an oppressive state-corporate alliance, but a fracturing of sovereignty and a decline in the pervasiveness of state power. What is emerging instead is a complex network of micro-systems of power, within which ultimate power is not wielded by a single subject. There is no central source of command and no practical centre of political life. In the future, governance is less likely to be monopolised by nation-states and more likely to be in the hands of either local communities or, even more likely, major corporations.

Another aspect of the privatisation of public space concerns changes in the design or use of what is clearly 'publicly-owned' space in order to give it the appearance of being private. The work of Oscar Newman (1973) and Alice Coleman (1985) has been influential in encouraging policy-makers to try to 'design out' crime. By manipulating physical features of the urban environment it is argued that people's opportunities, and even their propensities to commit offences, can be reduced. Although these hypotheses have been challenged, the practical recommendations have proved attractive to policy-makers anxious to find measures to reduce crime. One of the most influential ideas emerging within this school of thought has been that of 'defensible space' – the territoriality which leads people to protect places. This has had a significant impact on urban design, with sometimes subtle changes made with the aim of discouraging 'strangers' from moving into particular spaces. Contemporary designers have taken up this approach by, for example, increasing the use of 'cul-de-sac' developments intended to discourage people from using roads as a thoroughfare, or designing areas through which there is public right of way in such a manner that this right of way is disguised; the area looking more like private than public property, with the hoped-for consequence of discouraging 'outsiders' (see Jones and Newburn, 1998). A further development involves increasing the visibility of private security patrols in public areas. Arguably, the purpose of such patrols is to discourage access to the public space they are guarding, at least in the case of individuals or groups considered to constitute a threat.

Both these aspects of the privatisation of public space have strong resonance with Mike Davis's description of developments in contemporary Los Angeles (Davis, 1990). Davis argues that changes in the spatial configuration of many North American cities have undermined the concept of healthy public spaces. Many of the large public spaces in large cities were originally designed as 'safety valves', in which people from various backgrounds could interact in common places and recreations. According to Davis, the picture in many late modern American cities could not be further from this: 'today's upscale, pseudo-public spaces – sumptuary malls, office centers, culture acropolises and so on – are full of invisible signs warning off the underclass "other"'. In a similar vein, Reiss (1988) has argued that citizens are increasingly becoming 'prisoners' of privately-protected places and that public places are viewed as unprotected by the public police. He notes that in the late modern city, a place of anonymity and impersonality, private space is becoming increasingly controlled and tightly-defined. According to North American authors, the consequences of what has been termed the 'enclavisation' of suburban USA with the comparatively wealthy isolating themselves in privately-protected 'bubbles of security', are dire for the public spaces that remain. Davis (1992) argues that outside the 'gated communities' of the middle classes the increasingly militarised public police are left to deal with the criminalised poor in what have become 'places of terror'.

> The American city ... is being systematically turned inside out – or, rather, outside in. The valorized spaces of the new megastructures and super-malls are concentrated in the centre, street frontage is denuded, public activity is sorted into strictly functional compartments, and circulation is internalized in corridors under the gaze of private police. (Davis, 1990, p. 226)

Davis's vision is often held aloft as the prime example of the consequences of postmodernisation on both urban environments and on security arrangements in such environments. Indeed, we have been struck by the frequency with which commentators use Mike Davis's description of LA as a handy summary of what is emerging in the UK (see, for example, South, 1997). We are sceptical about this thesis and in the following section we consider the extent to which such developments in urban space can realistically be linked to changes in policing in late modern Britain.

LINKING SPATIAL AND POLICING DEVELOPMENTS IN BRITAIN

Both of the main elements of the 'privatisation of public space' argument have clearly struck a chord with commentators on this side of the Atlantic. In this section, we draw on our recent study of private policing (Jones and Newburn, 1998) and examine the evidence for the pervasiveness of these developments in the British context.

Although actual figures indicating the extent of growth of 'mass private property' in Britain are difficult to find, there is a widespread impression that the growth of these kinds of space has been substantial and that this has resulted in public policing being increasingly displaced by private security. Perhaps the most-cited example of Shearing and Stenning's mass private property concerns the growth of the private shopping mall, so visible in most North American urban areas, though little studied in the UK (for an exception, see Taylor et al., 1996). When we examine developments in the retail sector in Britain we find that they do display some parallels with the North American experience. For example, authors have noted the relative decline of 'high street' shops and expressed fears for the future of town centres in the face of what has been termed the 'Americanization' of British shopping (Poole, 1991). Figures show that over the past twenty years there has been a clear growth of mass private property in the retail sector (Beck and Willis, 1995). In particular, recent decades have seen a trend of concentration, and especially the growth of supermarkets or superstores, in out-of-town retail parks and large shopping complexes. These developments reached a peak during the 1980s. For example, in 1983 there were 1,270 superstores in Britain taking up 8.6 per cent of all retail space. By 1992 this had increased to 3,500 of these stores accounting for 19 per cent of retail space. The first shopping centres opened in Britain during the 1960s and by the early 1970s there were around 200 (Poole, 1991). This number multiplied around five times to nearly 1,000 such complexes by 1994. Out-of-town retail parks showed particularly rapid growth during the 1980s, with the first one opening in 1982. A decade later this number had grown to 260. By the mid-1990s, there were five 'giant' shopping centres in Britain, and they remain relatively rare, both in terms of total numbers and floorspace (British Council of Shopping Centres, 1993). All these developments have clearly impacted on traditional town centres and high streets, and in some areas they have contributed to what has been termed a 'dough-nut syndrome' (Beck and Willis, 1995), whereby consumers are lured to out-of-town shopping complexes rather than high-street shops.

Although such developments are undoubtedly significant we should be cautious about placing too much emphasis upon them. For example, from the early 1990s onwards there is clear evidence of a slowdown in some of these trends linked to official attempts to protect the traditional town centre. A policy of refurbishment of town centres has been adopted in many local authority areas, increasingly supported by central government policy. For example, the Department of the Environment announced new guidelines in 1994 which were intended to discourage further out-of-town complexes. Planning restrictions were tightened in response to recommendations from the House of Commons Select Committee on the Environment. By the mid-1990s only four out of the 50 giant shopping complexes planned during the 1980s had actually been built, and figures showed a steep fall in the proportion of supermarket planning applications that were successful. Overall, there have undoubtedly been important developments of mass private property in the retail sector which have almost certainly increased the degree to which the general shopping public are policed by private security rather than the public police. However, this growth had not been as extensive as has been the case in North America, and indeed has slowed significantly in recent years as a result of government planning controls.

Development of other kinds of mass private property has been far more limited in Britain than in North America. For example, in terms of large 'privately-policed' work complexes, the long-term trend in Britain is towards smaller rather than larger workplaces. The last twenty years have seen a marked decline in the proportion of total employment in larger establishments and people are increasingly likely to work for small firms (employing less than 100 people), which by the early 1990s accounted for about half of non-government employment in Britain (Department of Trade and Industry, 1995).

Shearing and Stenning suggest that it is mass private property in the form of residential accommodation – 'the row of single or double family dwellings [being] pulled down and replaced by a massive high rise apartment building, or a multiple condominium town-house complex' (1981, p. 229) – which provides one of the clearest examples of the decline in the sphere of the public police. There have undoubtedly been substantial developments of this kind in North America, and some sources suggest that the increase in privately-owned residential complexes has been so great that it probably accounts for the most significant privatisation of US local government responsibilities (ACIR, 1989). One of the most important kinds of development in this regard is the 'community association' in which each owner is a member of a property organisation, having to comply with its rules and also pay for a number of services provided collectively. However, such developments have been much more limited in Britain (Lavery, 1995). As Bottoms and Wiles (1994b) have argued, one of the significant differences between metropolitan development in many North American cities and those in post-war Britain, is the massive intervention by local government in housing markets. This perhaps prevented the pattern of 'enclavisation' appearing so obviously in Britain, although there are undoubtedly some places where elements of this process are apparent. In London, for example, such housing is visible in the newly developed Docklands areas, where many of the new riverfront developments are apartment-style dwellings, sometimes guarded by private security contracted by the property managers. There is little evidence, however, of any major transformation in popular residential dwelling patterns in Britain. For example, recent reports from the General Household Survey, show little change over recent years in the proportion of family units living in flats or apartments. The proportion of households in the Survey which were described as detached, semi-detached or terraced houses, was about the same in 1993 as it was in 1971. The main development of large residential blocks in British cities occurred during the 1960s, but these developments mainly involved public housing, and few of these developments, if any, were policed by private security.[2] Finally, although there may be a move towards more of these US-style developments in the future, this, as Lavery noted, 'would have limited impact as there is relatively little new development in the UK, especially when compared to the US'. Indeed, in our local study site a key aim of the local authority planning department's policy was to 'revitalise public space'. This was a direct example of the type of local government intervention which has shielded some urban areas in Britain from the worst effects of the unregulated property market. Through planning restrictions, the local council influenced the design of residential and leisure buildings, and actively used such influence to protect against cul-de-sac developments and other design features linked with enclavisation and 'deadened space'.

There are, therefore, important differences between the North American and the British context. In particular, there have been far fewer privately-owned developments in the housing and educational sectors. For example, in the USA the housing market has traditionally been free of government controls, and there has been very little public provision in the housing market (Boleat and Taylor, 1993). This has allowed a greater development of large privately-owned residential estates and complexes, and the development of 'gated communities' policed by private security rather than the public police (Benson, 1990). In North America, many universities are privately-owned, in contrast to the UK where this remains very rare.

Although elements of the mass private property thesis are undoubtedly detectable, the thesis does not provide a full explanation of what is happening to policing in Britain. In fact, it appears that the notion of 'mass private property' also does not capture the full and growing complexity in spatial forms that is visible. As our recent study of policing in Wandsworth found, it is impossible to divide the variety of spatial forms which exist within one locality into opposing categories of 'public' and 'private'. In fact, many publicly-owned areas are crucially 'private spaces', perhaps the best examples being military establishments. As we noted above, as well as more public life taking place on private property, more public spaces (in that there is full public right of way to or through them) are being 'privatised' by subtle design and surveillance techniques. As well as the increasing disjuncture between private ownership and private space, the range of institutional owners of property and providers of policing is becoming more complex. Recent reforms in education, health and other aspects of policy, have encouraged providers of public services increasingly to imitate aspects of commercial enterprise. Although most schools and colleges remain largely funded from taxation, they are increasingly required to operate within cash-limited budgets, meet set performance standards, and to raise their own income. Similar developments are visible in the 'social market' reforms of the National Health Service, leading to the establishment of independent Hospital Trusts and General Practice Fundholders. Many of the examples of 'mass private property' described by Shearing and Stenning have, in Britain at least, not been owned by private corporations. Rather, many educational institutions, leisure complexes and hospital sites have been owned and run by 'the state' – in some form or other – or other 'non-market' organisations. For this reason, we would argue that 'mass hybrid property' has been of greater relevance in Britain than 'mass private property'.

Though a complex web of spatial forms is appearing, the terms 'public' and 'private' are not redundant. We can postulate a model of public and private space with degrees of 'publicness' or 'privateness' on a continuum. At one end, there are large, open spaces, owned by the national or local state on behalf of all, accessible to large numbers of people with few restrictions. At the other – and more 'private' – end of the spectrum there is the individual household, smaller, less accessible, and largely hidden from wider society.

There is clearly a significant and growing amount of 'blurring' in the boundaries between policing bodies in late modern Britain (Jones and Newburn, 1998). Whilst much debate has focused upon what we have called the 'sectoral' elements of these boundaries, (i.e. whether bodies are publicly funded from taxation or by other means), our primary concern in this chapter has been the degree to which 'spatial' boundaries are also becoming blurred. A dominant theme has been the apparent growing spatial remit of 'private' policing bodies as compared with public bodies. However, we would argue that although the spatial blurring is detectable, it would be overly simplistic to argue that the trends move in one direction only, i.e. away from public police. Indeed, our local study provided a number of counter-examples to this theme.

The apparent decline of the 'natural habitat' of the public police, and simultaneous growth in 'spaces' more usually occupied by 'private police', is insufficient to explain the changes that are taking place in policing on the ground. Thus, as we saw above, although some national indicators suggest growth in mass private property, this has not been a dramatic transformation – certainly by North American standards. This leads us to question the adequacy of the 'mass private property' thesis. The growth of mass private property, though important, is not the fundamental source of change. We also need to be careful about drawing too clear a link between types of space and forms of policing. Not only did we find that the spatial forms appearing at the local level were far more complex than just public, private and 'public-private', but that in those spaces where private security guards are operating, in many cases it has not been the public police who have been replaced. Parks, hospitals and college sites – where private security is increasingly visible – arguably never formed part of the 'natural domain' of the public police. They were certainly not sites that were subject to routine patrol by public police. Security guards have been employed, not because of the disappearance of the public police from these sites, but often because of the perceived lack of effectiveness of what remained (largely as a result of cuts in government expenditure) of other agents of less formal social control, such as caretakers, receptionists and park-keepers. Thus, rather than presenting a picture of policing in Britain which is characterised by the progressive replacement of public by private policing bodies, the reality appears to be one of growth in both private security and public policing (albeit at different rates) with the primary consequence that policing overall has been significantly formalised. While these more formal kinds of control are more visible, it is possible that they are less effective than the informal controls exerted previously, but which appear to have broken down. This area of policing has important parallels with Hunter's arguments outlined above about the decline in the parochial sphere, and the greater pressure growing upon more formal agents of social control.

Another important finding from our local study is that although there has clearly been a substantial blurring of the spatial boundaries between policing bodies, this should not be exaggerated, for 'public' and 'private' bodies generally continue to operate in separate spheres. Furthermore, where blurring has occurred, it has by no means developed in one direction. Thus, whilst most criminological attention is focused on the increasing penetration of private policing bodies into public space, it is also the case that in some ways 'public policing' in late modern Britain is penetrating more into 'private space' than in the past. One notable example is the growth in police interventions in domestic violence and child abuse (Jones et al., 1994). Such investigations have taken them into the realm of the family to a degree that was unprecedented even 20 years ago. Police responding to calls from the public operate across a variety of types of space. Also, in other areas there have been attempts to extend the spatial remit of the public police. For example, following the murder of London headteacher Philip Lawrence, the government announced their intention of providing for a power of stop and search on school premises for police officers. Furthermore, the Criminal Justice and Public Order Act 1994 introduced a new criminal offence of aggravated trespass which extended the powers of the public police on private property. Finally, recent legislation has increased the powers of the police to tap telephones, bug premises, and so on, all of which arguably enhances their powers to work in private space. The focus upon the dichotomy between public constabularies and the private security also simplifies what is happening in terms of spatial remits. It is worth emphasising that some 'public policing bodies', such as Environmental Health Officers and Health and Safety Inspectors, have extensive rights of access to private property (far greater powers than the police do in this regard). In fact, the vast majority of the 'bread and butter' work of these bodies takes place in 'private space' in some form or other (in peoples' homes or businesses).

CONCLUDING COMMENTS: POLICING BEYOND THE MILLENNIUM

Clearly there have been fundamental changes in policing in Britain in recent decades. Moreover, some of these developments are related in complex ways to changes in the nature of urban space. Private security is now much more visible than was the case 30 years ago. The growth of mass private property has played a part in this development. While important changes have taken place, particularly in the retail sector, it appears that these are not nearly as far advanced as is the case in the USA (and show little likelihood of ever approximating the North American experience). As we have been at pains to point out, however, it is important not to over-emphasise this development in explanations of the rise of private security more generally in Britain. What empirical evidence there is suggests a gradual transition has been taking place rather than the 'quiet revolution' posited by Shearing and Stenning. There has been a tendency in much criminological writing to focus over-much on the guarding sector of the private security industry. As we move into the late 1990s and beyond, the focus will arguably shift away from staffed services – security guards in caps and uniforms. Current developments suggest that the electronic and physical security equipment sector will be of growing importance. It may well be that developments in such areas as home-shopping, home-working and, increasingly, home-based leisure activities, are 'privatising life' (for some social groups at least), and that the impact will be more significant than the changes brought about by the restructuring of urban space on which we have been concentrating here.

Where does all this leave us? We would contend that the relationship between changing forms of urban space and developments in policing cannot be adequately explained solely or even mainly by reference to the rise of mass public property. There are clear dangers in translating too directly from the North American experience. We are still some distance from the 'enclavisation' and privately patrolled domestic fortresses of Mike Davis's dystopian vision of modern Los Angeles. Crucially, in relation to urban space, there is both the process of fragmentation we referred to above and what we might refer to here as the progressive commodification of space (Jones and Newburn, 1998). One of the most significant trends associated with urbanism is the increasing extent to which life is lived in settings which are almost exclusively manufactured. The extent to which these settings can be considered to be 'public' or 'private' – and the process of fragmentation giving rise to the increasing visibility of what we have termed 'hybrid space' – form the backdrop to the key arguments about the nature of the contemporary city and the changing nature of the policing of urban environments.

The important point here is that the realities of space in late modern society are so complicated that they cannot adequately be captured by the private/public dichotomy. 'Hybrid spaces' – those which are neither unambiguously public nor unambiguously private – complicate the picture. Though it remains the case that the more 'private' space is the more likely it is to be policed by 'private' policing organisations (Jones and Newburn, 1988), and vice versa, this relationship is not straightforward or uniform. To this extent, changes in the nature of space are likely to affect the policing division of labour. However, other processes are at work. Fiscal constraint limits the ability of public policing organisations to meet public demands (Spitzer and Scull, 1977; Morgan and Newburn, 1997) and the functional and geographical breadth of public policing organisations further hamper them in the 'competition' with private providers with highly specific functional remits and geographical boundaries. The development of new technologies and the information society (Bell, 1973) has contributed to the progressive commodification of 'security'. The processes of globalisation and localisation which have been most associated with the notion of late modern social change (see Bottoms and Wiles, 1997) have placed new limitations on the 'Sovereign State' (Garland, 1996) and, as a consequence, on that body exercising the state's legitimate use of force. Explanation of changes in the policing division of labour cannot be reduced to issues of space, important though these are. Understanding the changing nature of space, particularly in the urban context, will continue to be central to understanding the nature of policing, but the spatial dimension of policing is interconnected with other dimensions of policing: the functional, sectoral, legal and geographical (for a full discussion see Jones and Newburn, 1998). Each of the dimensions has had a role to play in the changing policing division of labour, of which the growth of private security has been one highly visible part.

We would further argue that the above discussion should lead one to guard against any straightforward functional linking of changes in policing with what is happening to urban space in late modern societies. Urban space has changed and continues to change, as does policing. However, it appears that something more fundamental is happening, something which underpins developments in both urban space and policing. Although a comprehensive theory to explain what is going on has yet to be attempted – and we have not attempted to do so here – we would argue that a way forward is suggested by the raft of social, economic, cultural and political developments which have been associated with the 'late modern change thesis' (see Johnston, 1996 for a summary). The linked series of changes connected to globalisation, to the 'decline' of the nation state, commodification, social fragmentation and pluralism, provide a framework that captures much of what appears to be happening to contemporary policing. They help us to explain not only changes in property relations, but broader changes in the role of the state, its 'fiscal crisis', the commodification of security, and the development of a sense of 'ontological insecurity' (Giddens, 1990). Helpful though such work is, however, considerably more research is required to examine in greater detail the impact of these changes on policing and social life. The 'late modern change' thesis does not yet provide an adequate theory of changes in contemporary policing because it is largely unhelpful regarding possible mechanisms of causation. Indeed, there are times when the thesis sounds crudely deterministic. It has been noted, for example, that 'late modern' developments are appearing to different extents in modern societies (Lash and Urry, 1987). At the very least this suggests that 'sovereign states' are not passive reactors to unstoppable global forces. We must be careful in our assumptions about the relationship between structural social change and the nature of policing and security. It would certainly be a mistake to assume that policing organisations are merely empty vessels being tossed around on the seas of global social change.

NOTES

1. Although because of changes in occupational classifications and enumeration techniques over the longer period these figures should be regarded as approximate indicators of trends rather than exact estimates.
2. Recent years, however, have seen some local councils introduce private security patrols in council housing estates and blocks, and CCTV surveillance is increasingly installed in public housing estates.

REFERENCES

Advisory Commission on Intergovernmental Relations (1989) *Residential Community Associations: Private Governments in the Intergovernmental System?* ACIR: Washington, DC.

Arendt, H. (1963) *On Revolution*. New York: Viking Press.

Beck, A. and Willis, A. (1995) *Crime and Security: Managing the Risk to Safe Shopping*. Leicester: Perpetuity Press.

Bell, D. (1973) *The Coming of Post-Industrial Society*. New York: Basic Books.

Benson, B. L. (1990) *The Enterprise of the Law: Justice Without the State*. San Francisco: Pacific Research Institute for Public Policy.

Bittner, E. (1980) *The Function of the Police in Modern Society*. Cambridge, Mass.: Oelgeschlager, Gunn and Hain.

Bobbio, N. (1989) *Democracy and Dictatorship*. Minneapolis: University of Minnesota Press.

Boleat, M. and Taylor, B. (1993) *Housing in Britain*. London: The Building Societies Association.

Bottoms, A. E. and Wiles, P. (1994a) 'Crime and Insecurity in the City', paper presented at the International Course organised by the International Society of Criminology, Leuven, Belgium.

Bottoms, A. E. and Wiles, P. (1994b) 'Understanding Crime Prevention in Late Modern Societies', paper presented to the 22nd Cropwood Round Table Conference, Preventing Crime and Disorder: Targeting Strategies and Community Responsibilities, Cambridge: Institute of Criminology.

Bottoms, A. E. and Wiles, p. (1997) 'Environmental Criminology', in M. Maguire, R. Morgan and R. Reiner (eds), *The Oxford Handbook of Criminology*. Oxford: Clarendon Press.

British Council of Shopping Centres (1994) *Review of Activities 1993*. London: BCSC.

Bunyan, T. (1977) *The Political Police in Britain*. London: Quartet.

Coleman, A. (1985) *Utopia on Trial*. London: Hilary Shipman.

Davis, M. (1990) *City of Quartz*. London: Vintage.

Department of Trade and Industry (1995) *Small and Medium Sized Enterprise Statistics for the UK, 1993*. Small Firms Statistics Unit, DTI, June.

Evans, D. J., Fyfe, N. R. and Herbert, D. T. (1992) *Crime, Policing and Place: Essays in Environmental Criminology*. London: Routledge.

Garland, D. (1996) 'The Limits of the Sovereign State'. *The British Journal of Criminology*, 36 (4), Autumn, pp. 445–71.

George, B. and Button, M. (1994) 'The Need for Regulation of the Private Security Industry'. A submission to the House of Commons Home Affairs Select Committee, November.

Giddens, A. (1990) *The Consequences of Modernity*. Cambridge: Polity Press.

Hunter, A. (1995) 'Private, Parochial and Public Social Orders: The Problem of Crime and Incivility in Urban Communities', in P. Kasinitz (ed.) *Metropolis: Centre and Symbol of our Times*. Basingstoke: Macmillan.

Hutter, B. (1988) *The Reasonable Arm of the Law*. Oxford: Clarendon Press.

Jacobs, J. (1961) *The Death and Life of Great American Cities*. New York: Random House.

Johnston, L. (1992) *The Rebirth of Private Policing*. London: Routledge.

Johnston, L. (1996) 'Policing Diversity: The Impact of the Public-private Divide Complex on Policing', in F. Leishman, B. Loveday and S. Savage (eds), *Core Issues in Policing*. Harlow: Longman.

Jones, T. and Newburn, T. (1995) 'How Big is the Private Security Sector?' *Policing and Society*, 5, pp. 221–32.

Jones, T. and Newburn, T. (1997) *Policing After the Act*. London: PSI.

Jones, T. and Newburn, T. (1998) *Private Security and Public Policing*. Oxford: Clarendon Press.

Jones, T., Newburn, T. and Smith, D. J. (1994) *Democracy and Policing*. London: Policy Studies Institute.

Kasinitz, P. (ed.) (1995) *Metropolis: Centre and symbol of our times*. Basingstoke: Macmillan.

Lash, S. and Urry, J. (1989) *The End of Organised Capitalism*. Cambridge: Polity Press.

Lavery, K. (1995) 'Privatisation by the Back Door: The Rise of Private Government in the USA'. *Public Money and Management*, 15 (4), Oct.–Dec.

Loveland, I. (1989) 'Policing welfare: Local authority responses to claimant fraud in the Housing Benefit Scheme', *Journal of Law and Society*, 16, 2, 187–209.

McClintock, F. H. and Wiles, P. (eds) (1972) *The Security Industry in the UK: Papers presented to the Cropwood Round-Table Conference*, July 1971, Cambridge: Institute of Criminology.

McManus, M. (1996) *From Fate to Choice: Private Bobbies, Public Beats*. Aldershot: Avebury.

Miller, J. P. and Luke, D. E. (1977) *Law Enforcement by Public Officials and Special Police Forces*. London: Home Office.

Morgan, R. and Newburn, T. (1997) *The Future of Policing*. Oxford: Oxford University Press.

Newman, O. (1973) *Defensible Space*. London: Architectural Press.

Poole, R. (1991) *Safe Shopping: The Identification of Opportunities for Crime and Disorder in Covered Shopping Centres*. Birmingham: West Midlands Constabulary.

Randall, P. and Hamilton, P. (1972) 'The Security Industry in the United Kingdom', in F. H. McClintock and P. Wiles (eds), *The Security Industry in the UK: Papers presented to the Cropwood Round-Table Conference*, July 1971, Cambridge: Institute of Criminology.

Reiner, R. (1992) 'Policing a Postmodern Society'. *Modern Law Review*, 55(6).

Reiner, R. (1993) 'Police Research in the United Kingdom', in M. Tonry and N. Morris (eds), *Modern Policing: Crime and Justice: An Annual Review of Research*, vol. 15. Chicago: University of Chicago Press.

Reiner, R. (1995) 'Police Research in the United Kingdom: A Critical View', in M. Tonry and N. Morris (eds), *Modern Policing*. Chicago: University of Chicago Press.

Reiss, A. (1998) *Private Employment of Public Police*. Washington, DC: US Dept of Justice.

Shearing C. (1992) 'The Relationship between Public and Private Policing', in M. Tonry and N. Morris (eds), *Modern Policing: Crime and Justice: a review of research*, vol. 15, Chicago: University of Chicago Press.

Shearing, C. and Stenning, P. (1981) 'Modern Private Security: Its Growth and Implications', in M. Tonry and N. Morris (eds), *Modern Policing: Crime and Justice: An Annual Review of Research*, vol. 15. Chicago: University of Chicago Press.

Shearing, C. and Stenning, P. (1983) 'Private Security: Implications for Social Control'. *Social Problems*, 30(5), pp. 493–506.

Shearing, C. and Stenning, P. (1987) 'Say Cheese! The Disney Order that's Not so Mickey Mouse', in Shearing and Stenning (eds), *Private Policing*. Newbury Park, Calif.: Sage.

Skogan, W. (1990) *Disorder and Decline: Crime and the Spiral of Decay in American Neighbourhoods*. New York: Free Press.

South, N. (1988) *Policing for Profit*. London: Sage.

South, N. (1997) 'Control, Crime and "End of the Century Criminology"', in P. Francis, P. Davies and V. Jupp (eds), *Policing Futures: The Police, Law Enforcement and the Twenty-First Century*. Basingstoke: Macmillan.

Spitzer, S. and Scull, A. (1977) 'Privatization and Capitalist Development: The Case of Private Police', *Social Problems*, 25(1), pp. 18–29.

Stanko, E. A. (1988) 'Hidden Violence Against Women', in M. Maguire and J. Pointing (eds), *Victims of Crime: A New Deal?*. Milton Keynes: Open University Press.

Taylor, I., Evans, K. and Fraser, P. (1996) *A Tale of Two Cities: Global Change, Local Feeling and Everyday Life in the North of England*. London: Routledge.

Wall, D. (1997) 'Policing the Virtual Community: The Internet, Cyberspace and Cybercrime', in P. Francis, P. Davies and V. Jupp (eds), *Policing Futures: The Police, Law Enforcement and the Twenty-First Century*. Basingstoke: Macmillan.

Weintraub, J. (1995) 'Varieties and Vicissitudes of Public Space', in P. Kasinitz (ed.), *Metropolis: Centre and Symbol of Our Times*. Basingstoke: Macmillan.

6 Respectable, Rural and English: the Lobby Against the Regulation of Firearms in Great Britain

Ian Taylor

INTRODUCTION

In this chapter, I want to present some observations and analysis with respect to the organised pressure group that, for the first time in the post-war period, began in 1996 to attract significant public attention in Britain – the 'sports-shooters' and their friends and allies in the firearms trade, who collectively became known in press discussion as 'the gun lobby'. My concerns in this paper represent an exercise in the social scientific analysis of law-creation, in that the group concerned was engaged in a campaign of resistance against the passage of publicly proposed legislation. But, as I will argue later, the paper is also intended as a contribution to the fast-growing literature in what might be called 'cultural criminology', i.e. in bringing the insights of cultural theory to bear on critical issues in the unending and anxious public debate over law and order. In this instance, my attention is focused on the cultural connections between gun ownership, certain versions of masculinity, and notions of 'respectability' and 'Englishness'. My interest is also excited by the ways in which these connected discourses were firmly institutionalised in Home Office and parliamentary circles, in the period between 'Hungerford' and 'Dunblane', as sensible, rational and balanced sources of official discourse on guns.

My concerns in this paper do not extend to any detailed and formal analysis of the role of firearms in crime, trends in firearms crime, or, indeed, to the evaluation of the Firearms Amendment Act which eventually became law in February 1997 (or the revised legislation, promised by our new government, to extend the ban on handguns to pistols of over .22 calibre). Some of these issues have been treated elsewhere (Taylor, 1997) and others will hopefully be the subject of detailed research at some future date. It suffices, for the moment, to remember that the emergence of the 'gun lobby' was one of several features of the anguished public debate in Britain which followed the massacre of sixteen infants and their teacher at the Dunblane Primary School by Thomas Hamilton on 13 March 1996 – the second major instance of a so-called 'spree-killing' in England in nine years. The previous incident, on 13 August 1987, in the village of Hungerford in Berkshire, involved the murder of sixteen people and the wounding of eleven others, chosen mostly at random, by 27-year-old Michael Ryan, a member of a local gun club, wearing army fatigues. The Hungerford massacre gave rise to troubled public debate and the passage of a new Firearms Act, banning the ownership of certain automatic weaponry. But the 'Dunblane massacre', committed against pre-school infants, was the subject of international press coverage and the bipartisan response of the political leadership of the country. It also gave rise to a concerted movement, led by the Snowdrop Petition (based in Dunblane), the nationally organised Gun Control Network, favouring the radically improved regulation of firearms ownership. This crystallised around the successful demand for a ban on the ownership in private hands of all handguns (other than a small number which were claimed as Olympic pistols). This development occurred in the aftermath of a period of heightened public concern over what was widely

Table 6.1   Offences involving firearms reported to the police
(England and Wales, 1984–93)

Year	Homicides	Attempted murder and other acts endangering life	Other violence against the person	Robbery	Burglary	Criminal damage	Other	All offences
1984	67	322	2,330	2,098	93	3,417	49	8,376
1985	45	353	2,652	2,531	125	3,977	59	9,742
1986	51	363	2,015	2,629	96	4,140	89	9,363
1987	77	508	1,944	2,831	109	3,453	69	9,002
1988	36	531	1,816	2,688	107	3,235	80	8,524
1989	45	581	1,914	3,390	133	3,321	111	9,502
1990	60	663	1,855	3,939	154	3,544	118	10,373
1991	55	861	1,795	5,296	176	3,777	169	12,129
1992	56	866	1,893	5,827	182	4,318	163	13,305
1993	74	1,047	1,738	5,918	235	4,682	257	13,951

Source: *Criminal Statistics (England and Wales) 1994*, Cm.3010 (Table 3.1).

thought to be a significant increased use of firearms in crime. Throughout 1993, there were many reports in the local and national press focusing on an ominous and apparently relentless increase in the number of incidents being reported to the police (see Table 6.1).

In the period 1990–3, the number of firearms offences reported to the police in Scotland increased from 435 to 738. So, throughout Britain as a whole – a country which for years defined itself (in contrast to 'America') as a 'gun-free' and civil society – anxieties over the apparent increase in the use of firearms in crime and, perhaps, the increased availability of firearms, was voiced with great regularity, particularly in the local press (albeit in some urban areas more than others). A variety of theories began to be developed journalistically as to whether the firearms in use were mainly illicit firearms, finding their way into Britain as a result of the easing of border control within the European Community and/or the increasing prevalence of organised criminality in parts of Europe. Other commentators speculated on the rise of 'gangsta rap' culture, especially amongst Britain's black 'underclass' – the latest expression of an undesirable American influence. There was also periodic discussion, especially in police circles, of the possible development of a 'grey market' in firearms – the emergence of arsenals of weapons in Britain with an ambiguous and fluid relationship to the legal firearms market and the 'black economy' of illicit firearms possession and/or use.

The *ad hoc* development of these lay-theories of gun crime was slowed by the release of the criminal statistics for 1994, which showed a reduction in the number of offences involving firearms reported to the police to 12,977 and, although the 1995 return showed a one per cent increase to 13,104, popular concern over guns seemed, if anything, to have been replaced (in a culture suffused with fast-developing anxieties and panics of all kinds) by anxieties over knives. The massacre in Dunblane had the effect of resurrecting the anxieties over guns and firearms crime and the extent to which the firearms used in crime originated from legal owners. These anxieties were to play no small part in the parliamentary and public debates, and also in the enquiry into the Dunblane massacre conducted by Lord Justice Cullen. There is no question but that this theme – that legal ownership of handguns and shotguns was a contributory factor in firearms crime as such – attained a kind of master status in popular understandings of the issues during the debates around the Cullen Enquiry (Thomas Hamilton was, after all, a fully licensed firearms owner and an erstwhile member of a sports shooting club). In the event, this master argument was to prove impossible for the gun lobby to overturn, and the Conservative government, however reluctantly, was compelled to legislate against handguns as a matter of public safety.

The analysis of the movements that led up to the passage of this legislation is not our purpose here (cf. Karp, 1997). Our concern instead is with those who were moved to oppose this legislation.

THE POLITICS OF GUN LOBBIES

In his recently published re-analysis of *Masculinities*, Connell (1994) devotes five pages to the role of 'the gun lobby' in Australia and the United States, especially with respect to the defence of what Connell calls 'hegemonic masculinity' (the routine domination of men within the gender order, which he takes to be a defining feature of most modern societies). He argues that 'gun lobby' type politics emerge in circumstances of crisis in this routine gender order, and that three defining preoccupations of such politics can be identified – the routine monopoly of men in respect of violence (the male as *warrior*), the idea of an exemplary form of masculinity (the male as *hero*) and the role of the male in the management of social and personal relations (the responsible male in a *necessary* position of power and command). The first dimension of this reconstruction and reassertion of masculinity – the male as *warrior* – has also been the subject of powerful recent studies and analyses of male violence in the United States by Jeffords (1989) and Gibson (1994), tracing the continual unfolding of the 'Vietnam syndrome' in that country, not least in the spread of the militia movements (for a recent overview see Stern, 1996). Jeffords' study also draws attention to the role of Hollywood, in particular, in the active reconstruction and celebration of a version of American manhood – from John Wayne and Clint Eastwood to Bruce Willis – as a kind of modern-day frontiersman, albeit located on the urban rather than the Western 'frontier'. Spitzer (1995), amongst many others, draws attention to the influence of this kind of masculinism in the movements that have sprung up in the United States to oppose any attempt to regulate or restrict the ownership of firearms in the United States, especially, of course, the National Rifle Association (NRA). In alliance with a multitude of local organisations across the United States, the NRA has been extraordinarily successful in its recent campaigns – not least, in holding back demands for the national registration of firearms ownership in the US and in restricting discussion of firearms control in that country (as in 'the Brady Bill' of 1993) to the question of a five-day 'waiting period' during the purchase of lethal weapons.

One of the lessons of the movement for firearms control that developed in the aftermath of the Dunblane massacre in England, Scotland and Wales, and the debates which surrounded the passage, under the Conservative government, of the Firearms Amendment Act (1996) and its rapid revision (to extend legal prohibition to all handguns) under the New Labour government (1997), is that we do not have an equivalent electorally powerful and publicly recognised national organisation to the NRA (though there is in Britain a National Rifle Association, one of several organisations that in 1996 gave support to the political work undertaken on behalf of all shooters by the British Sports Shooting Council). In part, this is simply a reflection of the very different history of firearms ownership, and the general provenance or availability of firearms in England, Scotland and Wales compared with the United States (Squires, 1997). The estimate – apparently accepted by Lord Cullen in his Report – is that there were some 2.7 million legally held firearms in Great Britain in 1996 (Cullen, 1996, para. 9.5). According to the collation of existing national information rapidly undertaken by the Firearms Control Task Force of the Canadian Department of Justice in 1995, there were some 3,307 firearms owners per 100,000 people in Britain, compared to 85,385 in the United States, 42,857 in Switzerland, 29,412 in New Zealand, 24,138 in Canada and 19,444 in Australia. These statistics have been the subject of angry critique by Jan Stevenson (1996), who argues that these official estimates lack credibility to any knowledgeable sports-shooter, but they are largely consistent with another set of statistical comparisons collected by *The Observer* (see Table 6.2).

Whether or not one accepts either of these different sets of comparative data, it is clear that the prevalence of legally owned firearms in England, Scotland and Wales is very low on any international comparison. But, as the campaigns around firearms regulation in the aftermath of Dunblane made clear, this has not meant that there is no 'gun lobby' at all in England, Scotland and Wales. One objective of this paper is to identify and record the specific character of this 'gun lobby', and to comment on its political significance. A second objective is to offer some interpretative commentary on the public intervention of this lobby – with respect to the question of a certain, socially located form of masculinity (particularly in England), and the presence and continuing play of a particular lay-theory of the nature and

Table 6.2   Firearms Ownership (Percentage of households with guns)

Country	Percentage of households with guns
United States	48
Norway	32
Canada	29.1
Finland	23.2
France	22.6
New Zealand	22.3
Austria	19.4
Belgium	16.6
Italy	16
Sweden	15.1
Northern Ireland	8.4
Scotland	4.7
England & Wales	4.7

Source: *The Observer*, 18 August 1996.

source of violence and criminality advanced by that lobby during 1996–7. It is in this sense that this paper is an exercise in cultural criminology, with particular respect to firearms and guns. It is decidedly not an exercise in nineteenth-century positivist social science, of the kind which some members of the 'gun lobby' have been keen to resurrect in recent months, demanding attention only to 'the facts' made available on existing systems of policing and firearms licensing and registration. The acquaintance I have made with the system of firearms regulation in England in 1996 and 1997 is of a system that is in need of radical modernisation (not least in respect of computerisation of basic records on a national archive, as against the hard-copy (paper) records which currently do service across 43 police forces of England and Wales): it would be the most unwise commentator who drew any firm conclusions from such a set of records.[1]

References made to 'the gun lobby' in England in 1996,[2] in parliamentary debates and in the national press, were very often a response to the interventions made by the British Sports Shooting Council (BSSC). In the aftermath of Dunblane, the BSSC assumed a lead position, for example, in the presentation of evidence on behalf of sports shooting organisations to the Cullen Enquiry, and, more generally, in the campaigns which were waged in the press against what was described as panicky legislative response to the massacre itself. For most of 1996, the BSSC presented itself as an umbrella organisation, speaking on behalf of the British Field Sports Society, the National Pistol Association, the National Rifle Association, the National Small-Bore Association, the Clay Pigeon Shooting Association, the Gun Trade Association, the Muzzle Loaders' Association, the Shooting Sports Trust and the United Kingdom Practical Shooting Association. In its various interventions on television and in the press during 1996, it also made common cause with the Handgunners' Association and even the radically libertarian Shooters' Rights Association – until the secretary of this particular organisation, Richard Law, in December 1996 had his firearms license revoked by Dyfed Powys police after discovery of firearms and ammunition worth over £100,000 on his premises (which had hitherto also functioned as a Home Office-approved firing range) on the suspicion that these firearms could not all be for private use (*The Guardian*, 5 Dec. 1996).

The membership of these different organisations in England, Scotland and Wales in 1996 was said to comprise about 200,000. A significant number of these individuals made use of these guns in a sporting context, whether competitively or simply for 'leisure', at one of Britain's gun clubs, of which, according to the Cullen Report (para. 8.36), there were 2,118 approved by the Secretary of State in 1996. Significant numbers of these individuals also subscribed to, or were regular readers of, one or more of the eleven gun magazines which were regularly on sale in newsagents and railway bookstands in England, Scotland and Wales, and which an inquiring journalist early in 1994 estimated to have a combined circulation of just over a quarter of a million copies (Engel, 1994). Anecdotal evidence suggests that some of these magazines have lost circulation since 1994, and two have ceased publication. But there is no doubting the continued existence in England of a committed constituency of 'sports shooters': in May 1997, for example, the Sportsmen's Association claimed a membership of over 40,000 (*Shooting Times and Country Magazine*, 22 May 1997) and was able to organise three rallies in London against the new firearms legislation, with the largest attracting over 25,000 people. The Sportsmen's Association, which in the first months of 1996 was quite closely allied with the Shooters' Rights Association and the Handgunners, later shifted ground, and began to present itself as a close ally of the British Field Sports Society, which was beginning to develop an organised campaign to defend hunting and other aspects of what its Chief Executive referred to as the 'moral economy' of the countryside (*Shooting Times and Country Magazine*, 19 June 1997).

The use of shotguns and pistols in target-shooting may have some resonance for the rural economy, but it also echoes the military background of many of those routinely involved in sports shooting. During the parliamentary debates after Dunblane, members of parliament were themselves astounded to discover that the House of Commons had a shooting range, overwhelmingly, though not exclusively, patronised by Conservative members from the shire counties. Many MPs, including senior members of Labour's Shadow Cabinet, were equally surprised to discover the existence of a body known as the House of Commons Firearms Consultative Committee (FCC), established in the aftermath of the Hungerford shooting in August 1987 and the subsequent Firearms (Amendment) Act 1988. The FCC had been releasing annual reports ever since, and playing an influential advisory role in most governmental deliberations in the sphere of firearms policy. Membership of this Committee was a result of a process of identification and appointment of:

> those who appear to the Home Secretary to have knowledge and experience of either the possession, use (in particular for sport or competition) or keeping of, or transactions in, firearms or weapons technology; or the administration or enforcement of the provisions of the Firearms Acts. (FCC *Sixth Annual Report*, 1995 para 1.1)

It is clear that the FCC – for all that it was established in response to the 'amok killings' in Hungerford in August 1987 – is not a committee with any direct experience of victimisation by firearms crime, and was not appointed to any such purpose. The Committee was established, instead, as a way of drawing more directly on the knowledge of a specific interest-group with an experience of firearms in the routine governance of this field of activity, still largely understood, for all the horror of the Hungerford incident, as a sport. In this fashion – after the example of many such imperatively coordinated advisory committees in Whitehall which claim to provide the resource of expert knowledge – the FCC worked to give a more direct voice in government to representatives of the firearms industry and trade, as well as, in this instance, the *soi-disant* 'sports shooting community'. In this sense, the FCC helped to position firearms traders and sport shooters as an integral link in the policy consultation process, rather than leaving the trade and the sport shooters to operate primarily as an outside lobby or pressure group – an option that is not available, under such arrangements, to gun control organisations (like the Gun Control Network) or to organisations of victims of firearms violence (like the Hungerford parents' organisation or the Snowdrop petitioners). Putting this point another way, we can say that the FCC works to normalise the idea of firearms ownership and use (albeit within regulated circumstances) and therefore constitutes an important element in the 'firearms lobby' in England. A great deal of trust, for example, was placed in the sports shooting press in the work of the FCC during the Cullen Enquiry, particularly in respect of the arguments the firearms lobby were advancing *against* any kind of ban on private ownership of handguns. The 'sports shooters' were absolutely stunned by the decision taken by the last government, in the critical last few days before publication of the Cullen Report, to switch position and to go for a partial handgun ban (see the pained remarks of Sir Jerry Wiggin MP that the FCC was not consulted prior to publication of the Firearms Amendment Bill – *Hansard*, 18 Nov. 1996, col. 726).

THE DISCOURSES OF THE ENGLISH GUN LOBBY

In their agitated responses to the Dunblane massacre, and to the urgent public pressure for a renewed and strict regulation of firearms ownership in England, Scotland and Wales, spokespeople for the firearms trade and for sports shooting advanced a mix of six different discursive arguments. We shall review each of these in brief, before moving on to our main concern in this paper – to interrogate the meaning of the commitment to the gun that was being displayed by this body of organised (industrial, economic, cultural and social) interest. It is not my concern here to treat these arguments *on their merits*, i.e. as if they were themselves fully fledged quasi-social-scientific theories. My intention is to treat them as a 'discursive formation' – as the body of discourses that is emblematic and constitutive of the English 'gun lobby'.

i) 'Maniacs': the Proper Identification of 'Unfit Persons'

Perhaps the most frequently rehearsed of all the discursive 'gun lobby' arguments during 1996 was that which identified Thomas Hamilton, the perpetrator of the Dunblane massacre, as some kind of 'psychiatric Other'. Evidence given to the Cullen Enquiry by the BSSC placed an enormous emphasis on the responsibilities of Police

Firearms Licensing Officers in the identification of individuals as 'fit persons' to own firearms. In particular they argued for the enhancement of the role of GPs in this process of identification of disturbed or problematic individuals. The Cullen Enquiry devoted fully two chapters (41 pages) to a narrative on the life of Thomas Hamilton – one of which (Chapter 4, 'Events in the life of Thomas Hamilton') is a traditional piece of lay-theory on Thomas Hamilton's sexual psychopathology (his interest in young boys), with no clear account being offered as to how this sexual predilection might in itself connect to his interest in guns and the subsequent slaughter of young pre-school children of both sexes. In the parliamentary debates of 1996 around the Firearms Amendment Act, spokespersons for sports shooting argued repetitively and insistently that the key issue was not the firearm as such, but the person into whose hands a firearm might fall. The 'real problem' was the effective identification of 'maniacs' like Thomas Hamilton or Michael Ryan and the prevention of their gaining access to lethal weaponry.

There are three observations to make. First, this argument is the equivalent in the English context of that advanced in the USA, most famously by the NRA, that 'it is not guns that kill, but people'. The argument is open to the empirical objection arising out of a mass of sophisticated research (which the NRA has tried consistently to marginalise or suppress through putting pressure on funding agencies in the United States) – for example, by the Centre for Injury Control at Emory University, Georgia (e.g. Kellerman et al., 1993). Kellerman's work purports to demonstrate, *inter alia*:

> that homes where guns are kept are almost three times more likely to be the scene of a homicide than comparative homes without guns, even after the independent effects of victim age, sex, race, neighbourhood, previous family violence, anyone using illicit drugs, and any history of previous arrests were taken into account. (Kellerman, 1994, p. 615)

On the evidence of Kellerman, echoing earlier work by Cook (1983) and Zimring (1968), it is precisely the availability of guns – especially when kept in private households – which plays a major, determining role in the production of firearms violence (especially in the form of deliberate homicide, accidents, suicides). More recent research by American scholars working in the public health field makes powerful connections between the failure to regulate the spread of the 9 mm. handgun in America (the 'Saturday night special') and the continuing escalation of violent deaths amongst young Afro-Americans in America's inner cities. On the evidence, the issue *is* the prevalence of the gun, not the question of identification of fit or unfit persons.

Secondly, the argument that the psychiatric profession and/or GPs could be asked to play a more active role in the firearms licensing process is based on a curious, dated and highly individualistic psychopathological theory, namely that it is possible *a priori* to identify the existence of 'dangerous' individuals, and to anticipate, even on a probabilistic model, their later explosion into killing sprees. The British Medical Association (BMA), through its secretary, Mac Armstrong, gave evidence to the Home Affairs Select Committee in May 1996 indicating that there is no such predictive measure available with respect to murderous or other seriously anti-social behaviour, other than in the case of individuals who already have a 'strong history of psychotic illness linked to violent behavior' (see 'Gun Licence Tests "Are Pointless", *The Guardian*, 3 May 1996). In this respect, the BMA was simply giving voice to conclusions already well known to penologists interested in the reform of parole in the mid-1970s, namely, that there is no such thing as a reliable science for predicting 'dangerousness' (Bottoms, 1977).

Thirdly, insistence on identifying 'maniacs' or 'disturbed', 'strange', 'lonely' and isolated men unfit to hold a firearms licence was a necessary discursive response to the fact that Thomas Hamilton, like Michael Ryan, was a 'legal' firearms owner, that is, a person who had been identified, via the existing licensing system, as being fit and proper to own a private arsenal of firearms (the system makes no formal distinction, at this or any other point in the decision-making process, between the fitness of persons to own handguns or rifles). Moreover, many other firearms incidents appearing in the local or national press involve individual licence-holders of respectable backgrounds and/or in reputable occupations (rather than Rambo stereotypes like Michael Ryan).[3] As we shall see later, the defence of the idea of the responsible gun-owner, identified in terms of holding a licence, is not simply an empirical quasi-legal category, which can be more or less sensibly managed (the licensing of Thomas Hamilton was an example of mismanagement of the existing system): it is, much more importantly, a matter of ideological and social significance, especially in the sphere of masculinity.

ii) The Illegal Market: the 'Real Criminals'

A second popular refrain of spokespeople for sports shooting organisations and the gun trade in 1996 was that the legislation being proposed was wrongly targeted. The main source of the increased number of firearms in use 'on the street' was the illegal market in guns, dominated by 'the criminal fraternity' not least, in some accounts, by foreigners. References ranged from the Jamaican 'Yardies', who excited so much attention in the early 1990s, to Russian and Eastern European 'mafiosi' whose presence, recently, is thought to be on the increase in Western Europe as well as North America. This kind of account has a long history in the populist criminology of the mass media and everyday talk about crime. 'Foreign' corruption has always played a key role, for example, in mass media accounts of the drug trade. In recent discussions of firearms crime in Britain, however, we have been presented with a strong image of an underworld of organized criminals, heavily armed themselves and active in selling on such weaponry 'on the street'. The evidence presented in support of the existence of such a cartel of organized and professional criminality is rather thin. Van Duyne's (1993, 1996) close analysis of the structures of organized crime elsewhere in Europe and, in particular, the close relationship between the *ad hoc* and episodic business activities 'in crime' and the legitimate local economic markets, suggests that this is a relationship of interdependence rather than of binary opposition. We ought to be empirically interested in the process whereby guns do in practice move between legal owners, firearm traders, individual miscreants and/or local subcultures, rather than assuming, as the sports shooters want to insist, that all these actors live in hermetically sealed social worlds.

iii) 'Panic Legislation'

An insistent refrain from the 'gun lobby' in 1996 was that the proposed legislation was being carried through 'in panic'. The *Daily Telegraph* editorial of 17 October 1996 ('Making Law in a Panic'), for example, reacted in shock and anger at the decision taken by the Conservative government to change position and move towards a partial handgun ban, accusing the Cabinet of caving in to 'Labour self-righteousness and popular emotion'. It also carried a feature, by Allan Massie, in which the government's shift was eventually supported on strategic grounds (to keep the Conservatives in touch with popular

emotion), but which also argued that the proposed legislation arose
from the 'emotional blackmail' exerted by 'Middle Scotland'. In the
various papers written by Munday and Stevenson (1996) and presented to the Cullen Enquiry, the strategy adopted is that of eschewing emotion and 'special pleading' on behalf of the Dunblane families,
in order to ground the debate over firearms regulation in what these
authors take to be the self-evident 'facts' about firearms ownership
and rates of violent crime. Implicit in this strategy, of course, is a cold
certainty that these facts speak for themselves, in favour of firearms,
in the right hands, as an entirely normal and legitimate practice – that
is, for responsible, respectable men. I shall return to this theme of
rationality and masculinity. But it is important to note here how this
approach tries to valorise the kind of measured discourse (so characteristic, for example, of the Civil Service in England) in which the
'soundness' or 'reliability' of a policy proposal is identified in terms of
the absence of any clear or partisan moral or political purpose.

iv) Firearms, National Pride and Sporting Achievement

Another powerful theme for sports shooters in 1996 was the argument
that pistol shooting was recognised as an Olympic (as well as a
Commonwealth Games) sport in which Great Britain had 'traditionally' done well. This argument seems to have informed the compro-
mise position arrived at by the Conservative government, firstly, in
their refusal to extend the prohibition on handgun ownership to the
.22 calibre pistol and, secondly, the careful way in which the Home
Secretary outlined the arrangements to be made to allow Britain's
best pistol shooters to continue with their training (with police escort
being provided during transportation and storage of their guns and
equipment abroad). It is noteworthy how frequently the spokesperson
chosen to represent the sports shooting interest in debates on national
television in 1996 (including, for example, Jeremy Paxman's *You
Decide*) was Carol Page, Olympic team member and .32 calibre pistol
shooter, always appearing in the national tracksuit. The obvious discursive connection being constructed here was to 'national pride',
signified by Ms Page's achievement in the international Olympic
sphere. The attempt to connect sporting victories to ideas of national
honour, and, indeed, to the self-esteem of individual citizens
(all drawn together as 'the nation') continues to be a powerful aspect
of the coverage of different sports (in particular, international athlet-
ics or football) in the popular and quality press and on national

television. It has many troubling features at a time when tribal feelings are on the increase throughout the world. Some thirty years ago, two Conservative commentators with significant sporting experience, Philip Goodhart and Christopher Chataway (1968) – apparently resigned to the inevitability of such tribal sentiment – referred to international sports competition as a form of 'War without Weapons'. But sports-shooting matches involve the competitive use of firepower and in that sense specifically connect the idea of international competition and the acquisition and ownership of armaments in general.

A closely connected dimension of this appeal to the firearm as an essential piece of sports equipment was the insistence on shooting, generally, as a sport. Shooting, whether of grouse on a moor or targets on a range, was often identified, especially alongside archery, as a form of country or field sport, on a continuum of sports and leisure pastimes with angling, cricket and golf. Several important sub-texts (which is to say 'presences') and several issues which were left unsaid ('absences') arose in this particular discursive argument. The first spoken sub-text was that sports shooting was a popular and democratic form of sport in which, according to the BSSC in the evidence it presented to the Home Affairs Subcommittee in 1996, 'over one million' participate. Sports shooting, like angling, was presented as a significant participatory sport. This argument always invited critical empirical enquiry and attempts (on several audience-participation programmes in 1996) to equate sports shooting with angling, cricket or golf usually resulted in incredulous and angry audience responses.

A second sub-text worked to represent sports-shooting as the chosen and preferred sport of women (Carol Page acting almost as an iconic signifier of women's active and enthusiastic participation) and also of the disabled – especially disabled people confined to wheelchairs. This argument found some purchase in amendments to the Labour government's Firearms Bill in the House of Lords in September 1997, exempting disabled people from the overall ban on handguns. The effect of this discursive move was to emphasise the harmlessless of sports shooting and suggest that any criticism of the use of firearms by the disabled would be insensitive to the situation of disabled people. The show of solidarity with the disabled by defenders of sport shooting also opened up the kinds of arguments, so frequently rehearsed by the gun lobby in the USA, with respect to guns as an instrument for self-defence.

Whatever else might be said about the substance of these two sub-texts, they had the crucial effect of suppressing alternative arguments – specifically, the issue of 'arms and the man' (the sensuous and affectionate relationship of the sports shooter with the gun[4]), in the different expressions which this connection assumes in sports shooting and handgun clubs. Though no statistical evidence is available in the public realm, it is clear that the membership of the more than 2,000 gun clubs in Britain is overwhelmingly male. The forms of masculinity in evidence in these clubs will vary – from the 'protest masculinity' that, according to some investigative journalists and even to many sports shooters themselves, was in evidence in many handgun clubs – to forms of 'respectable' military masculinity in evidence among many committed sports-shooting enthusiasts. This particular inscription of respectable masculinity echoed the mix of attitude, behaviour and practice which the BSSC saw itself as representing, and therefore could never be subject to critical investigation (even in its particular and defining 'love of guns').

v) The Tutelage and Discipline of Sports Shooting

Another important sub-text of the discourses over firearms and sport was the emphasis often placed on the merits of the discipline and training involved in the introduction of novices and young people into use of firearms on dedicated firing ranges. This refrain was particularly marked in discussion of the use of firearms by Officers' Training Corps in secondary schools up and down the country. In 1997 it resurfaced in a debate within the Boy Scouts movement over the use of firearms training as part of the process of 'character-building' traditionally associated with the Scouts. This clearly echoed the discourses of 'harmless respectability' and evoked the notion that the *responsible* use of guns and the *commitment of individuals to training and practice* reflected other closely connected social values. The maintenance (and perhaps the effective reproduction) of social order, irrespective of party-political and other considerations, was suggested, as was training for leadership (for example, in the competitive new world of finance and commerce) of 'disciplined' individuals, attuned, we might say, to focusing on specific and dedicated targets. The specific construction being attempted here was to the idea of self-improvement through hard work and repetitive practice – a refrain which had enormous cultural purchase at a time when English society was becoming increasingly aware of the importance of skill and disciplined habits of work and personal lifestyle in competitive post-Fordist circumstances. But in England these refrains simultaneously carried powerful and

nostalgic references to 'tried and trusted' cultural themes: of defer-
ence to the good taste and sensibilities of the landed nobility, the
'English gentleman' no less, harmlessly carrying his shotgun across the
grouse moors, and relying on his retainers to collect the fallen quar-
ries; and also to a form of masculinity that, *by definition*, spoke of reliability in a world of great uncertainties and change.

vi) Guns for Self-protection, and the Right to Bear Arms

The analysis of discourses of the English gun lobby must pay attention
to 'absences' (suppressed or forgotten areas of talk and discussion) as
well as 'presences' in the chosen or approved forms. In this respect we
should be attentive to how the arguments which were voiced by sports
shooters or spokespersons for the firearms trade in England differed
from the discourses of the 'gun lobby' in the USA. In contrast to the
arguments that have become familiar in the US throughout the 1980s
and 1990s, for example (Kopel, 1992), little credence was placed
in England on the firearm as an instrument for self-protection and
none at all on the idea of 'the concealed weapon' which is now legal
in many different American states (see McDowell, Loftin and
Wiersema, 1995). Nor was there much display of another dimension
of the American debate, very effectively mobilised by the NRA, in
which the carrying of firearms by women was advocated as an extension of feminist discourse on the carrying of rape alarms. It is not that
these arguments are never voiced in England (the Paxman programme gave voice to an elderly Yorkshireman who had pistol-
whipped two local car thieves), but they were not taken up as
first-order arguments, with a high degree of public legitimacy or
appeal. There was also little evidence in the debates in Parliament or
on public television of the NRA argument about the right to carry
guns as a marker and an entitlement of full-blooded citizenship, protected by the Second Amendment of the US Constitution (for further
discussion of this currently pressing political and legal issue see Wills,
1995). This kind of argument was publicly advanced only by the
Shooters' Rights Association, although there is some evidence that
small numbers of other individuals, often of military background or
associated with fringe organisations of the far right[5] and far left[6] hold
them. For the shooting and firearms lobby as a whole, recognition of
some other notion of citizenship (we shall argue later, the nature of
Englishness) acted as a check on any such populist or libertarian
rhetoric.

INTERPRETING THE DISCOURSES OF SPOKESPERSONS
FOR THE ENGLISH GUN LOBBY

The analysis of discourses and/or ideological representation is one of
the most fertile and contested areas of social-scientific enquiry. This is
also an area on which literary theory (whether in the psychoanalytical
or Bakhtinian traditions) has a lot to offer. One of the fascinating
aspects of doing analytical work on issues of firearms ownership or
crime is the frequency with which one encounters the use of linguistic
references or metaphors deriving from the sphere of firearms: 'getting
a bead on the target', 'going off half cock', 'going ballistic', 'son of a
gun', and so on. The use of such metaphors seems especially common
in reports and commentaries on male-dominated sports – particularly
football. Only last week, the Chief Executive of Manchester United,
Martin Edwards, was quoted in the local newspaper, on his football
club's search for new players on the transfer market, as saying:

> There is one more transfer possibility. There is one more bullet in
> the gun and if we hit the target it will be a useful addition ...
> Sometimes you don't get what you want immediately, then if you
> keep your powder dry another opportunity will arise.   (*Manchester
> Evening News*, 10 July 1997, p. 76)

There is also evidence of a widespread use of militaristic and firearms
metaphors in the world of business and finance in competitive market
society: the routine talk, for example, of 'hits' or 'taking out the opposition', which could fruitfully be the subject of separate extended
study.

I wish to focus my analysis of the discourse of the English gun lobby
on three distinct themes. But I need first to clarify my position. I am
not arguing that public discourses against gun control had a constant
or unitary character. In fact the priorities of the 'gun lobby' changed
quite markedly at different moments in 1996: first, in relation to
the broad 'war of position' taking place in parliamentary or press
responses, especially in respect of daily reports from the Cullen
Enquiry; and, secondly, in relation to other initiatives taken by individuals or different sports-shooting organisations or representatives of
the gun trade, as well as in response to arguments amongst these
groups about the strategy of a common front (through the BSSC). Nor
am I arguing that one can understand the discourses of the English
gun lobby just through a close reading of what was said by their

spokespersons in the course of the long debates of 1996: there is, as I have said, a lot that was left *unspoken* and unattended, including the full horror of the event which gave rise to the firearms debate of 1996 in the first place. Dunblane was always deplored, but in a manner which suggested that there was need to move on from emotion to more 'rational' discourses ('the facts').

i) There was widespread resort by spokespersons for the gun lobby to the use of statistics and 'facts' and the denunciation of the movements for firearms control as being led by 'emotion' and 'panic'. The unspoken sub-text in these interventions is clear enough:

> A familiar theme in patriarchal ideology is that men are rational whilst women are emotional. This is a deep-seated assumption in European philosophy. It is one of the leading ideas in sex-role theory, in the form of the instrumental/expressive dichotomy, and is widespread in popular culture too. Science and technology, seen by the dominant ideology as the motors of progress, are culturally defined as a masculine realm. Hegemonic masculinity establishes its hegemony partly by its claim to embody the power of reason, and thus represent the interests of the whole society.   (Connell, 1994 p. 164)

So the submission made by Jan Stevenson, the founder of *The Handgunner*, to the Cullen Enquiry, we are told, was informed, with no false modesty, from 'four decades of study and experience' resulting from his working 'to the highest standards of scholarship' (Stevenson, 1996, p. 73). The Home Office evidence to the Cullen Enquiry is indicted, with great force, by Richard Munday, the military historian and firearms enthusiast, as having resulted from 'over-hasty compilation' and being 'full of unsupported statements, logical non-sequiturs and somewhat tortuous overlay of different strains of argument' (Munday, 1996, p. 227).

ii) This claim to masculinity having a close and definitive connection to rationality is closely tied up with an idea of men as exercising their rationality whilst in positions of power and authority, that is, whilst being *responsible*. In its pure form, this equates patriarchy with the Law of the Father, responsible for the safety and well-being of a dependent family and, of course, in many cultures at many times (the American frontier in the last century), this connects directly to the idea of the Man/Father/Head of Household acting as Guard against a threatening world of Nature and the human Other ('wild bears' or 'the Indians', for example).[7] In a culture in which there has been no generalised and legal popular access to guns since 1662, however, this kind of discourse has scant purchase.[8]

iii) England is also a distinctive culture in a very different sense. As Perry Anderson, Tom Nairn and E.P. Thompson made clear in their momentous political and theoretical debate in the 1960s, this is a society in which there still has not been a successful bourgeois revolution. In his classic essay on 'The Peculiarities of the English', Thompson (1965) argues that the slow process of social change inaugurated by the Settlement of 1688 produced no full-scale transformation of social relations (or bourgeois achievement of hegemony), but neither did it completely institutionalise the aristocracy or the lesser gentry in a permanent and secure position. Instead the eighteenth century and early nineteenth century were witness to a process of accommodation of landed gentry and mercantile interests at both national and local level, a process which Thompson, in order to highlight the murky character of the economic, political, personal and familial struggles that repetitively took place in the winning of position and influence during this period, chooses to call 'Old Corruption'. These struggles were nearly always played out, however, in the context of appeals to continuity, whether in the form of *national tradition* or *local custom*. It is remarkable how even the high points of England's commercial, industrial and imperial activities were accompanied, discursively, by appeals to ideas of 'the nation' expressed in terms of the traditions and practices of rural England and the quaint traditions of the rural gentry.

The sporting gun or the shotgun as an emblem of the landed gentry lifestyle found expression in the submissions made to the House of Commons Home Affairs Subcommittee and to the Cullen Enquiry by the BSSC: emphasis was placed on the use of firearms by field sportsmen and farmers (notably, in a phrase that would be of interest to linguistic analysts, in the control of vermin). In nearly all such representations, the more specific agendas of the different organisations affiliated to the BSSC coalition (like the National Pistol Association or the Gun Trade Association) were subordinated to the generalised 'master text'. This, as outlined earlier, carried a range of different allusions to: the self-evidently responsible moral character of firearms owners deemed fit to own such weaponry through the existing system of firearms licensing; the important role of such weapons in a recognised Olympic sport; and the importance of the kind of training and discipline involved in training young people ('future leaders') in the safe but effective use of firearms.

The social references operative in these discourses of the English gun lobby were *quite different* to the references mobilised in the rhetoric of the NRA in the United States, with the constantly repeated refrain about the constitutional 'right to bear arms' or to the NRA's alter egos, the armed militias, taking the paranoid themes in American politics to their logical extremes by taking up arms against an oppressive State. The English gun lobby's appeal, by contrast, was to an ordered and hierarchical world in which a limited number of respectable men, licensed to carry guns essentially on the basis of trust, would exercise their paternalistic responsibilities – like the gentry itself – with care and restraint. This sure and certain discourse was threatened less by individual incidents like the Dunblane and Hungerford spree-killings (which the discourse had firmly identified as the acts of 'maniacs' – *self-evidently* emerging from very different biographies than those of the typical – responsible and respectable – sports shooter) than by the various interventions made during the debates of 1996 by committed 'firearms-libertarians', echoing the arguments of the NRA for a *universal* entitlement to own and carry guns.

In the summer of 1996, some of these arguments began to be advanced on radio and television by Richard Munday and Jan Stevenson of the Handgunners' Association and Richard Law of the Shooters' Rights Association. These interventions were sometimes accompanied in newspaper feature articles on the gun clubs with pictures of handgun enthusiasts foregrounding knots of khaki clad young men in balaclavas (see, for example, Peter Beaumont, 'Dressed to Kill – Just for Thrills', *The Observer*, 12 Sept. 1993). These re-presentations provided critical visual evidence of the co-presence within the 'sports shooting fraternity' of the kinds of young men associated in the public mind with street-corner gangsterism in Los Angeles or the genocidal civil wars in Chechnia, Rwanda or Yugoslavia – young men *by definition* beyond control of the established hierarchies of power and status. There was visual confirmation, in other words, of handguns having fallen into the hands of 'the dispossessed'. The presence of such images paralleled the release of a series of press stories detailing the mayhem being caused in the United States as a result of the cheap and easy availability of the 9 mm. handgun (the 'Saturday night special').

But for most English readers the United States is a long way away, especially in terms of its constitutional libertarianism. The anxiety provoked by the press images was *social* and *political*: it was evidence not just of the existence in England of a large and angry underclass of dispossessed young men. The visual images provided a powerful empirical counter-factual to the public rhetorics of the sport-shooting 'community', and especially the refrain that firearms ownership was best understood in terms of the retrieval of the 'country way of life'. They may also have problematised the gun lobby's argument that there is no connection between the legal and illegal markets in firearms. The young men shown in many of these photographic images did not look like the kind who would pause to enquire about the provenance of particular weapons. The importance of such visual symbols in the public debate that led to the passage of the Firearms (Amendment) Act 1996 is incalculable. The quite momentous move towards heightened regulation of firearms in England in 1996 involved the kinds of deep-seated fears and anxieties that have historically underpinned life in a society still deeply divided by class and status. And finally, as Prince Phillip himself only belatedly understood, it also involved a fundamental misreading of the way in which any unqualified and obstinate appeals to the values of the English country-man (as if they were some kind of social and political solution to firearms problems in the late 1990s) had been undermined by the horror of Dunblane.

NOTES

Revised version of the paper presented to the British Society of Criminology Conference, Queen's University, Belfast (July 1997).

Acknowledgements: This paper benefits from very helpful suggestions from Ruth Jamieson and from both the editors of this volume, as well as from my continuing conversations with Tony and Judith Hill, Mick Moore and Gill Marshall-Andrews of the Gun Control Network.

1. Commentators frequently try to make use, for example, of existing statistical material in order to demonstrate the absence of any evidence for a link between the number of legal-owned firearms in private hands and the frequency with which firearms are used in crime (Munday and Stevenson, 1996, *passim*). I am as sceptical about these statistical exercises (on the basis of existing police data in England and Wales) as I am about those studies, like that of Corkery (1994), which try to demonstrate the existence of some such link and/or suggest that there is an increasing use 'by criminals' of firearms stolen from legal firearmsowners.

2. I have opted to identify the 'gun lobby' of England, Scotland and Wales as the English gun lobby. I am aware that the campaigns against the

Firearms Amendment Act in 1996 attracted some support in Wales and also, in rather more muted fashion, in Scotland. The bulk of my argument, especially in the second half of my paper, is that the politics of the gun lobby are rather closely implicated with the idea of the 'respectable English country gentleman'.

3. In 1996, for example, the press reported on a 66-year-old pensioner and retired cleaner from High Wycombe who allowed access to guns to young children visiting his home – which children then revisited his home and stole the guns for use in thefts (*The Guardian*, 19 March); a prison officer (arrested at Milton Keynes rail station when threatening a woman with a Magnum pistol), licensed for five of twelve guns found in his home (*The Mail on Sunday*, 9 June), and a London marketing executive found drunk in possession of an antique shotgun on a West Highland rail line (*Scotsman*, 3 October). These examples, alighted on through no systematic process of search, do not include the instances of use of firearms by licensed owners on their own families or themselves which are reported in the local press (for example, the murder of 12-year-old Dominic Bennici by his father, Vincent, who then committed suicide, in Oldham in 1997 (*Manchester Evening News*, 14 March 1997).

4. Even the most cursory examination of the firearms press provides a mass of evidence of discourses crying out for psychoanalytic and critical cultural interpretation. The August 1996 issue of *Guns and Shooting*, for example, had as its special feature the new 'Bianchi Beef Cake' Action Revolver, with the plaintive enquiry 'Is It Up to the Job?'

5. In October 1995, for example, the 64-year-old Mr Bannistre-Parker, who claimed to be a retired army Major, was arrested at his home in Preston after threatening two burglars with a shotgun. In court, it was revealed that Mr Bannistre-Parker was an active member of an organisation known as the Legion of Frontiersmen (European Command) (*Daily Telegraph*, 25 Oct. 1995).

6. In late 1996 and early 1997, for example, a curious alliance was struck between the BSSC and *Living Marxism*, the house journal of the Revolutionary Communist Party, in campaigning against New Labour's commitments to an extension of the ban of private handguns ownership. At a pre-election seminar in London in February 1997, one of the chief theoreticians of the RCP, Frank Furedi, argued that the proposed firearms legislation represented 'the new authoritarianism' of a crisis-ridden capitalist State, a descendant of the Firearms Act 1920, which he interpreted as an attempt by the capitalist state to disarm revolutionary fractions of the proletariat.

7. The NRA's *Book of Rifles* opens with the following words:

    The ability to shoot a rifle is an American tradition. Our country was established and its boundaries expanded westward by men with rifles in their hands. The rifle gave the settlers protection against the marauding Indians and other foes, and was an important means of securing food for the pioneer family. (Smith and Smith, 1948, p. i).

8. The Militia Act 1662 of Charles II authorized the King's agent 'to search for and seize all arms in the custody or possession of any person

or persons who the said lieutenants or any two or more of their deputies shall judge dangerous to the peace of the kingdom'. This statute was followed up by the punitive Game Act 1671 debarring all non-hunters from owning guns, on pain of severe fines. There have been periods since when small numbers of arms have crept back into civil society, usually via soldiers returning from wars (e.g. 1918–20), but generally English everyday life has been free from the threat of firearms owned and used by other citizens from the late seventeenth century onwards. (For an alternative interpretation, see Kopel, 1992.)

REFERENCES

Bottoms, A. E. (1977) 'Reflections on the Renaissance of Dangerousness', *Howard Journal*, 16, pp. (2) 70–96.

Canada, Government of (1995) *A Review of Firearms Statistics and Regulations in Selected Countries*. Ottawa: Department of Justice, Firearms Control Task Group (March).

Connell, R. W. (1995) *Masculinities*. Oxford: Polity Press.

Cook, P. (1983) 'The Influence of Gun Availability on Violent Crime Patterns', in M. Tonry and N. Morris (eds), *Crime and Justice*. Chicago: University of Chicago Press.

Corkery, J.(1994) *The Theft of Firearms*, Home Office Research and Planning Unit Paper no. 84. London: Home Office.

Cullen (1996) *The Public Inquiry into the Shootings at Dunblane Primary School on 13 March 1996* (The Hon. Lord Cullen), Cm. 3386, Edinburgh: Scottish Office.

Engel, M. (1994) 'Bang, bang, you're read', *The Guardian*, 14 March.

Gibson, J. W. (1994) *Warrior Dreams: Violence and Manhood in Post-Vietnam America*. New York: Hill and Wang.

Goodhart, P. and Chataway, C. (1968) *War without Weapons: the Rise of Mass Sport in the Twentieth Century – and its Effect on Men and Nations*. London: W. H. Allen.

Greenwood, C. (1972) *Firearms Control*. London: Routledge and Kegan Paul.

Jeffords, S. (1989) *The Remasculinization of America*. Bloomington: Indiana University Press.

Karp, A. (1997) 'Learning from Dunblane', Unpublished ms, Old Dominion University, Norfolk, Virginia.

Kellerman, A. (1994) 'Editorial', *Western Journal of Medicine*, 161 (6), pp. 614–15.

Kellerman, A., et al. (1993) 'Gun Ownership as a Risk Factor for Homicide in the Home', *New England Journal of Medicine*, 329, pp. 1085–91.

Kopel, D. (1992) *Gun Control in Great Britain: Saving Lives or Constricting Liberty?* Chicago: University of Illinois.

McDowell, D., Loftin, C. and Wiersema, B. (1995) 'Easing Concealed Firearms Law: Effects on Homicide in Three States', *Journal of Criminal Law and Criminology*, 86 (1), pp. 193–206.

Munday, R. A. I. (1996) 'Remarks on the Home Office and Scottish Office Statistical Surveys', in R. A. I. Munday and J. A. Stevenson (eds), *Guns and Violence: the Debate before Lord Cullen*. Brightlingsea, Essex: Piedmont Publishing.

Munday, R. A. I. and Stevenson, J. A. (eds) (1996) *Guns and Violence: the Debate before Lord Cullen*. Brightlingsea, Essex: Piedmont Publishing.

Smith, W. H. B. and Smith, J. E. (1948) *The Book of Rifles*. Harrisburg, Penn.: Stackpole.

Spitzer, R. J. (1995) *The Politics of Gun Control*. Chatham, NJ: Chatham House.

Squires, P. (1997) 'Firearms in Britain: the Irrelevance of America', Paper presented to the British Society of Criminology conference, Queens' University, Belfast.

Stern, K. S. (1996) *A Force upon the Plain: the American Militia Movement and the Politics of Hate*. New York: Simon and Schuster.

Stevenson, J. (1996) 'Evidence into Issues Concerning the Control of Firearms arising from the Dunblane Tragedy', in R. A. I. Munday and J. A. Stevenson (eds), *Guns and Violence: the Debate before Lord Cullen*. Brightlingsea, Essex: Piedmont Publishing.

Taylor, I. (1997) 'Firearms Crime – at the Time of the Cullen Enquiry', *Salford Papers in Sociology*, 20 (revised version of lecture to the Scottish Association for the Study of Delinquency, Edinburgh, 7 Nov. 1996).

Thompson, E. P. (1965) 'The Peculiarities of the English', in R. Miliband and J. Savile (eds), *The Socialist Register 1965*. London: Merlin Press.

van Duyne, P. (1993) 'Organized Crime Markets in a Turbulent Europe', *European Journal on Criminal Policy and Research*, 3, pp. 10–31.

van Duyne, P. (1996) 'The Phantom and Threat of Organized Crime', *Crime, Law and Social Change*, 24 (4), pp. 341–77.

Wills, G. (1995) 'The Right to Bear Arms', *New York Review of Books*, 21 Sept., pp. 62–73.

Zimring, F. E. (1968) 'Is Gun Control Likely to Reduce Violent Killings?' *University of Chicago Law Review*, 35, pp. 721–37.

7 Illegal Leisure: Alcohol, Drugs and the Regulation of Modern Youth
Howard Parker

INTRODUCTION

This chapter looks at the gradual reconstruction of the nature of leisure in adolescence and young adulthood and the increasing propensity for leisure to be packaged and purchased both through legal and illegal markets. There is no shortage of theoretical debate about the implications of postmodernity for growing up in the UK or Western Europe. Numerous persuasive commentaries looking at the increasingly lengthy and uncertain journey to adult citizenship (Furlong and Cartmel, 1997; Irwin, 1995) argue that marriage, parenthood and a confirmed career or occupation are increasingly deferred. Young Britons thus tend to remain in a semi-autonomous, semi-dependent or 'unsettled' phase until their mid-twenties (Chisholm and Bergeret, 1991). This period might be called post-adolescence (Jones, 1991) This one process in itself facilitates the development of a 'new' period when leisure, including illegal pleasures, are particularly prized. The purchase of leisure also affects not just adolescents but increasingly a clearly targeted niche children's market, thus even pre-teens are being captured by this process. For the outgoing young person, leisure is increasingly constructed around the youth market of designer clothes and shoes, packaged music, fast food, and public entertainment of infinite variety from concerts to raves to holidays in the sun. This MacDonaldisation process has led some commentators to argue that, in an era of individuation (Roberts et al., 1994), one's biography is constructed less by social class, gender or race and more by skilful and indeed lucky navigation through modern times. Furthermore one's very social identity is increasingly defined by consumption, by what one wears, listens to, and generally purchases (Roberts, 1998).

With the compression of time and space through global travel and an increase in the pace of life, the eternal desire to mediate the bad times with the good takes on even greater importance. Windows of opportunity to take 'time out' from being stressed-out are often small. Time to wind down is constrained and the demand to relax quickly and efficiently is thus increased. In modern times a significant minority of UK youth look to purchasing this time out through alcohol and drugs. If cosmetic surgery can deliver a better appearance pharmacology can deliver a better experience. 'Getting out of it', 'buzzing', being 'off yer face', 'blasted', 'totally stoned', whatever, can be a reward for one's success or a pick-me-up when things are not working out.

The roles of alcohol and illicit drugs have changed significantly during the 1990s for both adolescents and young adults but not in the way that public discourse has assumed. The endless criticisms levelled at young Britons throughout the decade particularly via the media's coverage of their political condemnation by Conservative ministers is built on both misunderstandings and misrepresentation of the nature of illegal leisure. This chapter looks at how alcohol 'misuse', by those under 18, and illicit drug use right across adolescence into young adulthood has developed during the decade. It juxtaposes the known epidemiological patterns and what young people actually say and do, with official constructions of their behaviour and fate. In particular this paper discusses two very high-profile regulation 'strategies' triggered by the Alcopops saga and the war on drugs rhetoric of both Conservative and Labour governments. They illustrate how informed governance has been undermined by allowing social policy to be shaped by media-led misconceptions and the desire to present clear, simple solutions to the public. In turn this shows how the current political imperative to *regulate* youth and *prohibit* their illegal leisure activities is built on misconception and misunderstanding of both process and outcome in respect of drinking and drug taking.

BLAMING YOUTH

There is nothing new about blaming youth for the ills of society. Scape-goating and stereotyping in this way has a distinguished tradition (Cohen, 1973; Pearson, 1983). The 1990s has been a decade when blaming others has been a routine political activity. The blaming of a small group of 'persistent' offenders under the age of 14 for a rise in crime rates, community fear of crime and moral breakdown was repeatedly articulated by the Conservative Home Secretary, Michael Howard. He not only read the tabloids but provided them with regular copy, particularly at each Conservative Party Conference between 1993 and 1996.

> We're all sick and tired of reading about young hooligans who've endlessly stolen cars, burgled houses and terrorised communities. We'll set up separate secure centres for 12–14 year olds who can't be locked up at all and we must get on, pass the legislation, build these centres, get these thugs off the streets, that's what we've got to do.   (Michael Howard, Home Secretary, 1993)

The attempted introduction of secure training centres for under 15s, the extension of the length of custodial sentences for under 18-year-olds, the reduction in the use of cautioning as a diversion from court proceedings, the encouragement of school exclusions, were all measures aimed at 'dangerous' youth during the 1990s.

Indeed, 1990s youth have been able to do little right. Each summer when GCSE and A level results are published and show improved overall standards the adult response is that 'they're getting easier'. Modern youth are weak-willed as evidenced by their fast-food diets, obesity and lack of exercise. On the moral front young women from poor communities are accused of getting pregnant to jump problem housing lists. All this of course is before Ecstasy and raves are mentioned.

ALCOHOL AND YOUTH

Expressing concern about the 'abuse' of alcohol by the young is a long-standing professional activity (e.g. Royal College of General Practitioners, 1986; Royal College of Psychiatrists, 1986). Evidence that some young people drink dangerously can always be gathered because some do. The tendency is to produce this evidence, suitably endorsed by experts, whenever troublesome youth are high on the political agenda. At the end of the 1980s the *lager louts*, young employed men from the Home Counties who were said to disrupt town-centre life each weekend with drunken disorder, had their few minutes of fame (ACPO, 1988; Tuck, 1989).

Although young people's alcohol consumption rose during the 1960s and 1970s it plateaued during the 1980s. The picture by the mid-1980s was of a stable spectrum of drinking patterns with a small minority of teenage abstainers, a majority of moderate drinkers and a minority of heavy, frequent young drinkers. Young men drank more than young women. Drinking levels rose from about 15 years of age tending to peak in early adulthood (Marsh et al., 1986; May, 1992). Heavy drinking tended to be defined as over the then safe limits of 14 units for women and 21 for men, and it was generally agreed that 10–15 per cent of the youth population drank excessively and well beyond even today's upwardly revised safe limits (Plant and Plant, 1992). It was also agreed that far more young people would get drunk on a fairly regular basis (Plant et al., 1985).

During the first half of the 1990s the drinking habits of British adolescents and young adults received scant attention, and no government interest and the subtle but important changes underway in this normalised social habit were missed – more of which later. However, in the political and moral climate of the 1995–7 period it was perhaps inevitable that alcohol and youth would be twinned. And so it was. The arrival of alcoholic lemonades in 1995, led from Australia by *Two Dogs* and soon dominated by *Hooch*, made by Bass in the UK, produced the catalyst for another spotlight to be turned on the social behaviour of young people. The success of these fruit-flavoured 'alcoholised' lemonades set off a fierce public debate which lasted into late 1997. The Alcopops Saga had begun.

THE ALCOPOPS SAGA

The Regulation Panic

The 'debate' began sensibly enough with serious concern being expressed about the drinks manufacturers' perceived unethical and mercenary behaviour in respect of targeting the youth market, thereby encouraging young people to break the law through underage purchasing and break a code of expected behaviour by excessive, premature drinking. Children and teenagers are already troublesome enough, went the thesis, we don't need to make matters worse by encouraging them to drink alcohol before their time. The three sustainable and well made objections to Alcopops (Alcohol Concern, 1996) were:

- The collapse of the distinction between alcoholic and soft drinks
- The promotion of alcohol potent drinks attractive to a teenage market
- The masking of the taste of alcohol with sugary flavourings

This initial theme became a 'regulation panic', although once it had been run and re-run it had a tired look about it. The media, however, feeling Alcopops and Youth had more mileage in them, created a second theme. It constructed a moral panic about the drinking delinquent. Alcopops would lead modern youth into crime and disorder which in turn would undermine the moral fabric of the UK. In short, the media purposefully linked Alcopops to the broader youth-blaming discourse discussed earlier. It spawned a moral panic from a regulation panic.

The Drinking Delinquent

The moral panic was constructed by linking Alcopops to early drinking, disorder, drunkenness, delinquency and poor parenting. The archetypal story was created by the *Sunday* and *Daily Mirror* group. Their thesis was contained on a double-page spread (8 Sept. 1996), when they reported on the results of a commissioned survey. Alongside pictures of teenagers swigging from bottles their headlines were clear:

> Britain is in danger of raising a generation of young people who first become hopelessly drunk at the age of 14, whose easy access to alcohol proves that the licensing laws are an ineffective joke and whose behaviour begins in a downward spiral leading to crime, underage pregnancies and social breakdown.

The 'drinking delinquent' was reconstructed as another folk devil to run alongside those already in place to be blamed. For several months this imagery was repeated both by television (e.g. BBC2, Close Up North's *Closing Time*) and in particular by local media throughout the country, who made the connection between Alcopops and under-age drinking, local street drinking networks, weekend gatherings of local youth, disorder, drunkenness and violence. Thus at regional level

> 'Teenage drinking blamed on alcopops'. (*Leicester Mercury*, 19 April 1996)
> 'Police back fears about alcopops'. (*Yorkshire Evening Post*, 20 June 1996)
> 'Alarming rise in drink abuse by youngsters ... seminar told of harmful effects of trendy alcoholic lemonade'. (*Press and Journal Aberdeen*, 21 June 1996)

The Alcopops saga confirmed the intellectual fragility of the final days of the Conservative administration. Whilst happy to condone the blaming of the drinking delinquent and to link it to their pre-election law and order campaign, they were conspicuously silent on intervening to regulate a 'successful' drinks industry. The media did not forget this.

Alcopops after the General Election

From just after the announcement of a General Election early in 1997 through to polling day in May the Alcopops stories simply disappeared. The media had other things on their journalistic minds. However very shortly after the election and with the new Labour administration quickly making it clear that it would be more interventionist, the media campaign began again, but by this time reverting back to demands for regulation. The dominant theme was that the under-age and thus illegal consumption of Alcopops was continuing unchecked. Two key stories, one about a boy who set fire to a school after consuming a variety of alcohol products including Alcopops, and another story about a young man's death on a railway line, were covered throughout the media.

> 'Publican banned after train kills alcopop boy: under-age drinker's death brings more calls for control'. (*The Times*, 26 June 1997)

The push for regulation continued as several police forces and local authorities courted regional and national publicity for their checks on off-licences by utilising 'underage' teenagers, under supervision, to attempt to buy Alcopops. Where there were illegal sales the headlines followed:

> 'Police trap for alcopop youngsters'. (*The Express*, 6 June 1997)
> 'Underage alcopop buyers beat store safety check'. (*The Times*, 22 July 1997)

The new Labour administration set about strategically defusing this 'third leg' of panic by insisting it would take firm action. It happily speculated about banning Alcopops at off-sales to kill off the media coverage in order to give it time to deal, or not, with a very fraught policy dilemma. In the end the solution was to give *ad hoc* regulation another try. In July 1997 the government agreed to give the drinks industry, through the Portman Group, the manufacturers' own regulatory council, another chance. The industry was required to improve and toughen its code on product promotion and retailing, expand 'proof of age' card schemes and improve training for off- and on-sales staff. The government decided to implement the Confiscation of Alcohol (Young Persons) Act of 1997 which allows the police to confiscate alcohol from young people they believe to be under 18. It also promised to introduce legislation to make it an offence for adults to knowingly purchase alcohol for under 18s. Finally, government agreed to clear the bureaucratic way for more intensive off-licence test-purchasing to entrap licensees selling to the under 18s. This was coupled with further encouragement to magistrates to be tough on granting and reviewing local liquor licences.

This considerable package of new regulation was classically underpinned by threat of far more draconian action if the drinks industry did not put its house in order. All this clearly differentiated the new Labour administration from the Conservatives' hands-off approach to any profitable, productive sector of the market economy. The previous government had introduced all-day opening for pubs and bars, deregulated Sunday licensing laws, encouraged family rooms in pubs and raised the recommended safe drinking limit. One might say the Conservatives had encouraged personal choice and freedom in respect of alcohol use certainly when compared with the more interventionist, perhaps paternalistic, stance of Labour.

YOUNG DRINKERS IN THE 1990s

We can now compare and contrast this public and political debate about young people and alcohol with what has actually happened to drinking patterns during the 1990s.

The continuity and stability in drinking patterns of the 1980s has in fact been dislocated during the 1990s by four shifts: major changes in the alcohol products young people drink; a probable increase in the proportion of non- and light drinkers amongst 1990s youth; an increase in the amount young weekly drinkers consume and an increase in the amount consumed per session or episode amongst regular young drinkers.

This said, and before outlining these shifts, we must note that much remains stable and unchanged. There is a robust back-cloth of continuity in young people's alcohol profiles.

DESIGNER DRINKS AND COMMODIFICATION

Commodification is part of the global process of diversification in variety, range and specificity of products and services associated with postmodernity. This process is found full blown in the promotion of alcohol to the youth and young adult market. Thus *what* young people drink has changed radically with designer drinks now dominating their repertoires. These bottled and canned, increasingly strong in alcohol by volume, branded, image-laden products are those now favoured by young people. Premium strong lagers, strong white ciders and fortified fruit wines are particularly popular (McKeganey et al., 1996; Measham, 1996; the Scottish Council on Alcohol, 1996; Hughes et al., 1997; Brain and Parker, 1997). In short, young people's drinking, particularly away from dinner table wine, is dominated by brand name designer drinks. The most popular brands are, for example, for cider Diamond White (ABV 8 per cent), for premium lagers Becks, Fosters' Ice, and Budweiser (all ABV 5 per cent) and for fruit wines Mad Dog, 20/20, Ravers and Thunderbird (all over ABV 13 per cent). Alcopops are, in reality, extensions of the process whereby image, strength and easy taste are all carefully blended into a branded alcohol product with youth appeal.

An Increase in Light and Non-drinkers?

There has always been a small minority of Britons in every age group who never drink alcohol at all. Their abstention is motivated by ethnic or religious expectations or simply personal choice. A large group of light drinkers who only indulge on special occasions is also identifiable and they, in fact, have much in common with abstainers whereby alcohol plays almost no role in their lives.

Whilst there is no strong, clear shift identifiable, it does appear that very light and non-drinking young people are increasing as a proportion of the overall age group (Foxcroft and Lowe, 1995). We are talking about a small shift in a minority group, but nevertheless in the world of leisure consumption this rejection of alcohol by a minority is important to acknowledge as an identifiable pattern (Balding and Regis, 1996).

Weekly Drinkers in Adolescence

There is a corollary to this increase in light drinking in that we have clear evidence that those one in five of 11 to 16-year-olds who drink weekly (Measham, 1996) and particularly the third of 14 to 16-year-olds who do so, are drinking more each week. The most impressive evidence of this comes from Exeter University's young people's lifestyle surveys. Balding and Regis (1996) refer to this process as 'more alcohol down fewer throats'.

Getting Drunk: More Alcohol per Session

Sticking mainly with the weekly and more than once a week minority, there is good evidence that they are drinking more per session than was found in the 1980s. The mean number of units of alcohol consumed 'last time' by regular young drinkers a decade ago was 4–5 for girls and 6–7 for boys (15–16 years). This figure seems to have risen significantly during the decade to 6–7 units for girls and 8–9 units for boys (Measham, 1996; Miller and Plant, 1996). Even this average hides an increasing tendency for over 11 units to be consumed each episode by the heaviest young drinkers. This heavy sessional drinking is particularly marked in Scotland and Northern Ireland (Dean, 1990; Loretto, 1994).

ALCOPOPS' IMPACT ON YOUTH DRINKING PATTERNS

Alcopops and Risk Takers

Where, if at all, do Alcopops fit into this picture of continuity and change? Do they, as the public discourse would have it, encourage inappropriate drinking and related deviant behaviour?

In a study in north-west England involving a survey of 727–13 to 16-year-olds, interviews with 55 outside drinkers and an observational study of 3 street drinking networks in different urban neighbourhoods, an attempt was made to identify the significance of Alcopops on young people's drinking habits. The main findings of the study were all consistent with much of the earlier work. The drinking spectrum was in evidence as was the increase in alcohol intakes through adolescence. In particular, by asking young people to nominate exactly what they drank (e.g. range and brand), this study identified both a commitment to designer drinks in general and to a personalised range in particular, whereby, young drinkers had several favourites which they interchanged.

This study (Brain and Parker, 1997) showed that Alcopops, particularly Hooch, had indeed quickly penetrated the drinking repertoires of teenage consumers. However, this was not because young people had simply followed the publicity trail to a new product. The investigation discovered that young drinkers use an identifiable formula of *price*, *strength*, *taste* and *image* to decide what to drink. This cost-benefit assessment was most pronounced amongst young drinkers with limited financial resources.

Heavy frequent drinkers, those who begin to conform to the 'drinking delinquent' identikit were far more likely to drink lagers and ciders and less likely to drink Alcopops regularly. These heavier drinkers did indeed tend towards being more 'risk taking', being far more likely to have been recently very drunk, tried drugs and been arrested. Alcopops drinkers on the other hand were, according to the survey results, predominantly 13 to 14-year-olds, female, middle class and light occasional drinkers, hardly the profile portrayed by the media.

Motivational Accounts for Young Street Drinkers

By purposefully interviewing and observing young public street drinkers who hang out and consume alcohol in local meeting places (e.g. the cemetery, the park, the canal bridge) the drinking delinquent became the research focus. What did those very individuals whom both the national and local media pathologise think of Alcopops?

For this group 'getting wrecked' and 'buzzing' were very important. This state was primarily achieved through excessive drinking, with illicit drug use being a secondary alternative. Fifty-three of the 55 street drinkers had tried an illicit drug, with cannabis and amphetamines dominating their experience.

One local drinking network contacted and observed had a clear favourite drink – a strong white cider, Pulse, typically bought from late shops in 2 litre bottles for around £2. Pulse could offer one unit of alcohol at a quarter of the price of a bottle of Hooch. It was acceptable by taste, by strength at 8.4 per cent ABV, and was extremely good value if getting drunk was the primary goal, which it usually was.

> Drinking gives me a high, I don't talk unless I'm pissed.   (Des, male, 15 years)

> I'd drink everyday if I had the money, it's just a buzz, I love it the buzz when you get pissed.   (Bill, male, 16 years)

> A good time ... drinking at the weekend, I drink for a buzz, it puts me in a good mood, because friends doing it ... nearly every

weekend we walk around the streets spend about £1.20 [each] on
Pulse.   (Ken, male, 14 years)

Pulse, interestingly had an acceptable masculine image for this particular street network. In another network, Effes Pils, a strong, but cheap,
premium lager was the primary product at the time of the fieldwork.

Effes Pils is good value for money. You get 4 bottles for £2.50, go
halves with someone and you can get 8 for £5. (Dek, male, 15 years)

I stick to about four different types, stick between 5 and 6%, stay
with Stella, Effes and Carling, they all slide down, lagers on offer
and have a decent percentage.   (Bill, male, 15 years)

The importance of product image emerged as a key issue more from
the qualitative fieldwork rather than the survey, and it is here, with
imagery, that designer lagers and ciders left Alcopops behind.

Hooch and that, I've tried them, they're more for women than guys
... guys I know don't really drink them. (Mark, male, 16 years)

They [girls] drink shit like Hooch, it's a girl's drink. Hooch is alright
at the end of the night when I've had a pure beer like Stella.   (Bill,
male, 15 years)

REGULATING THE 'DRINKING DELINQUENT'

The 1990s almost passed by without any new regulation of young
drinkers. The development of increasingly strong, smooth-tasting,
image-laden designer drinks, aimed at the youth market, was ignored
by government and opposition politicians alike. The linkage between
these beverages and increased sessional drinking and thus drunkenness was not made. And yet suddenly a regulation panic about
Alcopops and teenage drinkers arrives, turns into a moral panic and
produces an enormous media-led regulatory drive against under-age
drinkers and the so-called drinking delinquent. The political process is
this malleable and this fickle.
   Yet in truth Alcopops, whilst they most certainly demonstrate the
sophistication and determination of the drinks industry to capture
youth market drinkers, are merely an extension of the designer drinks
phenomenon which developed throughout the 1990s without official

criticism. The 'problem' under-age drinker has little time for Alcopops, preferring the good value and appropriate image from premium lagers and ciders and fortified fruit wines. When we look at the meaning and value given to 'buzzing' amongst young street drinkers, we can quickly see the gulf between the simplistic discourse about youth crime and Alcopops and their actual motives and strategies. The youth formation who will be least affected by the new raft of regulation will be those specifically targeted for control.

RECREATIONAL DRUG USE AMONGST YOUNG BRITONS

The Upward Trends

The 1990s have seen an unprecedented rise in the number of adolescents who have been involved in illicit drugs. Whichever research technique is utilised, be it household survey (Leitner et al., 1993; Mott and Mirrlees-Black, 1995) school administered questionnaires (Balding, 1997) or school surveys administered by independent researchers, the upward trends are apparent and in all four country regions of the UK (e.g. Roberts et al., 1995; Craig, 1997; Miller and Plant, 1996).

The north-west longitudinal study reported here involved tracking the same group of young people for 5 years of their adolescence (14–19 years), looking at how their drinking and drug use developed, or not, through the 1990s (see Newcombe et al., 1995; Parker and Measham, 1994; Parker et al., 1995; Parker et al., 1998). In this paper only very brief reference can be made to what has been a mammoth investigation. The data presented will suggest that illegal leisure through drug trying and, for a significant minority, more regular drug use is becoming 'normalised' or accommodated and accepted within youth culture. This makes its rapid prohibition or regulation in a democratic market economy almost impossible.

Table 7.1 looks at the offer rates for the first four years of the study. It describes how by the age of 17 each annual sample and the cohort (those tracked successfully for all four years) have been in situations where drugs have been on offer, for free or to buy. By age 17, 9 in 10 young people have reported being in such situations or settings. However, what even these figures hide is that such scenarios are encountered on numerous occasions as young people move in their own social space.

Table 7.1   Drug offers for samples and cohort (ages 14–17 inc.)

	Year One	Year Two	Year Three	Year Four
Sample	(n = 776) 59%	(n = 752) 71%	(n = 523) 76%	(n = 536) 88%
Cohort	(n = 240) 56%	(n = 240) 68%	(n = 240) 77%	(n = 240) 88%

In Table 7.2 we can see that the proportion of respondents who disclose ever having tried an illicit drug has increased annually through adolescence, whereby over half this fairly representative sample have tried a drug by the end of compulsory schooling. Table 7.3 shows which drugs are involved. Cannabis clearly dominates drug trying, with

Table 7.2   Lifetime prevalence (trying) for samples and cohort
(ages 14–17 inc.)

	Year One	Year Two	Year Three	Year Four
Sample	(n = 776) 36%	(n = 752) 47%	(n = 523) 51%	(n = 536) 57%
Cohort	(n = 240) 27%	(n = 240) 39%	(n = 240) 45%	(n = 240) 57%

Table 7.3   Lifetime prevalence of illicit drug trying, annual samples (%)

	Year One	Year Two	Year Three	Year Four	Year Five
Cannabis (Draw, Pot)	32	41	45	54	59
Nitrites (Poppers, Rush)	14	22	24	31	35
LSD (Trips, Acid)	13	25	24	27	28
Solvents (Butane, Glue)	12	13	10	10	9
Magic Mushrooms	10	12	10	10	9
Amphetamine (Whizz, Speed)	10	16	18	25	33
MDMA (Ecstasy)	6	7	5	13	20
Cocaine (Coke, Crack)	1	4	2	4	6
Tranquillisers (Tranx)	1	5	2	4	5
Heroin (Smack, Skag)	0	3	1	1	1
Steroids	N/A	N/A	N/A	1	1

nitrates, amphetamines, LSD and, in later adolescence, Ecstasy being the key drugs. These rates, although slightly higher than most other early 1990s studies, are now being replicated in mid-1990s surveys (e.g. Barnard et al., 1996; Miller and Plant, 1996).

It is unwise, however, to rely on lifetime 'trying' rates as the key measure of the significance of illicit drug use in youth populations. Such figures may be based on only one or two brief, perhaps regretted, experiments in early adolescence. This hardly describes a leisure/pleasure activity or the way young people make decisions about illegal drugs.

Drugs Pathways in the 1990s

Using the core cohort of 240, a complex analysis of their four years' questionnaire returns plus interviews with 86 of them allowed distinctive decision-making journeys to be identified and four robust drugs pathways to be created (Aldridge et al., 1996). These four pathways were:

Abstainers, who had never tried a drug and had no intention of doing so in the future.

Former triers had tried one or more drugs, usually experimentally, and had no intention of using another illicit drug in the future.

In transition refers to a group who may or may not have tried illicit drugs but who believed they might do so in the future. They were keeping their options open.

Current users were those who used drugs regularly and expected to continue their drug use. Most had used several drugs, some were poly drug users.

Abstainers made up 35 per cent of the cohort. *Former triers* made up 10 per cent. Both these groups tend to hold anti-drug attitudes and what also binds them together is their declared intention not to try drugs in the future. Three-quarters of the 33 per cent *in transition* had tried a drug and a quarter had not. This pathway group tended to hold pro-drug attitudes and expected to try an illicit drug in the future. *Current users* held strong pro-drug attitudes and intended to use drugs again in the future. They made up 22 per cent of the cohort.

TALKING HEADS ONE

In Transition

Male, 17, sporty, alcohol and amphetamine 'experimenter' (Case 8):

> Just to experiment really. That's it. Just to experiment, just to try them. I suppose the atmosphere of clubs makes me want to try them ... not really because my friends are doing it, its because I want to experiment myself. I mean, my friends never ever pressure me at all no peer group pressure at all, its basically my choice.

Male, 18; Left school 16 (Case 44) (He's tried a lot of drugs from 14 onwards):

> [In the future?] I can see it changing. It's changed already. This is what I hope to do ... when I'm older I do want to continue smoking weed but not everyday. Just cannabis.

> I feel I know what's what. I know what drugs I would take and what I wouldn't, the amounts of drugs I would take and so on. [You say you don't use LSD anymore.] Yes I think I've matured with drug use. At first I was into anything, now I know what I like, what I don't like.

Drug Users

Female, 17, A level student (Case 64):

> Favourite drug, E ... because you feel so different, it's just, I can't explain, it's just such a wonderful feeling. You see everything in a different light, everyone seems so nice, and everyone's dead friendly. When everybody else is having it as well, you can do what you want and nobody thinks your stupid, everyone's the same, you can do what you want and no one thinks you're a dick.

Male, 17, amphetamine user (Case 65):

> It's sort of, when you go out and try and enjoy yourself and it's a sort of way of bringing on the enjoyment I suppose. It helps you relax. It's just something to do. It's sort to basically getting a bit of a buzz really.

TALKING HEADS TWO

Former Triers

Female, 17, tried cocaine when 15. Now 'anti-drugs'. Took cocaine via a boyfriend. (Case 13):

> Because I've tried it and I know I won't take it again ... Because I wouldn't normally take it apart from the fact I felt under pressure ... Just the fact I don't really want to use them. Things my mum said from when she was younger, and just that I don't particularly want to use them. [Other reasons?] Fear of consequence, the danger that it could lead to something else.

Male, 17, girlfriend died from drugs overdose. He was a regular poly drug user previously. (Case 42):

> My girlfriend. She just dehydrated, just collapsed ... She was drinking beer, and you know beer, it doesn't actually quench your thirst, does it? She just collapsed.

Abstainers

Female, 17, goes pubbing and clubbing, doing A levels and part-time work (Case 17):

> I've had it drummed into me even since I was little how bad it is and what it does to people [who by?] My mum and dad. Watch documentaries on it. I've seen how its affected friends. I've seen people get into debt. I think if you're the kind of person that can enjoy yourself you don't need it. I don't think anyone needs it. And, just the fact I'd be too scared.

Male, 18, sports trainer, occasional drinker (Case 28):

> You see lots of things on the news, on the television, in the papers, and personal experience as well. Well, what do I mean, you go out to a club and you see people smashed out of their brain and you think what's the point of doing that, you know, they can't stand up, they just look out of it, its just a joke.

... I'm quite a sporty person. My aim really is to do PE as a job or go into the army, so it doesn't appeal to me. My family as well, they own a business, at a pub. If I was caught drug dealing it would get my parents into trouble, they'd probably lose their business, can't do it.

These pathways are not describing static absolutes (see Talking Heads One and Two). They conceptually represent decision-making journeys, and the proportions of young people in each will continue to change as they do, predictably, at Year Five (Parker et al., 1998). However, we can see quite clearly that current regular users make up just under a quarter of the cohort. Their drug use will continue and with others, in transition, expecting to try or re-try drugs in the future, the incidence and prevalence of illicit drug use will continue to climb for this sample.

Decision-making Journeys

Most young people in this study demonstrated a fair degree of sophistication, particularly in later adolescence when making decisions about whether or not to try drugs. *Abstainers* were involved in all this because they had to negotiate through offer situations, friends and acquaintances taking drugs and often romantic partners being users. Whilst some 'hard-line' abstainers would have no truck with drugs or drug users, others were able to accommodate their peers' right to self-administering a drug recreationally. It seems increasingly difficult for abstainers to self-select peer groups which are totally drug free. This is a sign of the times.

Drug triers and users routinely applied a cost-benefit assessment in deciding whether to try or re-use particular drugs, each of which they judged separately on its own merits. The assessment formula took in immediate health risks, the implication of discovery, particularly by family or employers, the cost of the drugs as against other consumption options (e.g. alcohol), the after-effect of drug use in mood and performance, and the propensity of the drug to provide relaxation, energy, a 'buzz', etc. Very often this was all talked about in a very matter of fact way. Whilst former triers had clearly decided drugs were not worth it, the in-transition (trying majority) and current users were quite clear that they obtained far more positive experiences than negative ones from their drug use. With over 70 per cent of the Year Four users sample defining their last drugs experience as 'very good' or 'mostly good' and only 7 per cent feeling the experiences were 'very bad' or 'mostly bad' (Measham et al., 1998), drugs like cannabis, amphetamines and Ecstasy were rated highly. Only LSD, because of its propensity to induce 'bad trips', was assessed critically.

TOWARDS THE NORMALISATION OF RECREATIONAL DRUG USE

Illicit 'recreational' drug use has grown far more rapidly and extensively during the 1990s than at any other time. The availability of a large range of drugs, extensive drug trying and an increasing proportion of regular young drug users form the basis for the normalisation of recreational (i.e. non-dependent, occasional) use. With far more young women and young people from all social classes trying drugs, and higher education students demonstrating an enormous appetite for them (Webb et al., 1996), it is not difficult to conclude that the prohibition of this component of illegal leisure is a formidable task. It is made the more difficult by the accommodation of drug use and drug users in almost all the social space young people frequent from car, bus, train to pub, club and friends' bedrooms. Abstainers, whilst disappointed at witnessing this behaviour around them, are becoming increasingly pragmatic and reluctantly accepting the 'right' of their peers to indulge.

CONCLUSION

There is nothing new about attempts to regulate the consumption of alcohol and illicit drugs by young people. The significant issue for the 1990s is that despite quite enormous efforts and resources being put into prevention and prohibition there are no signs that illegal leisure is doing anything but growing in popularity.

When we pull together the regulatory attempts we find a large collection of *ad hoc* prohibition measures. On the alcohol front the new Labour administration seems particularly keen on introducing regulation. It is implementing the Confiscation of Alcohol (Young Person's) Act 1997 and preparing legislation to make the purchase of alcohol by an adult for someone under 18 an offence, along with legitimising the 'testing' and further prosecution of licensees and off-sales outlets.

Unfortunately all this regulation stemmed not from a carefully thought-out comprehensive alcohol policy but from a bizarre moral panic about Alcopops and the drinking delinquent prior to a General Election. The measures will have least impact on their intended target, young 'risk taking' street drinkers, because they fail to grasp what they drink and why, and pay no attention to the unintended consequences of such a 'zero tolerance' approach. In the unlikely event that such regulation will actually be implemented by the police in urban neighbourhoods, this type of surveillance and intervention would increase the alienation of local youth and quickly stimulate more devious drinking strategies, or as likely a transfer to illicit drugs.

Whilst there is little doubt that the drinking delinquent exists he is usually already damaged by his life and educational experiences, not by his psycho-active excesses (Rutter and Smith, 1994; Carlen, 1996). It would seem far more appropriate to discuss such young people as part of a debate about social exclusion, poverty, inequality and the causes of crime than to pander to tabloid opinion with sound bites about zero tolerance and curfews.

The gradual normalisation of recreational drug use over the 1990s has quite simply outwitted and outstripped official intervention delivered under the 'war on drugs' banner. Thus hundreds of millions of pounds have been spent on drugs education and prevention programmes which appear to have made precious little difference. It is predictable that instead of questioning why this is so, that is, questioning current policy, the new Labour government has merely redoubled its efforts by restating the war on drugs strategy but ensuring the blame for its continued failure will be shared with a new Drugs Tsar intent on further prohibition and regulation efforts, extending to prosecuting ravers. It is significant that senior police officers are far more sceptical about current policy than politicians, who appear willing to continue to publicly support a failing policy which is increasingly being called into question. *Tackling Drugs Together* (HMSO, 1994) illustrates the institutionalised misconceptions about youthful recreational drug use held in government. It assumes, indeed openly declares, that young people try drugs because of peer pressure, think that all drugs are the same and that drug use leads young people into crime. And yet when we explore young people's accounts and behaviour through time they clearly, particularly in later adolescence, make rational decisions about drugs. They are usually clear about their own limits and are not led into either drug use or crime by demonic forces. Moreover, they judge most drug experiences as positive and pleasurable.

Taking drugs is increasingly an act of consumption, a calculated risk decision to produce or induce 'good times' and 'time out' in a fast moving, uncertain world. The demand for psycho-active miracles is increasing in modern times and it is unsurprising, given these powerful social processes, that drugs education, public health messages and hectoring from an adult world, like *ad hoc* enforcement, have little effect.

What is most worrying about current drugs policy is that because it is cloaked in war-on-drugs rhetoric it cannot contemplate fully guarding the health and safety of young drug users. Drug taking is not always safe and the excessive drinking and drug-taking repertoires of some young people are indeed health damaging. Yet harm reduction measures are barely sanctioned in government policy, being left to local inter-agency initiatives. Combination dance drug night clubbers in particular need far more advice and direction about their drug repertoires. Street drugs also remain quality unassured. This is because the reality of youthful drug use must be denied and condemned. To accept there is a need for and provide public health intervention is to condone drug use according to the drugs warriors.

This unreality in drugs policy, its siting in the law and order 'youth blaming' discourse, will continue for some time yet. Unfortunately the social and epidemiological trends in illegal leisure will need to continue unchecked before the hegemony of the war on drugs discourse will be muted. 1990s youth have, unwittingly, by becoming the first chemical generation, also become objects of distorted debate. They have experienced more control than care, more blame than apology, and had far more restrictions and regulations heaped upon them than rights, positive status and personal freedoms bestowed. It serves them right of course: nothing good ever comes from getting stoned.

REFERENCES

ACPO (1988) *Public Disorder Outside Metropolitan Areas*. Association of Chief Police Officers.

Alcohol Concern (1996) *Pop Fiction: The Truth about Alcopops*. London.

Aldridge, J., Parker, H. and Measham, F. (1996) *Drugs Pathways in the 90s. Adolescents' Decision Making about Illicit Drug Use*. Home Office Drugs Prevention Initiative. (unpublished).

Balding, J. (1997) *Young People in 1996*. Exeter: Exeter University.

Balding, J. and Regis, J. (1996) 'More Alcohol Down Fewer Throats'. *Education and Health*, 13, 4, pp. 61–4.

Barnard, M., Forsyth, A. and McKeganey, N. (1996) 'Levels of Drug Use among a Sample of Scottish Schoolchildren'. *Drugs: Education, Prevention and Policy*, 3, 1, pp. 81–90.

Beck, U. (1992) *Risk Society: Towards a New Modernity*. London: Sage.

Brain, K. and Parker, H. (1997) *Drinking with Design: Alcopops, Designer Drinks and Youth Culture*. London: Portman Group.

Carlen, P. (1996) *Jigsaw – A Political Criminology of Youth Homelessness*. Buckingham: Open University Press.

Chisholm, L. and Bergeret, J. (1991) *Young People in the European Community*. Report to the Commission of the European Communities Task Force on Education, Training and Youth, Brussels.

Cohen, S. (1973) *Folk Devils and Moral Panics*. London: Paladin.

Craig, J. (1997) *Almost Adult*. Belfast: Northern Ireland Statistics and Research Agency.

Dean, A. (1990) 'Culture and Community: Drink and Soft Drugs in Hebridean Youth Culture'. *Sociological Review*, 38, pp. 517–65.

Foxcroft, D. and Lowe, G. (1995) 'Teenage Drinking: a Four Year Comparative Study'. *Alcohol and Alcoholism*, 36, 6, pp. 713–19.

Furlong, A. and Cartmel, F. (1997) *Young People and Social Change*. Buckingham: Open University Press.

HMSO (1994) *Tackling Drugs Together*. London.

Hughes, K., Mackintosh, A., Hastings, G., Wheeler, C., Watson, J. and Inglis, J. (1997) 'Young People, Alcohol and Designer Drinks'. *British Medical Journal*, 314.

Irwin, S. (1995) 'Social Reproductional Change in the Transition from Youth to Adulthood'. *Sociology*, 29, pp. 293–315.

Jones, G. (1991) *From Dependency to Citizenship: Transitions to Adulthood in Britain*. Paper given at Moscow Youth Institute.

Leitner, M., Shapland, J. and Wiles, P. (1993) *Drug Usage and Prevention*. London: Home Office.

Loretto, W. (1994) *Licit and Illicit Drug Use in Two Cultures*. London: Harwood.

Marsh, A., Dobbs, J. and White, A. (1986) *Adolescent Drinking*. London: HMSO.

May, C. (1992) 'A Burning Issue? Adolescent Alcohol Use in Britain'. *Alcohol and Alcoholism*, 27, 2, pp. 109–15.

McKeganey, N. et al. (1996) 'Designer Drinks and Drunkenness amongst a Sample of Scottish School Children'. *British Medical Journal* 313, p. 401.

Measham, F. (1996) 'The Big Bang Approach to Sessional Drinking: Changing Patterns of Alcohol Consumption amongst Young People in North West England'. *Addiction Research*, 4, 3, pp. 283–9.

Measham, F., Aldridge, J. and Parker, H. (1998) 'The Teenage Transition: From Adolescent Recreational Drug Use to the Young Adult Dance Culture in Britain'. *Journal of Drug Issues*, Special Issue, forthcoming.

Miller, P. and Plant, M. (1996) 'Drinking, Smoking and Illicit Drug Use among 15 and 16 Year Olds in the United Kingdom'. *British Medical Journal*, 313, pp. 394–7.

Mott, J. and Mirlees-Black, C. (1995) *Self Reported Misuse in England and Wales*. Research and Planning Unit Paper 89, Home Office, London.

Newcombe, R., Measham, F. and Parker, H. (1995) 'A Survey of Drinking and Deviant Behaviour among 14/15 Year Olds in North West England'. *Addiction Research*, 2, 4, pp. 319–41.

Parker, H., Aldridge, J. and Measham, F. (1998) *From Subculture to Drug Culture*. London: Routledge.

Parker, H. and Measham, F. (1994) "Pick 'n' mix": Changing Patterns of Illicit Drug Use amongst 1990s Adolescents'. *Drugs: Education, Prevention and Policy*, 1, 1, pp. 5–13.

Parker, H., Measham, F. and Aldridge, J. (1995) *Drugs Futures: Changing Patterns of Drug Use Amongst English Youth*. Institute for the Study of Drug Dependency, London.

Pearson, G. (1983) *Hooligan: A History of Respectable Fears*. London: Macmillan.

Plant, M., Peck, D. and Samuel, E. (1985) *Alcohol, Drugs and School Leavers*. London: Tavistock.

Plant, M. and Plant, M. (1992) *The Risk Takers: Alcohol, Drugs, Sex and Youth*. London: Tavistock–Routledge.

Release (1997) *Release Drugs and Dance Survey*. London.

Roberts, C., Moore, L., Blakey, V., Playle, R. and Tutor-Smith, C. (1995) 'Drug Use among 15–16 Year Olds in Wales 1990–94'. *Drugs: Education, Prevention and Policy*, 2, 3, pp. 305–17.

Roberts, K. (1998) *Leisure: Consumption, Lifestyles and Identities in Post Industrial Society*. Forthcoming.

Roberts, K., Clark, S. and Wallace, C. (1994) 'Flexibility and Individualisation: a Comparison of Transitions into Employment in England and Germany'. *Sociology*, 28, 1, pp. 31–54.

Royal College of General Practitioners (1986) *Alcohol: A Balanced View*. London.

Royal College of Psychiatrists (1986) *Alcohol, Our Favourite Drug*. London: Tavistock.

Rutter, M. and Smith, D. (eds) (1994) *Psychosocial Disorders in Young People: Time Trends and Their Causes*. Chichester: John Wiley.

Scottish Council on Alcohol (1996) *Young People and Alcohol in Scotland: A Survey of Brand Preferences of 15–17 Year Olds*. London.

Stares, P. (1996) *Global Habit: the Drug Problem in a Borderless World*. Washington, DC: Brooklyn Institute.

Tuck, M. (1989) *Drinking and Disorder: a Study of Non-metropolitan Violence*. HORPU Research Report 108, London: HMSO.

Webb, E. et al. (1996) 'Alcohol and Drug Use in UK University Students'. *Lancet*, 348, pp. 922–5.

8 Bodybuilding, Steroids and Violence: Is there a Connection?

Russell P. Dobash, Lee Monaghan,
R. Emerson Dobash and Michael Bloor

INTRODUCTION

In the late 1980s the British media discovered a new and apparently widespread social problem – 'roid rage'. The phenomena of 'roid rage', uncontrollable malevolent aggression and violence, was reputedly linked to the use or abuse of anabolic androgenic steroids. As in the classic moral panic, the media, institutions of the state and various 'experts' identified bodybuilding steroid users as a new group of 'folk devils'. A by-line in the *Guardian* (13 Oct. 1992) made this explicit: 'Many bodybuilders abuse steroids, leading to the violent conduct known as Roid Rage.' The police added an authoritative voice with one Manchester detective inspector proclaiming: 'the abuse of anabolic steroids makes a mild man a monster' (*Manchester Evening News*, 15 June 1997). The culmination of this interest was the amendment of the Misuses of Drugs acts in 1996 which made 'possession with intent to supply' steroids a criminal offence. Yet, the scientific evidence for the link between anabolic steroids and violence was far from conclusive.

In 1994 we began an investigation of the supposed link between bodybuilding, steroids and violence by carrying out a two-year ethnographic in-depth interview study of bodybuilding and steroid use in South Wales. Locating bodybuilding in the context of changes associated with late modern society, we argued that South Wales, with its declining economic and social base, constituted a location where young men might turn to bodybuilding and steroid use as one means of maintaining self in the face of significant social change. The study was located in the context of several empirical and theoretical traditions, particularly, proposals regarding the structural and cultural changes occurring in late modern societies, the emerging work on the sociology of the body and the traditional investigations of drug cultures. It was, and is, our view that the media and biologically oriented experts had made generally exaggerated claims regarding the steroids/violence connection on the basis of very weak evidence, and, most importantly, that existing research paid scant attention to the impact of the cultural and social aspects of bodybuilding on steroid use. The research sought to locate steroid use in the everyday world of bodybuilders, investigating their shared understandings, beliefs and perceptions. Here we consider how steroid use is an integral part of the bodybuilding culture and explore the links between aggression and violence. We begin with a consideration of the biologically oriented literature on steroid abuse and violence.

BIOLOGY AND STEROIDS

The physiological and psychological effects of anabolic steroids have long been the subject of investigation (Kashkin, 1992). There is little doubt that, when combined with appropriate training regimes, anabolic steroids can enhance physical performance and alter the appearance of the body through the acquisition of greater muscularity (Kennedy, 1993; Brower, Blow and Hill, 1994). What is more contentious are the supposed negative effects of these substances. Reported long-term consequences of the use/abuse of anabolic steroids include: liver damage, arteriosclerosis, hypertension, changes in personality, lowered sperm counts in males and masculinisation in females (Kashkin, 1992). Of particular relevance to the research reported here is the supposed relationship between steroid use and increased irritability, aggression and violence (Choi, Parrott and Cowan, 1989; Choi, 1993; Pope and Katz, 1994). Pharmacological approaches to the steroid violence connection posit a direct, reductionist link. In these accounts, steroids are thought to produce undesirable side-effects such as uncontrollable outbursts of anger – roid rage – by stimulating central nervous system androgen receptors and/or altering brain morphology (Giannini, Miller and Kocjan, 1991; Kashkin, 1992). The strongest claims in this domain posit a direct, invariant relationship between anabolic steroid use and violence, suggesting that the drug-taking activities of bodybuilders 'pose risks not only to consumers ... but also to the general public by increasing the odds of violent and antisocial behaviour'. Pope and Katz (1990, p. 28) appear to have uncovered several cases of homicide and 'near-homicide' associated with the use of steroids. They claim steroids affect 'the central nervous system' and can cause users to develop 'manic and psychotic symptoms, culminating in violent crimes'.

The medical and behavioural science literature tells a consistent story: steroid use/abuse is the significant or sole causal agent in the genesis of aggressive and violent behaviour among steroid users. However, the research upon which these claims are based suffers from a number of methodological shortcomings and has generated a great deal of contradictory evidence. At best the research is equivocal, as Kashkin (1992, p. 389) concluded after an extensive review of the available evidence, 'the few available systematic surveys with semi-structured interviews with anabolic steroid users have produced conflicting results'. The research often suffers from inadequate methods and rash claims. On a conceptual level, the majority of the literature conflates aggression and violence, failing to distinguish between assertive, forceful acts and physical violence. Aggression may certainly have untoward consequences, but a distinction needs to be made between various types of aggressive acts and the perpetration of malevolent violence. No such distinction appears in this literature. There is also a failure to distinguish between the various substances labelled 'steroids'. As Riem and Hursey (1995, p. 236) and their colleagues observe, steroids come in various formulations, 'often exhibiting considerable differences in potency or biological activity'. The most important limitation is a failure to consider potential mediating effects at the biological and social levels. Biologically, it is clear that individuals may absorb and assimilate steroids in a variety of ways. In short, it is not possible to assume consistent or identical pharmacological effects on all steroid users. Of particular significance for the study considered here is a near absence of research on the social and cultural context of steroid use/abuse. Only recently have researchers begun to investigate the way social and cultural factors may intersect with steroid use (Goldstein, 1990; Bjorkqvist et al., 1994).

The research reported here investigated the supposed steroid–bodybuilding–violence link by conducting a two-year ethnographic and in-depth interview study of the culture of bodybuilding (for details see Dobash et al., 1996; Monaghan 1997). The ethnographic investigation and the vast majority of the interviews were conducted by Monaghan, who at the time was a practising bodybuilder. Although the ethnographic work was carried out in several locations, including bodybuilding contests and well-users' needle exchanges, the bulk of the fieldwork was conducted in bodybuilding gyms in South Wales. After an extensive investigation of fifteen gyms, four were chosen as 'strategic' locations for the intensive fieldwork. These gyms were included because bodybuilders identified them as 'hard core', meaning they had the requisite equipment and atmosphere associated with the serious business of creating the perfect physique.

In order to supplement and expand the knowledge gained through the ethnography, we also carried out 67 in-depth structured interviews with bodybuilders and weight-trainers. All interviews were tape-recorded, transcribed and analysed using ETHNOGRAPH. It should be noted that although training with weights is an essential element of bodybuilding, not all weight trainers are bodybuilders. For example, some people lift weights to keep fit while others are engaged in preparation for competitive sports. There were 43 self-identified body-builders in this study, three-quarters reporting using steroids (see also Korkia and Stimson, 1993). Young adult males predominated in the interview sample (mean age 30), there were only eight women. Most of these young men were employed – only 16 per cent told us they were currently unemployed – in traditional working-class jobs (ware-houseman, steel erector), skilled manual or clerical positions (mechanic, joiner), and a few were professionals (solicitor, computer programmer). On the basis of evidence gathered in the ethnographic fieldwork, we judge the sample to be reasonably representative of the bodybuilding and weight-lifting community of South Wales.

We will draw on these interviews and ethnographic field notes to explore the dietary regimes and orientations of bodybuilders showing how they are linked to attempts to create the 'perfect' body, examine how these orientations and 'lifestyles' are associated with the use of steroids, and investigate the possible links between the culture of bodybuilding, the use of steroids and acts of aggression and violence. We begin by locating this investigation in the wider theoretical context of work on the significance of the body in late modern society.

LATE MODERN SOCIETY AND THE BODY

The work of Michel Foucault has created a burgeoning interest in the sociology of the body and personal identity (Foucault, 1977; 1978). His work on the 'genealogy of the modern subject' alerted scholars to the processes associated with the creation of the human subject. Historically, these mechanisms involved 'dividing practices' and 'scientific classification' aimed at the body and 'soul', which were usually embedded within institutions and associated with the emergence of the 'discipline society'. In this century the process of 'subjectification' of individuals has meant the development of self through cultural practices, often, though not always, guided by an authority.

The process of 'subjectification' is exemplified in the proliferation of self-improvement movements in modern European and North American societies. In North America, improvement of the 'soul' is guided by the dictates of a therapeutic society in which 'all social phenomena ... are converted into matters of personality in order to have meaning' (Sennett, 1977). Every year millions of Americans consult a psychologist, psychiatrist or other 'psych' professional in a quest to improve and enhance self (Castel, Castel, and Lovell, 1982; Bellah et al., 1985; Dobash and Dobash, 1992) The body is also a target for self-improvement. As Bordo (1993, p. 25) points out, European and North American societies appear obsessed with the body and these obsessions are the 'logical (if extreme) manifestations of anxieties and fantasies fostered by our culture'. Bordo observes how feminist analysis of the 'politics of appearance' precedes Foucault's accounts. Her nuanced feminist analysis of anorexia nervosa accordingly focuses on practices aimed at training 'the female body in docility and obedience to cultural demands' (Bordo, 1993, p. 27). Weight-lifting and bodybuilding, with their emphasis on cultivation of the physique, mind and 'spirit', can be seen as exemplars of these developments. Bodybuilding is not some strange incomprehensible aberration. Like anorexia nervosa, it is merely one of a range of cultural 'obsessions' aimed at improving, perfecting and 'conquering' the body. Through bodily and dietary regimes men and a few women seek to 'form and transform themselves'. Bodybuilding is deeply embedded in the 'culture of self' associated with late modernity in which relationships of 'self-to-self' are 'intensified and valorised' (Foucault, 1978).

Giddens (1991) has attempted to identify the social and cultural processes linked to these emergent 'obsessions'. Late modernity, he argues, is associated with a number of unique social processes, including the 'disembedding' of individuals from the 'hold of specific locales' and globalisation which has diminished the impact of traditional forms of social organisation in the spheres of production, the family and the community. These changes may lead to a reduction in indigenous types of social control and an increasing emphasis on self-discovery through a multiplicity of 'lifestyle' choices. He is critical of Foucault's account of 'subjectification', arguing that it places too much emphasis on the objectification of the body and self through externalised authority. For Giddens (1991, p. 218), the body is 'reflexively mobilised' and available to be 'worked upon' by the influences of high modernity. Self-reflexive processes generate lifestyle planning and 'bodily regimes' which are, he argues, 'generic to the circumstances of day-to-day life' (ibid., p. 105).

Giddens' approach to these developments is primarily positive and encouraging – with late modernity offering a proliferation of lifestyle choices to all. Lasch (1980) has written in a highly critical manner of the consequences of late modernity, the therapeutic society and its attendant culture of narcissism. He argues, contrary to Giddens, that such a society has untoward consequences for the individual, family and community. Echoing de Tocqueville, he claims that individuals have retreated from community and family into purely personal concerns associated with psychic and bodily self-improvement. Lasch links the culture of narcissism and personal insecurity to an 'evaporation of history', a loss of feelings of belonging to a succession of generations. A break with the past is, according to Lasch, associated with an absence of authentic relationships with others.

Personal Insecurity, Masculinity and Location

In contrast to Giddens' account, Lasch's approach is deeply historical. Giddens' appears to assume that the current obsession with health and the cultivation of the body are unique. Historically, and still today, the adornment and 'shape' of the female body has been the object of the normalising gaze and cultural practices of men and women alike, albeit different for each (Bordo, 1993). Historical evidence further suggests that periods of social crisis are often associated with an emphasis on the corporeal, expressed through cultural movements concerned with health and healthy bodily practices (Shilling, 1993). In the US, the period 1880s to the 1920s was characterised by unease and insecurity associated with the demise of a rural society and the rise of a national and international economy. These changes generated a number of self-improvement movements oriented to enhancement of mental and physical health (Castel, Castel and Lovell, 1982; Bellah et al., 1985). Some observers claim that the social and economic changes associated with the present era have created a personal insecurity leading to a crisis of masculinity. South Wales is a location exemplifying the social and economic changes that are thought to be associated with such a 'crisis'.

Traditional forms of working-class employment in South Wales, notably mining and steel production, have been powerful determinants of masculinity and class and gender relations (Harris, 1987). Throughout the 1970s and 1980s, South Wales steadily moved toward a 'post-industrial' economy with a shrinking manufacturing base, the overwhelming proportion of employment growth in government funded and private sector service arenas, leading to a consequent diminution of traditional male working-class patterns of employment and a marginal, though socially significant, increase in the employment opportunities for women (Cooke, 1987). The economic and social conditions associated with this localised manifestation of late modernity may have broken the traditional connections: male employment, community, family and personal identity.

The sparse research literature on bodybuilding locates it within the context of a late modern society in which men are suffering an identity crisis (Klein, 1993, 1995; Gillett and White, 1992). Klein, echoing the work of sociologists such as Giddens, but adding a psychoanalytic gloss, characterises bodybuilding as a symptom of 'masculinity in crisis'. This 'dialogue with muscles' is a postmodern reflection of a trans-historical, possibly cross-cultural, equation of 'muscles and masculinity'. In the past such an equation was functional: the body was used in the productive process. Today, muscularity is emblematic of the crisis in masculinity, masking 'shortcomings' and insecurity while symbolising masculine power and invulnerability. Utility – use value – is replaced by representation. Being healthy, as signified by a muscular body, is replaced by the urge to 'look healthy'.

Steroids and Violence

Locating bodybuilding in the context of the structural and cultural changes associated with late modernity may be one route to understanding. It is crucial, however, to go beyond the structural to investigate how personal and interpersonal relations may be shaped by the conditions of late modernity and how these, in turn, may be linked to aggression and violence. One example is the possible relationship between an expanding culture of male narcissism and acts of violence. Studies of violent men have persistently shown that they are unable to take the role of the 'other' or to empathise with the concerns of others. Instead their own interests 'must invariably prevail' (Toch, 1992). Such men elevate the fulfilment of their personal desires to the status of a 'natural law', operating on the premise that their own welfare/needs are or should be of primary concern over those of others (Dobash et al., 1996). An inability to empathise with others, and the belief that others fail to meet perceived needs, often characterise men who use violence. These orientations may not be unique to violent men but rather integral to masculine beliefs and orientations to others. Whatever the fundamental source of these orientations, the narcissism associated with bodybuilding may accentuate the potential for violence.

Understanding the cultural context of the bodybuilding 'gym' is crucial to an explanation of aggression and violence. A parallel may be drawn with Macandrew and Edgerton's (1970) classic study of 'drunken comportment'. Just as the relationship of alcoholic intoxication to various forms of drunken behaviour is variable and mediated through different local cultural frames of reference, so too the aggression and violence of steroid users. It would appear that the relationship is not a direct result of 'chemical changes in the brain', but rather one that is mediated through local cultural and situational contexts which give primacy to violent responses in a range of social encounters. It is important to ask if the culture of gyms accepts or promotes steroid use as well as fosters beliefs that feed into exculpatory accounts of the violence. The culture of steroid use may promote the view that aggressive and/or violent acts are connected to its use. Bodybuilding magazines certainly reflect this belief. Thus the lived and written culture may play a socially disinhibiting role, creating a context for a 'self-fulfilling prophecy' and/or providing exculpatory discourses for those who are already predisposed to violence.

Finally, it is important that social scientists do not dismiss the potential effects of the use of such substances. At least since Wolfgang's (1958) classic study of homicide, social scientists have explored the possible links between the ingestion of alcohol and drugs and the commission of crime and violence. Despite the years of research and the voluminous literature on the subject, there is still no consensus, although Goldstein (1990, p. 16) concluded after an extensive review of the literature that 'drugs and violence are strongly related'. However, the same review indicated that much more systematic and rigorous research was needed. Although media and pharmacological accounts frequently posit a 'direct' relationship between steroid use and violence, the relationship appears to be more complicated. While some substances may have 'direct' pharmacological connections with aggression, they may also interact with personal, social and cultural forces to promote violent inclinations and/or self-fulfilling prophecies and techniques of neutralisation. It may be of some significance that steroid use has been used in US and Australian courts in pleas of mitigation where lethal violence as been used. While not successful, psychiatrists have none the less been called as expert witnesses (Pope and Katz, 1990); suggesting the possibility that an authoritative 'vocabulary of motives' for violent acts may be reinforcing everyday accounts of such events. Let us examine some of the elements of the bodybuilding culture that may be linked to violence, particularly the pursuit of the perfect body, the use of steroids, insecurity, narcissism and aggression.

CREATING THE PERFECT BODY

The bodybuilders interviewed in this study exhibited an extraordinary obsession with the routines associated with creating the perfect body. While these bodily regimes vary, most focus on pumping iron and preparing and eating food. Endless hours are spent in the gym four to six days a week. Like boxers, bodybuilders relish the intense exertion and 'pain' associated with strenuous weight-lifting and push themselves beyond their achieved limits (Wacquant, 1995). In this process the body is segmented and objectified. Specific days are devoted to exercises intended to develop distinct areas of the body: for example, Monday – legs, Wednesday – arms, Friday – back and Sunday – chest. Routines remain sacrosanct until a plateau is reached and the routine is changed. Training regimes structure their daily existence.

> 'when you know there's nothing else on your mind bar training, you can gear your whole day around training, and that's how it's got to be to progress, I think. You know, everything else you do other than training is detracting from training ... apart from maybe socialising a little bit which I think is good to relax you. Apart from that, work [paid employment] ... gets in the way.'

Obsessive commitment to routine is displayed in the order of training regimes in gyms, as trainers move from one apparatus to the next without variation. The discipline of 'training' is very apparent in the gym and is one of the important determinants of gym culture.

The intense, dedicated lifestyle evident in the bodybuilding culture is usually linked to internalised forms of self-regulation. For many, failure to adhere to self-imposed routines provokes feelings of guilt leading to reassessment and realignment. Through this process of subjectification, they become the arbiters and regulators of their own bodies, but do so in the context of a culture of scrutiny and surveillance (Aycock, 1992).

'I'm not happy if I don't train. I don't feel like going out, you know, put it that way ... if I haven't trained for a few days and then I go out, I think, "I'm having a drink, I'm abusing my body, and I haven't even trained", you know, I feel really shitty. It's psychological ... but you feel all weedy and flat.'

In order to maximise the impact of weight training, most bodybuilders adhere to rigid dietary prescriptions dictating high protein, low fat and daily caloric intake. Training and the preparation and ingestion of food take precedence over all other activities, shaping daily routines and determining relationships with others.

'Yeah, I was making sure you [I] get so much protein in every meal. Protein every two hours – my body weight was about 220 so I was aiming for about 220 grams of protein a day. And knowing that you can only take in about thirty grams at one sitting, I'd have to split it up so I was having 25 to 30 grams every two hours right throughout the day.'

Male bodybuilders, appear to have little patience for the routines and concerns of others – wives, girlfriends, children, family and friends – who must accept and accommodate the lifestyle. Complaints of insensitivity or rigidity are dismissed or ignored in the belief that tacit or explicit agreements have been made and that others must adhere to the strictures of these commitments.

'No, other people don't understand. Like, my girlfriend's mother do phone up on the weekends and do say come on we'll go to the beach. She done that last Sunday ... and I said "hang on we can't just get up and go. I got to cook my dinner now", and, it took me two hours to get ready like, and that's just cooking food just to make sure you got stuff to eat cause, ... you're going to end up eating chips, pies, whatever, cause you can't get nothing tidy out [to eat].'

The Ideal Body

Bodybuilders are clear about their intentions. They seek the ideal body primarily as a representational resource, and there is considerable agreement about what constitutes the ideal.

> 'Oh, bigger the better. More muscular, it's going to get to the stage when the biggest who walks out is going to win. ... The biggest man should win. ... not sort of blown up and just fat, the biggest muscles.'

> 'Too muscular? No. Well, that's my idea of bodybuilding. Massive, freaky body builder. I don't like these sort of slimmish looking body builders, all grace and that shit. ... I see bodybuilders, huge bodybuilders like and I think "that's good", right, and I'd like to be like that, I'd like to be big ..., I'd like to look like that.'

The pursuit of the ideal is relentless yet elusive. Many are perpetually dissatisfied with their bodies. Like anorexics who believe they can never be too thin, many bodybuilders think they can never be too big or too muscular.

> 'I compare it with when people talk about bulimia and anorexia and people say, "I don't understand how they can do that". It's exactly the same as bodybuilding, I think. Same mental problem, and it's you've got this phobia about being thin, so you want muscle. You don't want to be fat obviously. You want muscularity ... if you feel thin and you're clothes are hanging on you, flipping hell, it's so uncomfortable. It's nothing more, no lovelier feeling than clothes fitting you well, which they do when you've got a stack of muscle on you.'

For the majority, the goal was increased size and muscularity and for this they were willing to spend a great deal of time, energy and resources (gym fees, food supplements and steroids) and, like competitive athletes, to adhere to a rigid asceticism of 'rituals of restraint and every day routines of oblation' (Wacquant, 1995, p. 76). Unlike the aims of competitive athletes, those of bodybuilders are primarily aesthetic.

SELF–OTHER RELATIONSHIPS AND INSECURITY

The pursuit of the aesthetic is extremely self-oriented, and others become adjuncts, supporters or impediments to achieving their goal.

'when we first met she [my wife] did actually ask me if I had to choose between her and bodybuilding what would it be, and I gave her the answer, "bodybuilding". And, she got a bit upset by that but now she knows what I want out of bodybuilding and she knows like I've got to put that first, because of what I want out of it.'

Wacquant's (1995, p. 85) observations on the culture of boxing equally apply to bodybuilding: 'the boxing universe constitutes a closed world, a self-contained web of social relations and cultural meanings that acts as a prism refracting outside information and judgements according to its own logic'. The culture of bodybuilding similarly constitutes an insular social and symbolic universe. Within it men and a few women inhabit a culture where the interpretations of 'outsiders' are generally irrelevant and a narcissistic orientation prevails (not in the pathological but in a social sense (Klein, 1993)), with an extreme emphasis on self and personal appearance. Many were strikingly candid about the self-centred nature of their world.

'It is very selfish, very selfish … It makes you a bit arrogant and I think it brings out the arrogance in people. It makes you vain, very vain.'

Q. What do you think about the way female body builders look?

'I think it's got to be an improvement on what they look like otherwise because most women look like shit. I mean, put it this way, I prefer looking in the mirror at myself than looking at them.'

Extraordinary determination and self-centredness were evident throughout the interviews. Occasionally, and, particularly with more mature men and some of the women, self-reflection led to questioning of these orientations.

'God I lived for it! I wouldn't take a job because of my training. I would not get a job. I thought, how am I going to train [if I worked]? It ruled my life completely. It ruined my marriage. I wouldn't take a job. It literally overtook my life.'

Other researchers have remarked on the insecurity that drives men to pursue such perfection of the body. Klein (1993) locates this insecurity within a psychoanalytic framework, arguing that it often arises from the traumas of childhood. While bodybuilders interviewed in this study endorsed the idea of insecurity leading to an 'addiction' to weights, few located the source of anxiety in childhood. It may be that our research was not able to penetrate the resistance associated with revealing childhood experiences but we are generally sceptical of Klein's emphasis on childhood trauma. None the less, some body-builders did cite personal insecurity as a strong motive for their pursuit of the 'perfect body', and a fair proportion agreed that in-security was a strong generalised motivation for participating in bodybuilding.

Q. Why did you start bodybuilding?

'Insecurity I think, if I was to admit it.'
'There's very few people that would admit it but I'll be honest and say yeah they do [feel inadequate], but I don't feel inadequate because I train. I probably would if I didn't.'

Q. So before you trained?

'Yeah, I did feel a bit thin, and I just don't like feeling thin. I just had a real phobia about being thin.'

Whatever the basic motives for participating, bodybuilders remained unswerving in their commitments and the perfect physique is prized above all else. When asked whether they would prefer a good job or a good physique, they were almost unanimous: 'Oh, the physique! Straight off.' For most, the appearance of the body was more important than economic and social status, even physical health, and they contrasted physical appearance to other more conventional markers of masculine achievement.

'You've got this body and it doesn't matter how wealthy [you are] and they can drive the best [car] in the world, the Ferrari, they step out of it and they're a bag of shit and you're still looking good [laugh].'

In the eyes of participants the display of the body produces consid-erable cultural capital.

USING STEROIDS

An emphasis on size was one of the prime motives in the decision to use steroids. This was particularly the case for those involved in competitive bodybuilding: 'Just to help me get bigger. Mainly, just to help me get bigger – cause they definitely work.' For the majority of bodybuilders, the decision to use steroids was not profound or difficult. Many saw steroid use as a natural extension of the culture of strict dieting and food supplements: 'you use supplements – I mean that's not natural, is it? So, I'd say the other drugs [steroids] would be along the same lines.' Introduction to steroid use seemed natural, almost inevitable for most, particularly those intending to enter competitions, although a few seriously deliberated their use.

> 'once I started training and I got talking to the boys who had used them and they were on [about] how much good gains you could gain on them, how big that you could get ... then I thought well I'd like to compete so I talked it over with the boys in the gym and they said to compete you're going to have to use them because everybody, all the other competitors, are using them. So I bought a course off one of the boys in the gym, tried that to see how much gains I got off it straightaway and I thought, I'll just carry on. You know, keep progressing.'

Steroid use was the norm, and most respondents estimated that 90 to 100 per cent used them: 'Yeah, [in] the last ten years or so it's common knowledge, everyone's doing it and everyone's aware of it in the sport.' Steroid use is not a deviant activity among bodybuilders, and as with all cultural practices, normative standards were apparent. Respondents were clear that serious bodybuilders must earn the right to use steroids – it should be purposeful and utilitarian. Months, if not years of intensive training and deprivation were necessary before earning this right.

> '[They should] build a foundation, build some strength and muscle first, before they use the drugs.'

> 'I think people that don't compete or anything but use steroids are junkies because I really don't see the reason to do it. I honestly don't. Must be a competitor. It's their career. They want to win. They want to win badly enough. They've made their career on it.

They've made a lot of money on it. They're not going to do it forever, so that's why I class the difference.'

Most distinguished between use and abuse:

'I think that's something that's quite often overlooked. People say if you're on steroids you're on steroids. Well you're not are you? You're on steroids on a sensible level [or] you're on steroids on a ridiculous level.'

Even those who were not involved in steroid use were very knowledgeable about the supposed effects of different types of steroids. Through experimentation and the accumulation of knowledge, bodybuilders have created a rich ethno-pharmacology of steroid use (Bloor et al., 1998). Equipped with this knowledge, most plan and monitor their steroid use. A regime of multiple steroids taken in a cycle called 'stacking' was common.

Q. Can you describe to me the current cycle?

'Right. At the moment I'm doing a nine-week bulking cycle. Do you want to know what I'm taking? [Yes please] Deca for three weeks, Heptylate for three weeks. Testoviron for three weeks. And then the last four weeks I'll stack them with Pronabol. Weeks one to three is just Deca on its own. Weeks four to six will be Heptylate. But on week six I'll start the Pronabol as well.'

Deliberate planning was important, and its absence was an indication of abuse. Exceeding planned dosages was also defined as abuse. Both were seen as lack of self-discipline.

'"Abusing" is over dosing on them, taking way over the top every day and not having breaks, and just keeping on taking them. And "using" is using what you are supposed to use, just taking a bit training and taking it in the right dosages.'

Bodybuilders were generally unswerving in their praise of steroids for improving size and as an essential part of the preparation for competition. Other positive effects included enhanced libido and 'aggression' associated with weight-lifting.

'I don't think I'm going to reach any goals without steroids. It doesn't matter what side effects it gives me, nobody's gonna be able to convince me not to take them.'

'To achieve that size and everything and to even to be able to lift those, those sort of weights, you got to take it cause it just makes you stronger.'

'I could have competed without them but I probably wouldn't have done as well as I did do. But they improve you that much. They give you the edge.'

The potential negative effects – moodiness, irritability, aggression (see below), acne, and physiological changes – were recognised by most, but judged insignificant and/or inconsequential in comparison to the benefits.

'Yeah, severe acne. Yeah, it's got worse [on steroids]. You see I'm starting to get it on my arms and it's all across here now as well … I'm not worried about it. I'm not. I could have been worried about spots and things but I'm not bothered. As long as I get and achieve what I want to achieve, I don't care.'

Given the credibility gap between the medical community and athletes (Bahrke, Yesalis and Wright, 1996), it is not surprising that bodybuilders were generally unimpressed with health warnings issued by experts and quick to reject attempts to regulate and/or criminalise steroid use.

'So in other words the medical [profession] and the law givers have shit on us again and given us the shit end of the stick like [by creating new legislation]. What do they care? They never use 'em [steroids], because the average law giver is a big, fat balding, old man sitting down and he's probably a pervert as well.'

BODYBUILDING AND AGGRESSION

During interviews, respondents were asked if they thought aggression was essential to bodybuilding and whether bodybuilding might sometimes attract aggressive individuals. Aggression was considered essential for training, and most emphasised its disciplined, positive nature.

A few preferred to characterise it as determination. According to our respondents, bodybuilding did attract aggressive individuals.

> 'There's a bit of a subculture attached to it and all. I mean you go to the gyms and you've doorman in there. There's a big doorman scene with the gyms, I don't know whether you've noticed. And then you've got the martial arts side of it. It's an aggressive sport anyway. It is you know. The people you're in there with, half the times it's all rogues. I'm not being horrible, but you know what I mean? So you are rubbing shoulders with aggressive people.'

Most respondents coupled aggressive orientations to other attributes they felt were either promoted through the culture of bodybuilding or enhanced through participation. Self-confidence and arrogance were identified as important traits of bodybuilders by a fair number of participants. While a modicum of these attributes was deemed appropriate, the same traits, if exaggerated, could lead to aggression or violence . There was considerable agreement on this issue.

> 'Yeah I'd say the confidence aspect would make you change your attitude especially if you stand out in a crowd and you're bigger and better than somebody else. [This] would make you feel, 'look at me I'm big', do you know what I mean. Yes, I think their attitude would change.'

> 'And with the testosterone [released through bodybuilding] I found that makes you aggressive anyway. I mean bodybuilding makes you aggressive. Any type of weight training makes you aggressive, that's what I reckon. It just releases natural testosterone in your body. When you finish training if you're trying to drive home and you're in a traffic jam, you're much more likely to blow your top after a training session, have a "roid rage".'

STEROIDS, AGGRESSION AND VIOLENCE

Although bodybuilders believed that aggression (or determination) was integral to training and might be heightened through the physiological and social effects of training, this aggression was seen as positive. It helped to train harder, to lift more weights and increase muscle mass. The impact of steroids on one's disposition was viewed less positively. Almost all steroid-using bodybuilders thought steroids increased their irritability and aggression, although there were a few dissenting voices.

> 'There's no difference about how I feel whether I'm on or off [steroids]. I just feel the same. The only difference is that I can lift heavier.'

> 'I'm a passive sort of person, laid back. It doesn't change that. I think "roid rage" is used as an excuse, the papers like to exaggerate.'

These views were atypical. More typically bodybuilders thought steroids increased aggression. A recurring theme was that steroids shorten one's fuse, make one more temperamental and ready to display anger.

> 'Your fuse gets a bit shorter ... shortening their fuse rather than anything else. Whereas some people are quiet mellow, all of a sudden they're quite snappy. You can see the change over a few years I suppose.'

> 'Yeah, they don't help. They bring on more aggression. Definitely.'

> 'I don't know. They say the steroids make you aggressive and all that. I've taken them for years and it's made me slightly, perhaps it's made my fuse a little bit shorter but not much ... When I'm taking the gear and I'm very, very strong and all that, I won't take any nonsense from anybody – right!'

A few respondents were quite specific about the effects of steroids. They were convinced that if taken in 'excessive' amounts certain steroids were more likely than others to amplify aggressive and violent tendencies.

> 'Halotestin is much worse. In fact some people asked me about it? And they say they want to take Halotestin and all that and I know that they're aggressive anyway. And I say to them, "Don't bother, don't bother cause they'll get locked" ... It is bad. It's the only one that really changes me.'

While they generally associate steroids with aggression, most respondents did not think steroids made them more violent. There

were a few reports of a greater propensity to violence, particularly
from women bodybuilders speaking about male steroid-using bodybuilders with whom they lived.

> 'He's got a very short fuse and he snaps at the slightest thing ... he's
> very possessive normally. If we've been out and somebody's looked
> [at me], normally he wouldn't say anything. But if he's been to the
> gym and he's back on steroids ... [and] somebody looks he'd be over
> there straightaway and, "smack", that would be it.'

> 'I've seen quite a few violent outbursts cause I lived with two body-
> builders ... The worst episode – there was quite a few – I suppose
> [was] when I was attacked, insulted myself, my family for no reason.
> That's why I've got holes in the wall. He had me in the corner by
> there. Hitting me in the corner by there, my God ... Couldn't
> handle them [steroids], couldn't cope with them. He'd be like that
> with them – oooh, you know, it's frightening me ... He was really an
> intimidating, frightening person when he was angry ... He, changed,
> he never used to be like that.'

> Q. So you think it was the steroids then?

> 'Oh, definitely.'

Very little violence was reported by respondents and only a few
attributed violence to the use of steroids. For some, the violence
seemed inexplicable, and only one was prepared to invoke steroids as
an excuse. Exculpatory discourses such as the one that follows were
rare.

> 'I wouldn't have complete control over myself on steroids. From my
> experience, when I got steroids in my system, in my body, there's no
> other resolve, and then violence comes to a head. There's no
> calming the situation. You're so hyped and so motivated with the
> drug inside you, I think it switches off something that says like, "just
> be friends", and it happens to result in a fight.'

Most respondents were unsympathetic to exculpatory accounts and
thought that steroid use was not an excuse for violent behaviour.

> 'I think the people who really explode and do something like a
> murder would do it anyway. I mean that type of person is a bomb

waiting to go off. The steroids might be a fact of lighting your fuse but something would have set them off eventually anyway.'

'Help them get off with it, that's all, cause like ever since I've used them I've always known what I've been doing. Even, if you maybe do have a bad temper, you still know what you're doing. You still know you're having a temper. You still know that you're getting aggressive with someone.'

The general perception is that if one has a propensity toward violence then steroids might exacerbate these tendencies but will not turn a 'reasonable person' into an aggressive and violent person. It is generally believed that most bodybuilders are 'reasonable people' and that violent inclinations are independent of the bodybuilding culture and steroid use.

'It doesn't turn Peter Pan into an animal but it's people who are fairly aggressive anyway, you know like bouncers, etc. and those sort of people. There is no way if you are really timid and shy in your own natural life that you'll start bashing other people around.'

'Going back to the violence, I think it is all hyped up by the media. But ... there are people that abuse the stuff rather than use it properly. So if someone is naturally aggressive I think they [steroids] will enhance that and make them worse.'

'In my point of view, if you're a nutter and you take 'em, you'll just be a nutter worse. If you're a normal average person who takes 'em, you'll just be a little bit snappy, ... That's all, you wouldn't turn a normal average person into a nutter, a natural born killer. They don't actually change people's personalities.'

The majority of those interviewed saw little direct relationship between violence and steroid use and most thought that violence was a thing apart from steroid use, although the two could sometimes be related.

'The people I know ... half of them train and half don't, and there's no difference in the ones who train and the ones who don't, and there's any amount of people within each group who are punchy anyway, do you see what I mean.'

Even the two women bodybuilders quoted above who associated steroids with the violent outbursts of their partners also pointed to other factors that might contribute to the violence.

> 'but he told me he'd had psychiatric treatment as well cause he had problems with his background, hangups here, there and everywhere. I used to say to him, "You don't love yourself, you don't. You're not happy are you with yourself? So how can you be happy with any [one else]?".'

> 'When we've been out, it probably all goes in with his possessiveness but this hasn't helped. And he's admitted it then later, you know, it's the steroids.'

CONCLUSION

The in-depth interviews and ethnographic fieldwork reported here demonstrate how bodybuilding with its emphasis on the representational aspects of the body is an exemplar of the late modern condition. Whether this study can be seen as confirming the supposed link between the diminution of traditional sources of masculine identity, insecurity and an 'urge' to look healthy is open to question. It could be argued that confirmation of that link is dependent upon the individual insecurity associated with unemployment. Certainly insecurity seemed apparent in some of those interviewed, but unemployment did not feature among those in this sample. Analysis of interview materials did, however, reveal the insignificance of jobs in the lives of these men. Although most were employed they did not look to their job for fulfilment, status or esteem. Rather it was the sculpting of their bodies that led to self-esteem and recognition in the eyes of those who 'counted', other members of the bodybuilding culture.

The strength of the research reported here was in its intense concentration on the lifestyle and culture of bodybuilders. Not surprisingly, the appearance of the body was valued above all else with a consequent heightening of narcissistic orientations. In pursuit of the perfect physique – large and muscular – most bodybuilders were prepared to use steroids and this was not considered to be a deviant activity within that community. Steroid use was learned within the context of a rich ethno-pharmacology developed through experimentation and accumulated knowledge. Within this cultural context, steroid users drew fine distinctions between the use and abuse of steroids. Excessive use beyond the culturally defined limits was considered to be abuse. Abuse was also defined as a failure to regulate intake and/or to demonstrate appropriate commitment to a rigid regime of diet and weight-training. The use of steroids without appropriate levels of exertion and sacrifice was considered deviant.

Almost all users agreed that steroids increased irritability and 'aggression', although few accepted that there was a connection between steroid use and acts of violence, and few incidents of violence were reported. Although it is necessary to distinguish between aggression and violence, in order to support this claim (see also Goldstein and Lee, 1994), most of the bodybuilders repeatedly made such a distinction. They noted the importance of 'positive aggression' (seen as essential to bodybuilding and the determined training session) and generally condemned 'negative' aggression and acts of violence. Their accounts tell a common story of few acts of violence within this community and the rejection of exculpatory discourses about steroids and violence.

Locating these interpretations within a wider explanatory framework and recognising the limitations of 'self-report' studies, a number of risk factors for violence might be identified: a fair amount of aggression (often exacerbated by dieting and steroid use); intensified self-centredness (narcissism) with a concomitant lack of empathy toward others; individual insecurity among some bodybuilders; and, for a few, a history of violence, sometimes linked to occupations such as 'bouncing' and sometimes present in intimate relationships with women. Within the general literature all of these factors have been linked to violent inclinations and incidents.

Whatever interpretation one gives to this evidence, one conclusion to be drawn from this study is that no clear or direct connection can be made between the ingestion of steroids and the use of violence. The aggression and violence that was identified in this study was not invariably linked to the ingestion of steroids. Contrary to popular beliefs, bodybuilders did not recount 'uncontrollable' outbursts of violence produced by 'roid rage'. Instead, when bodybuilders told us about their own aggression and violence they talked about incidents where these acts were often moderated through rational deliberations. Furthermore, their accounts of the usual sources of conflict – sexual jealousy and defence of male 'honour' – leading to aggression and violence paralleled those found in research on other groups of young males. We judge the nature and levels of violence reported and observed in this study as generally parallel to what one would expect from a group of young adult males.

NOTES

Acknowledgements: The research reported here was supported by the Economic and Social Research Council. We gratefully acknowledge the participation of our many anonymous research subjects, of numerous service providers in South Wales (not least Dick Pates, Huw Perry and Andrew McBride) and of Sam Edwards, who carried out some of the interviews.

REFERENCES

Aycock, A. (1992) 'The Confession of the Flesh: Disciplinary Gaze in Casual Bodybuilding'. *Play and Culture*, 5, pp. 338–57.

Bahrke, M., Yesalis, C., and Wright, J. (1996) 'Psychological and Behavioural Effects of Endogenous Testosterone and Anabolic-Andorgenic Steroids: an Update'. *Sports Medicine*, 22, 6, pp. 367–90.

Bellah, R. N., Madsen, R., Sullivan, W. A., Swidler, A. and Tipton, S. M. (1985) *Habits of the Heart: Individualism and Commitment in American Life*. New York: Harper and Row.

Bjorkqvist, K., Nygren, T., Bjorklund, A. and Bjorkqvist, S. (1994) 'Testosterone Intake and Aggressiveness: Real Effect or Anticipation?' *Aggressive Behaviour*, 20, 2, pp. 17–26.

Bloor, M., Monaghan, L., Dobash, R. P. and Dobash, R. E. (1998) 'The Body as a Chemistry Experiment: Steroid Use among South Wales Bodybuilders'. In S. Nettleton and J. Watson (eds), *The Body in Everyday Life*. London: Routledge.

Bordo, S. (1993) *Unbearable Weight: Feminism, Western Culture and the Body*. Berkeley, Calif.: Univesity of California Press.

Brower, K., Blow, F. and Hill, E. (1994) 'Risk Factors for Anabolic Steroid Use in Men'. *Journal of Psychiatric Research*, 28, 4, pp. 35–40.

Castel, R., Castel, F. and Lovell, A. (1982) *The Psychiatristic Society,* trans. A. Goldhammer. New York: Columbia University Press.

Choi, P., Parrott, A. and Cowan, D. (1989) 'Adverse Behavioural Effects of Anabolic Steroids in Athletes: A Brief Review'. *Annals of Clinical Psychiatry*, 6, 1, pp. 183–7.

Choi, P. (1993) 'Alarming Effects of Anabolic Steroids'. *The Psychologists*, June, pp. 258–60.

Cooke, P. (1987) 'Wales'. In P. Damesick and P. Wood (eds), *Regional Problems, Problem Regions and Public Policy in the UK*. Oxford: Oxford University Press.

Dobash, R. E. and Dobash, R. P. (1992) *Women, Violence and Social Change*. London: Routledge.

Dobash, R. P., Dobash, R. E. and Bloor, M. (1996) *Steroids and Violence. Unpublished End-of-Grant Report*, ESRC project: L210252008, available from the ESRC and the authors.

Dobash, R. P., Dobash, R. E., Cavanagh, K. and Lewis, R. (1996) *Research Evaluation of Programmes for Violent Men*. Edinburgh/London: HMSO.

Foucault, M. (1977) *Discipline and Punish*. New York: Pantheon.

Foucault, M. (1978) *The History of Sexuality*, vol. 1. New York: Pantheon.

Giannini, A., Miller, N. and Kocjan, D. (1991) 'Treating Steroid Abuse: A Psychiatric Perspective'. *Clinical Pediatrics*, 30, 9, pp. 538–42.

Giddens, A. (1991) *Modernity and Self-Identity*. Oxford: Polity.

Gillett, J. and White, P. (1992) 'Male Bodybuilding and the Reassertion of Hegemonic Masculinity: A Critical Perspective'. *Play and Culture*, 5, pp. 358–69.

Goldstein, P. (1990) 'Anabolic Steroids: An Ethnographic Approach'. In G. Linn and L. Erinoff (eds), *Anabolic Steroids*. Rockville, Md.: US Department of Health and Human Services.

Goldstein, P. and Lee, C. (1994) 'Anabolic-Androgenic Steroid Use and Violence: A Preliminary Analysis'. Paper presented at the American Public Health Association Annual Meetings, Washington, DC, October.

Harris, C. C. (1987) *Redundancy and Recession in South Wales*. Oxford: Blackwell.

Kashkin, K. B. (1992) 'Anabolic Steroids'. In J. H. Lowinsohn (ed.), *Substance Abuse*. Baltimore: Williams and Wilkins.

Kennedy, R. (1993) *Hard-Core Bodybuilding: The Blood, Sweat and Tears of Pumping Iron*. New York: Sterling.

Klein, A. (1993) *Little Big Men: Bodybuilding Subculture and Gender Construction*. Albany, NY: State University of New York Press.

Klein, A. (1995) 'Life's Too Short to Die Small: Steroid Use among Male Bodybuilders'. In D. Sabo and F. Gordon (eds), *Men's Health and Illness: Gender, Power and the Body*. London: Sage.

Korkia, P. and Stimson, G. (1993) *Anabolic Steroid Use in Great Britain: An Exploratory Investigation*. London: Centre for Research on Drugs and Health Behaviour.

Lasch, C. (1980) *The Culture of Narcissism*. London: Abacus.

Macandrew, C. and Edgerton, R. (1970) *Drunken Comportment: A Social Explanation*. Norwich: Fletcher and Son.

Monaghan, L. (1997) 'We're Not Druggies, We're Athletes: Boydbuilding, Polypharmacology and Self-Identity'. Unpublished Ph.D. dissertation, University of Wales, Cardiff.

Pope, H. and Katz, D. (1990) 'Psychiatric effects of anabolic steroids'. *Psychiatric Annals*, 22, 1, pp. 24–29.

Pope, and Katz, (1994) 'Psychiatric and Medical Effects of Anabolic-Androgenic Steroid Use'. *Archives of General Psychiatry*, 51, 5, pp. 375–82.

Riem, K. and Hursey, K. (1995) 'Using Anabolic-Androgenic Steroids to Enhance Physique and Performance: Effects on Mood and Behaviour'. *Clinical Psychological Review*, 15, 3, pp. 235–56.

Sennett, R. (1977) *The Fall of Public Man*. Cambridge: Cambridge University Press.

Shilling, C. (1993) *The Body and Social Theory*. London: Sage.

Toch, H. (1992) *Violent Men,* rev. edn. Washington, DC: American Psychological Association.

Wacquant, L. (1995) 'Pugs at work: Bodily Capital and Bodily Labour among Professional Boxers. *Body and Society,* 1, 1, pp. 65–93.

Wolfgang, M. (1958) *Patterns of Criminal Homicide.* New York: John Wiley.

9 Regulating Crime Control
Rod Morgan and Pat Carlen

> Global unemployment has now reached its highest level since the great depression of the 1930s. More than 800 million human beings are ... unemployed or under employed in the world (ILO, 1994). That figure is likely to rise sharply between now and the turn of the century as millions of new entrants into the workforce find themselves without jobs.   (Rifkin, 1995, p. 3)

The last quarter of the twentieth century has seen an unprecedented increase in lifestyle diversity accompanied by a radical deregulation of financial markets on the one hand and a new agnosticism in knowledge production on the other – social changes occasioned primarily by the fundamental revolution in information technology brought about by the development of the silicone chip. However, these late twentieth-century innovations in culture, economy, science and technology, though frequently characterised as being 'postmodern', have been accompanied by widespread demands for, and several steps toward, harsher criminal justice and penal systems whose mooted or actual severity might almost be characterised as 'pre-modern'. (We think in particular of the 'short, sharp shock' programmes of the 1980s, the boot camp debates of the 1990s, the MP who in 1995 called for the televised flogging of offenders, the 1990s manacling of women prisoners during labour and childbirth, and the perennial insistence, notwithstanding all evidence to the contrary (see Prison Reform Trust, 1993; Currie, 1996), that 'prison works' (Pitts, 1992; Rutherford, 1996)). Meanwhile, despite the stridency of their claims, publicists such as Murray (1997) advance no real evidence in support of the 'prison works' thesis.

What has produced these contradictory social trends, and what effects have they had on criminal justice?

In an increasingly globalised economy investment flows are beyond the effective control of sovereign states. Domestic markets have had to become more competitively attractive for inward investment by multinational companies foraging for ever-lower production costs. The conclusions drawn, and their related policy injunctions, have been that all player-states should tighten their belts and re-order their spending priorities. More and more governments have engaged in leapfrogging initiatives to control public expenditure and deregulate their domestic markets. The resultant more 'flexible labour markets' are not only characterised by higher levels of unemployment, but also by widening income gaps between unskilled, part-time or unemployed workers, and the highly paid and geographically mobile managerial and professional elites.

Not all areas of public spending are being cut, however. The so-called 'law and order' services in most advanced societies are being rapidly expanded, and not, as with social security budgets, by default (as a result of the rising costs of increased unemployment), but by design. As the fissures open between rich and poor, between the educationally advantaged moving into the sunrise zones and the multiply disadvantaged trapped within the rust belts, rising crime levels add to the general sense of personal insecurity characteristic of post-industrial societies. They also threaten the stability which multi-national commercial providers of goods and services seek. Yet the changes have not been solely technological and economic. Nor have the apparently insatiable demands for better state protections (though explicitly framed in the language of law and order) been provoked solely by fear of crime. For, underlying the traditional crime and punishment discourses have been the age-old anxieties about the *new* (in particular, the novel phenomenon of widespread, long-term youth unemployment) and the *strange* (evidenced today, as previously, in fearful suspicions of ethnic minorities and foreigners). Very specific fears of crime, together with more nebulous terrors about the new and the strange have thus been conflated in an all-enveloping anxiety about the multiple risks seen to be embedded in all contemporary social relations. Furthermore, some pre-modern fears about some postmodern cultural innovations have facilitated the translation of global concerns about risk and insecurity into newly nagging personal anxieties about physical and social threats to individual life-chances. In postmodern societies the generalised anxiety about the risks inherent in new physical, economic and knowledge environments has been aggravated beyond all reason by the narcissism emanating from the unexpected alliances between the extremely conservative political philosophies of the 1980s and the deregulatory anti-epistemologies which came to the fore during the same period. Although in part based on opposed ontologies, between them they have produced the distinctive late twentieth-century grammars of individualism, free choice and loneliness, together with their accompanying catalogues of personal therapies and actuarial calculations of individual and social risk. Not unexpectedly, the flip-side of such a lonely self-consciousness of personal responsibility and risk is an accentuated culture of blame; and one distinctive feature of the 'blame culture' is the attribution of value to each according to their sins – rather than to each according to their needs and rights as citizens.

Exploited by political parties anxious to capitalise upon such easily dramatised and emotive issues as crime, risk, blame and punishment, and amplified by a monopolistic and avariciously 'dumbed down' press, the quest for increased security of life, limb and property has been swiftly translated in 1990s Britain into an expansion and tightening of both private protections and state corrections. The expansion in provision of security by the private sector has been parallelled by an increase in 'law and order' spending by the state. Thus, at the same time that it was being claimed that the state was being 'rolled back', its core function – as the guardian of internal order through the legitimate use of coercive force – was actually being pumped up by increased police powers, enhanced technological surveillance and crackdowns on targeted offences or offenders. But that is only part of the story. The traditional way of turning the regulatory screw (by use of legitimate force) has, in the last two decades, been buttressed by a strengthening of the legal/bureaucratic controls governing the main areas of public sector provision. In particular, agencies which previously gave some measure of protective nurturance to the young and poor (in the areas of accommodation, work and education) have been forced by a series of financial restrictions and legislative changes to take a more punitively critical stance towards claimants and clients.

In the short term at least, the so-called crackdown on crime (and 'welfare') has enjoyed a good deal of popular support. And especially in Britain, where the lives of the two-thirds of citizens who are prosperous are tinged principally by the fear that they may suddenly be propelled into the ranks of the unemployed. For, at base, it is the terrible prospect of being cast out from work (with all the accompanying exclusions that a personal world without work entails) that prompts the apparently inelastic demand for governments to strengthen the 'thin blue line' presumed to hold anarchy at bay. The Conservative and Labour parties have outbid each other to be tough on crime (Downes and Morgan, 1997).

The patterns of increased physical and bureaucratic repression, though widespread, are not universal, however. In the same way that some governments are resisting pressure to deregulate their domestic markets or make radically more flexible labour laws, so some jurisdictions, as part of a broader inclusionary welfare strategy, are continuing to make parsimonious use of exclusionary punishment. And, even in Britain, where the punitive response has received such popular support, there is, none the less, a strong and informed penal affairs lobby which continues to suggest that in order to control crime *effectively*, we need to have a wider and more holistic vision of dynamic social regulation which would see the whole apparatus of police, courts and prisons as but one important part in a complex parnership of productive and protective practices aiming to create and maintain less socially divisive systems of distributive and restorative justice.

The ironies and unintended ill-consequences of present fragmented policies on social and criminal justice have been well-documented (e.g. Brake and Hale, 1992). Three examples will suffice to support the point here. First it may be noted that strategies of risk reduction, pursued so that safe zones are established where commercial enterprises may flourish and employees feel safe, have, concomitantly, produced areas of exclusion where the unemployed or strangers (on any definition) are at increased risk of regulatory surveillance and suspicion. Secondly, drastically reduced social provision in housing and welfare support has impacted with extremely deleterious exponential effects on those excluded youngsters already most at risk of offending (see Carlen, 1996). And finally, worryingly, and most salient to any analysis of rising prison populations, it should be recognised that the focus of the most recent punitive obsession has not been restricted to suspected or already-convicted criminals. Instead, it has been widened to include the young in general (especially in Britain) and ethnic minorities in particular (throughout Western Europe).

There are clear political choices to be made. We have come to the conclusion that it is time (once more) to argue *against* the currently dominant '*anti-social*' conception of criminal justice which targets for further punishment those who have already suffered social exclusion by virtue of being unemployed, homeless or of ethnic minority or foreign national status; and argue (yet again) *for* a more *socially relevant, just* and *effective* notion of social regulation. The overall argument of the chapter will therefore be that: as there is overwhelming evidence to support the view that 'prison does *not* work' (and may even actually increase the likelihood of recidivism), it might well be worth developing social policies based on an alternative assumption: that new conceptions of distributive justice, social interdependency and public civility might be more effective than the penal system in promoting greater citizenship-security and reducing crime.

The rest of this chapter will be divided into two parts.The first will examine and critique the reasons and justifications for rising prison populations; the second will make a plea for a new ethics of social regulation which, rather than denying either individual or social responsibilities, would prioritise the values of social interdependency (as realised through 'family', work, 'education' and 'community'); and which, in recognition that informal social control is more effective than the formal criminal justice system in reducing crime, would also promote and cherish public civility by an increased regulation and enhancement of public space, transport systems and communal services.

PUNISHMENT UNLIMITED

We focus on imprisonment as a response to crime because we maintain, first, that imprisonment stands at the apex of social exclusionary policies generally and, secondly, because reliance on imprisonment implies an analysis of what the problem of crime involves.

Let us begin with some facts which are largely beyond dispute. What is happening to the rate of imprisonment and how do countries compare in this respect?

Rates of imprisonment can be calculated in many ways: in relation to crime conviction rates generally; according to the incidence of particular serious crime convictions; in relation to that age section of the adult population that typically commits most crime; and so on (Pease, 1994). For present purposes we shall confine ourselves to the crude measure of the number of persons in custody at any one time per 100,000 population. This measure is flawed in that it does not discriminate between states which send many offenders to prison for a short time, or a few offenders for a long time. Moreover, since the measure is unrelated to the number of convictions, it does not necessarily indicate punitiveness. However, since all official measures – official crime reports, apprehensions convictions and so on – are complex social constructs – the incarceration rate per head of population has one great merit. It is a fairly precise measure of populations locked up, for whatever reason. In the Northern Hemisphere this method of classifying countries brings together interesting penal bedfellows. At least three groupings are clearly discernible.

At the high end of the incarceration continuum is the Russian Federation and the United States, the old Cold War adversaries, both continuing to exercise powerful international influence, the former through territorial infrastructural networks and the latter in terms of ideology and global market forces. Both the Russian Federation and the United States imprison over 600 persons per 100,000 citizens, though Russia is contemplating a huge amnesty which may sharply reduce its reliance on custody, and the fifty states that make up the American Union are characterised by incarceration rates almost as divergent as those found within Europe.

At the opposite end of the incarceration continuum are the countries of Western Europe, ranging from the Scandinavian states, with around 60/65 per 100,000 to the old allies, England and Wales and Portugal, both now at 120 per 120,000 or above.

The third group of nations comprises the newly liberated former Warsaw Pact states confronted, it might be said, with a clear choice as to whether to pursue the penal path still being taken by Russia or that of their new Council of Europe partners in Western Europe. This group of states ranges from the Ukraine and Belarus with 400/500 prisoners per 100,000, to the Baltic states with figures in the 275–375 range, to countries such as the Czech Republic, Poland and Romania with prison populations in the 150–250 per 100,000 range.

It should be noted that these groupings are becoming less and less uniform and discrete. Some countries formerly within the Soviet sphere of influence have already reduced their prison populations below the level now prevailing in many Western European countries. By contrast the prison populations of several Western European countries are moving in the opposite direction, in the case of the United Kingdom influenced by policing and penal fashions from across the Atlantic, and in the case of the Netherlands as a consequence of what appears to be a hardening climate of public opinion combined with pressure from European Union neighbours that liberal domestic drugs policies be trimmed to come into community line.

In most countries reliance on imprisonment, in terms of the proportion of convicted offenders imprisoned, has fallen dramatically during the twentieth century. The reason why prison populations have generally grown during the same period is that the number of offenders brought before the courts has risen. In some countries, such as Britain, longer sentences have typically been meted out to them also. Pre-trial custodial populations have grown for similar reasons: more prosecutions, more remands in custody and longer periods awaiting trial. But these trends have been uneven over time and between countries. There is no straightforward relationship between incarceration rates and crime rates, nor is the relative size of a country's prison population easily explained by changing fashions in the philosophy of punishment, demographic factors, levels of economic activity or other public policy considerations (Zimring and Hawkins, 1991). This is not to say that factors subsumed by these headings – the occurrence of some outragious crimes inflaming public opinion, the level of unemployment or the supply of prison places, for example – do not have a short-term bearing on a country's rate of imprisonment. They do. But ultimately the number of persons sent to prison, and the average time they stay there, is a matter of political choice not the mechanical outcome of a universal law-like relationship.

That incarceration rates are a matter of political choice is well illustrated by the wide variations within federal states such as the USA. Texas currently has an incarceration rate of 686 per 100,000 – and coincidentally executes more offenders than any other state in the Union – whereas several states – North Dakota, Maine and Minnesota, for example – have rates in the 100/120 per 100,000 range and have abolished capital punishment. Texas has not achieved a notably safer environment for its citizens than have other American states. Moreover, the use of incarceration in the USA is not closely related to recorded crime rates. The overall US crime rate stabilised in the mid-1970s *prior* to a remarkable rise in the US prison population. The number of persons in prison in the USA has more than tripled since 1980 from 0.5 then to 1.6 million today. Moreover, in addition to the 1.6 million in prison there are between 3.5 and 4 million persons on probation or parole – that is a total of well over five million people, or over 3 per cent of the adult population, living under the supervision of the criminal justice system (Donziger, 1996). Were prisoners included among the ranks of the unemployed, which they are not, then the nation's jobless rate would be almost 2 per cent higher than its current much vaunted low rate (Western and Beckett, forthcoming).

The long-term trend throughout most of Europe may be for reduced reliance on imprisonment, but that trend is currently being thrown into reverse. The data for those European countries for which comparable data are available over the period 1984–95 indicate that though the pattern is far from universal, the overwhelming trend is neverthless upward. This can be seen clearly from the figures in Table 9.1. Of the 22 countries listed, 15 had in 1995 significantly

Table 9.1   Incarceration rates (prisoners per 100,000 population)
for Council of Europe member states for selected years for which data
are available

Country	Year				
	1984	1987	1990	1993	1995
Austria	114	102	82	91	85
Belgium	72	69	66	65	75
Cyprus	39	38	38	25	25
Denmark	70	69	63	71	65
Finland	–	–	62	62	60
France	74	88	82	86	90
Germany	104	84	80	81	80
Greece	40	40	49	68	55
Iceland	32	37	41	38	45
Ireland	47	54	–	60	60
Italy	76	57	57	89	90
Luxembourg	78	90	94	109	115
Netherlands	31	36	44	51	65
Norway	48	50	56	60	55
Portugal	68	85	87	111	125
Spain	38	66	85	106	105
Sweden	5	57	58	66	65
Switzerland	62	–	77	81	80
Turkey	171	100	82	72	90
England & Wales	83	94	90	89	100
Scotland	89	109	109	115	110
N/Ireland	–	121	109	118	105

higher incarceration rates than a decade earlier, in several instances –
France, Greece, Iceland, Ireland, Italy, Luxembourg, the Netherlands,
Portugal, Spain, Switzerland, England and Wales and Scotland – very
considerably higher, albeit from different base figures. Moreover, the
figures for several countries since 1995 show a further sharp trend
upwards.

England and Wales exhibits one of the most dramatic examples of
this upward trend. At the time of writing, the prison population in
England and Wales has risen above 63,500 and the surge in numbers
shows no signs of abating – a rise of no less than 56 per cent since the
most recent low population point of 40,600 in December 1992, when
the Criminal Justice Act 1992, premised on the sparing use of custodial sentences, came into force. The prison population today represents an incarceration rate of 123 per 100,000 and it is clear from the

criminal statistics that this rise reflects both an increase in the proportionate use of imprisonment as a penalty (in 1996 higher for all offender age groups than for many years past) *and* a rise in the length of sentences passed. That is, the increased incarceration rate during the 1990s reflects greater punitiveness.

This English experience is not unique. In Belgium the prison population has risen to over 8500 this year, representing an incarceration rate of 85 per 100,000. In the Netherlands, a country which ten years ago had almost the lowest incarceration rate in Europe, the prison population has now reached 14,000, representing an incarceration rate of 89 per 100,000. This is a truly astonishing rate of growth. If the Dutch fill all the additional prison places they are currently building – and it is to be expected that they will – then by the millennium they will have an incarceration rate of 98, well above the average in northwest Europe.

Part of the explanation for the rising number of prisoners in Europe lies in the phenomenon of 'Fortress Europe'. The attempt to stem migration flows, particularly from Eastern Europe, Africa and Asia, has led, *inter alia*, to widespread accounts of harassment, by the police and generally, of ethnic minorities, many of whose members are long-term residents in the countries concerned (for a report on Germany, for example, see Human Rights Watch, 1995). The elimination of border controls between most of the European Union States has also fuelled the demand that 'organised' crime, particularly the trade in drugs, be cracked down on by other forms of surveillance and intelligence gathering, the brunt of which effort appears disproportionately to be visited on vulnerably visible ethnic minorities, 'foreigners' or otherwise (Sim, Ruggiero and Ryan, 1995). At the deep end of the social exclusion continuum both processes have generated a massive increase in the number and proportion of foreigners imprisoned. Table 9.2 shows the magnitude of the increase. 'Foreigner' is a poor guide to the heterogeneous population so designated and imprisoned: it includes second-generation migrants and long-term residents as well as short-term visitors and recently arrived migrant workers.

Analysts, not surprisingly, vary in the degree to which they attribute over-representation of foreigners and ethnic minorities in criminal justice statistics and prison populations to stereotyping and discrimination at all the crucial decision-making points within the criminal justice system, as opposed to over-representation in offending (see Smith, 1997). But in a sense such arguments miss the important underlying point. The mere fact that some ethnic minority groups are

Table 9.2   Percentage of foreigners in selected prison populations for selected years for which data are available.

Country	Year					
	1983	1985	1987	1989	1991	1995
Austria	7	8	9	14	22	27
Belgium	22	28	27	31	34	41
France	25	26	27	28	30	28
Greece	12	16	19	27	22	–
Italy	8	9	9	9	15	17
Luxembourg	27	43	39	41	40	54
Netherlands	23	15	19	24	25	–
Norway	6	8	11	–	11	14
Spain	8	11	13	15	16	16
Sweden	17	21	22	22	20	26
Switzerland	32	35	36	41	44	57

grossly disproportionately incarcerated – in England and Wales, for example, the incarceration rate for all black citizens is eight times that for whites (Home Office, 1997a, Figure 9.8) – is evidence in its own right that ethnic minority members are excluded from mainstream opportunities. They represent an extreme example of a broader point about prison populations generally. Prisoners are disproportionately drawn from the ranks of the multiply disadvantaged (Walmesley et al., 1992), and in Europe the ethnic minorities fall overwhelmingly within the socio-economically dispossessed. This is reflected in the crimes in which they engage and on which the police concentrate, and in their vulnerability in the exercise of discretion within the criminal justice system (for examples of all these processes see the essays on France Germany, the Netherlands, Sweden and Switzerland in Tonry, 1997). The development of more 'flexible' labour markets, combined with immigration and 'organised' crime 'crackdowns', inevitably makes the existence of marginal social groups even more precarious and promotes their over-representation in police actions. As the welfare safety net shreds, the criminal justice keep net tightens.

One more fact is striking about Europe's rising prison populations and the conditions in which they are held. Given that countries in Western Europe do not appear to have dramatically different crime rates or types of crime (Mayhew and van Dijk, 1997) one might expect countries with relatively low incarceration rates to keep relatively high proportions of their prison populations in conditions of high security, reflecting that these are indeed persons from whom the public need absolutely to be protected. But it is not so. The Netherlands and the Scandinavian countries have traditionally employed small, relatively open establishments with generally rather liberal regimes from which it is both relatively easy and common to abscond (see Council of Europe, 1997, Table 8). By contrast, countries with far higher incarceration rates typically place a far higher premium on security. That is, they rely on a greater 'depth' of imprisonment as well as a higher rate.

By the same token, the evidence suggests that Europe's rising incarceration rates are being accompanied by intensifying prison security quotients that are well publicised by politicians, thereby signalling governments' commitment to being tough on crime. England, once again, provides a dramatic case in point. Despite the fact that the English Prison Service has achieved (if achievement it be) an improved security record in recent years (Prison Service, 1996, paras 5.1–5.3), the high-security escapes from Whitemoor and Parkhurst Prisons in 1994/5 therefore being an aberration, the resulting official inquiry reports (Woodcock, 1994; Learmont, 1995) nevertheless set aside the balance which had previously been favoured between 'security', 'control' and 'justice' in prisons and recommended that such 'confusion' be avoided by making custody the Service's 'primary purpose'. A whole raft of security enhancing measures were proposed, most of which have been adopted, thereby increasing the proportion of prisoners subject to high-security regimes and reducing that part of the prisons' budget available for prisoner programmes (for extended discussion, see Morgan, 1997).

The scale of the transformation in British penal policy over the past decade can scarcely be underestimated. In the late 1980s, in the years preceding the adoption of the Criminal Justice Act 1991, a degree of consensus, well supported by research evidence, emerged. It might have been termed 'new realism'. It was agreed that the prospect of imprisonment, or a sentence of imprisonment of marginally greater duration, does not act as a significant deterrent to crime in the individualistic calculative sense of the term (Home Office, 1991, para 2.8). It was also agreed that if the object of sentencing is to repair some deficit in offenders' make-up, prisons are the worst place to make the attempt (Home Office, 1990, para 2.7; Home Office, 1991, para 1.28). It followed that imprisonment should be used more parsimoniously, and this was the spirit, if not the letter, in which the 1991 Act was passed.

Half a decade later the mood has changed dramatically. Michael Howard, the outgoing Conservative Home Secretary, pronounced that 'prison works', both as a deterrent and incapacitant, and began the process of ensuring that prison regimes were made suitably 'austere' before being given the security excuse provided by the escapes of 1994/5. Moreover – and here the British policy thread differs some-what from that of its neighbours in Western Europe – Michael Howard took all his lessons from across the Atlantic, a borrowing which, given the penal disaster zone which most observers take the USA to represent, seems extraordinary. 'Truth' or 'honesty' in sen-tencing has been achieved by the Crime (Sentences) Act 1997 through provisions for the abolition of parole, mandatory minimum sentences for two not 'three strikes and you're out' candidates, and modest early release, in effect 'good time', earned through compliance with prison regime requirements as moderated by prison officers on cell-block landings. The 1997 Act is grounded on a *planned* further increase in the prison population (Home Office, 1996a, ch. 13).

It is still too early to say to what extent this Conservative legacy will be retained by the incoming Labour government. When in Opposition the Labour front bench did not oppose the 1997 Act, and in office have so far disavowed suggestions that the surging prison population could or should be reduced. Moreover, the Home Secretary, Jack Straw, has repeatedly endorsed the concept of 'zero tolerance' polic-ing – another import from across the Atlantic – and announced forth-coming legislation which will introduce 'community safety orders' and fast-track provisions for repeat juvenile offenders who have already gone byond what in future is to be a 'final warning'. It is difficult to see how these proposals, if implemented, will not further ratchet up the incarceration rate. In the case of juvenile and young adult offenders this will boost a disturbing trend already apparent since 1992. Between 1982 and 1992 the number of offenders under 21 receiving immediate custodial sentences more than halved. But juvenile and young adult custodial numbers are now rising once again. New Labour and Old Conservatism appear to have formed a coalition which sees early police intervention and swift, certain and severe punishment as the appropriate accompaniment for the deregulated market which both parties maintain will best lead to national prosperity.

What do these trends signify? What analysis of the crime problem do they imply?

Imprisonment is a popular response to crime because it suggests that the public is made safe by it – that the risk of further offending is eliminated. The measure removes the offender from the community and shuts him or her off behind a fence or a wall. Of course the victim in particular, and the public at large, is to some extent made safe – *while* the offender is in custody. In the vast majority of cases, however, imprisonment is a relatively transitory phenomenon. Most prisoners are in custody for days, weeks or months rather than years – the average period under sentence served by prisoners released during 1996 in England and Wales was a little over six months (Home Office, 1997a, Tables 4.12 and 5.11) – and when they are released prisoners typically return to the communities from whence they came. So, to the extent that imprisonment offers a respite from the offences of those offenders for which it is typically used, the respite is short-lived. If offenders who have been imprisoned continue to offend, and the majority do (almost three-quarters of all young offenders and approaching half of all adults are reconvicted within two years of release – see Home Office 1996b, ch. 10), it is more accurate to say that their offending is postponed rather than prevented. Of course a minority of very serious offenders go to prison for life, which in a few cases may literally mean life. But such cases are rare.

All of which means that a good deal of the paraphernalia of prison security is little more than a fetish. When prisoners abscond from the few open prisons, or fail to return from the declining number of home leaves, or, more rarely, escape from closed prisons, there is often well-publicised outrage and scare-mongering. It is clearly important that suspects or offenders committed by the courts to custody not be able to thumb their noses at the authorities. But it is in most cases ludicrous to suggest that these breaches represent a threat to the public which they would not otherwise face. This fiction is the product of increasingly elaborate prison perimeters and prisoner restrictions when in fact the absconders and escapees are usually only anticipating a social reality which, were it not for their impatience, would shortly have come to pass anyway.

Of course public safety could be secured more permanently by the use of imprisonment. There are several possibilities. Existing sentences could be made longer. Even if they were doubled, however, lifting the prison population to 125,000, the typical period of respite would still be only twelve months, the evidence suggests that released prisoners would be no less likely subsequently to commit further offences, and prison costs would almost certainly be more than doubled because of the need to construct over one hundred further prisons. Or imprisonment could proportionately be used more often for those offenders whom the courts convict. However, even were this done the proportion of offenders who are apprehended, prosecuted and convicted would remain dismally small: clear-up rates would be unaffected and the number of offenders at large would be relatively little affected. Moreover, it is worth noting that some market-related offences – drug trading, for example – attract a supply of potential offenders that may be almost unlimited. Imprisoning those responsible for these sorts of offences may serve only to create market opportunities for substitute offenders.

The popular attractions of imprisonment – taking out the offender, shutting him or her away, reducing the individual to a stripped-down common denominator thence to be worked on through whatever behaviourist processes are currently in vogue – is congruent with the individualised processes of responsibility and guilt employed by the criminal justice system. But in fact the custodial environment makes offending behaviour much more difficult to deal with and opens up counter-productive, possibly criminogenic, processes. Prisons are quite unlike the environments in which crime takes place – families, workplaces, neighbourhoods where social networks are generated and sustained. Prisons, almost by definition – this was part of Goffman's seminal characterisation of them as 'total institutions' – are places within which offenders, despite the current emphasis on cognitive behavioural programmes for anger management and sexual offenders, are largely deprived of personal responsibility for anything. Prisoners are fed, clothed and housed, told when to rise and go to work, are subject to constant surveillance, and are managed to the smallest degree. Which is why, not surprisingly, most enforced prisoner programmes delivered within prison exercise little influence on behaviour post-release. Imprisonment inculcates the ultimate 'dependency culture' and what learning takes place is largely from fellow offenders.

SECURING THE DYNAMIC SOCIETY

The large-scale use of imprisonment is a form of political escapism. Politicians hope that prisons comfort the populace but the desire is never fully realised because ever-rising prison populations are seldom seen as evidence that crime is being reduced. Instead they tend merely to confirm, and magnify, people's anxieties that even more criminals and ex-prisoners lurk around every corner. Then, caught in the inevitable spiral of their mutual amplification, the fears of crime and the demands for more prisons escalate. In one sense, these are not irrational responses. When prisoners are released they are indeed less capable of leading law-abiding lives. Their family ties have been fractured, their accommodation prospects are more precarious, their employment possibilities are further reduced, and their attitudes to law and its agents are more hostile. This process, as Lord Woolf argued in his 1991 Report, is not best designed to decrease crime.

Yet what alternatives are there? Can we ever secure more peace of mind about the safeguarding of our persons, private property and the public proprieties without multiplying these seemingly self-defeating incarcerationist policies still further? And, even if we accept the argument that prisons in themselves reduce neither offending nor fear of crime, are there really any achievable alternatives which might reverse these spirals of crime, fear and punishment, these social cankers which are so corrosive of citizen well-being and social cohesion?

We think there are. We will, therefore, now sketch out an alternative model of social regulation, one that would depend less on the rather narrowly targeted (and socially divisive) repressive penality presently favoured by politicians; and one that would, instead, promote the type of dynamic security that should emanate from a more holistic approach to social justice and social regulation.

The plea for a more holistic approach to social regulation which we make here is rooted in, and takes its arguments from, three slightly different perspectives on social order.

First, it draws on a long and classical tradition in social theory that argues that the majority of people are law-abiding not because they fear the strong arm of the law but because they are 'tied-in' to society by family, education, job, and cultural artifacts such as religion and ideology. It is the fear of weakening (or even destroying) these ties through bad behaviour (rather than through fear of official punishment) which – so the story goes – keeps people on the straight and narrow. Secondly, the quest for an holistic regulatory strategy is influenced by an environmentalist approach that argues for maintaining high standards of public civility via the organization and informal (civil) regulation of public space. Thirdly, and as might be anticipated, holism in relation to social and criminal justice necessitates a critique and rejection of the presently fragmented and haphazard approach to social and criminal problems which has, in recent years, resulted in programmes adopted to address one set of social inequalities being simultaneously subverted by contradictory strategies attempting to ameliorate others.

The first perspective invoked in support of a holistic approach to law and order is one that conceives of primary social regulation as an inherent quality and dynamic of social relationships based on respect and mutual interest, a dynamic, in short, of the type of society that has been referred to as a *stakeholder* society. In such a society the numbers of people excluded from participation by racism, unemployment, lack of training and homelessness would be reduced by social policies designed to 'define' people in (Dahrendorf et al., 1985). The fundamental starting point for such an holistic approach might well be rooted in a recognition that, because of the virtual collapse of the youth labour market, there is a real conflict of world-view and interests between today's youth and their parents and grandparents. The only way to reduce that conflict would be to develop and adopt a new theory of distributive justice. For despite all the theories of citizenship and communitarianism that are currently being peddled, there is a crashing silence about the ways in which the distribution of youth education, training, work, consumption and status might be rethought. Certainly, in a world where satisfying work is becoming scarce, a more appropriate conception of redistributivist justice would have to reject competition as being the best way to distribute the available work, education and other social goods. Of central importance, also, would be a redistribution of income and time in favour of children and young people, i.e. those most vulnerable to exclusion as a result of turbulent social change (see Young and Halsey, 1995). The overall aim would be to reduce (or at least limit) the numbers of people currently living in such destitution that they have nothing (or very little) to lose by committing crime.

The second main plank in any holistic approach to social regulation would be the tightening of informal or civil controls on public probity and civilities by the restoration of the thousands of jobs recently lost in public transport, public parks, council estate maintenance, environmental services, and education and health. Previously, these posts, whatever their explicit job descriptions may have entailed, also effectively (and silently) fulfilled the functions of informally policing public and semi-public space without the confrontational apparatus often accompanying (or at least necessarily implicit in) formal policing activities. We think in particular of the regional railway and London tube stations that at certain times of the day and night are nowadays utterly empty of any kind of officialdom – porters, ticket collectors or information providers of any kind. We think of the buses that do not seem safe to many people since they have become singly operated by a driver and without the traditional bus conductor. We think of the vast tracts of public park areas which are now without park keepers on foot and often also without motorised patrols. We think, too, of the massive and modern public institutions with their downsized staffs; of hospital and educational institutions denuded of porters, receptionists, lift staff and cleaners; and of the long, empty corridors inside buildings and the vast derelict spaces surrounding them – too frequently occupied only by that thieves' delight – an unmonitored carpark, full of expensive vehicles. All of these landscapes of public sector neglect and urban de-socialisation not only heighten the unease of the remaining skeleton staffs and the stranger-citizens going about their legitimate business, they are also a godsend to those whose business is less legitimate or even downright criminal. It therefore seems ironical to us that, in a society where two of the major social problems are unemployment and crime, so many of the jobs recently lost have been ones whose twin functions of reducing both fear of crime and the propensity to commit crime cannot be so adequately performed by technological devices.

And so we come to the third and essential component in any holistic approach to social regulation – the requirement that policies adopted in pursuit of a more effective system of criminal justice not be simultaneously subverted by policies pulling in an opposite direction. Nowhere has this tension been more apparent in recent years than in the areas of youth justice and community safety. We will therefore conclude this final chapter by discussing some of the requisite elements in a holistic approach to both youth justice and community crime prevention strategies.

Although policy-makers have, throughout this century, acknowledged that both youth justice and crime prevention are too important to be left to the criminal justice system, successive governments have shown a failure of nerve about relying on totally non-punitive measures of regulation. Repeatedly, they have not been prepared to allow time for new, non-penal regulatory measures to work independently of criminal legislation providing back-up measures. One consequence has been that, through a too-hasty resort to penal measures, Janus-faced policies of 'support but punish' have regularly weakened or destroyed any of the bourgeoning relationships of trust essential to ameliorative social compacts and relationships of dynamic security.

At the end of her excellent book on punishments in the community, Anne Worrall (1997, p. 151) asks:

What is wrong with widening the net of skills and knowledge, including social skills and self-knowledge? What is wrong with widening the net of self esteem, attachment and commitment to the future? What, in short, is wrong with widening the net of inclusion?

And the answer is, of course, that there is nothing wrong with widening the net of inclusion – so long as there is a recognition that the previously-excluded will need time to be convinced that they are at last being invited 'in' to enjoy something worthwhile. For as Worrall (1997, p. 150) also points out, more punishments in the community will not of themselves reduce the prison population. Only strictly enforced controls on the use of custodial sentencing will do that (see Carlen, 1983, 1989, 1990). But, a buttressing of informal social control mechanisms directed at the prevention of child abuse and neglect (a major cause of youth crime), increased educational facilities, and intensive working with young people already in trouble (see Currie, 1996, pp. 16–17), together with the resocialisation of our public spaces might both reduce the number of young people who feel that crime is the best option on offer, *and* reduce their opportunities for getting into criminal trouble. Easier said than done. The interrelated problems of child and young person poverty, fear of crime, and the new punitiveness are deep-rooted. None the less, recent statistics on child poverty and youth homelessness give further support to our contention that holistic, complex and comprehensive action needs to be taken before more young people's lives are laid waste by neglect and lack of opportunity.

'The percentage of children living in households with less than half of the average national income, after housing costs, rose from 16 per cent in 1981 to 33 per cent in 1992' (Audit Commission, 1996, p. 60). Between 1987 and 1992 the proportion of young men in Britain between the ages of 18 and 24 who were working fell from 86 to 73 per cent, whilst the proportion of young women working remained at 65 per cent (Barclay, 1995). The relative wages of those under 25 have continued to fall, and it has been estimated that about 150,000 young people are homeless. At the same time, and while welfare benefits have been slashed right across the board, a new punitiveness has resulted in ever more novel ways of policing young people: government hotlines have been set up so that the malevolent can snitch on their neighbours by telling the authorities that they suspect them of fraudulently claiming welfare benefits; more punitive sentencing has resulted in a steeply rising prison population – with the female section increasing more rapidly than the male; and there have been proposals to electronically tag child offenders under the age of 16, and, additionally, to ensure that, in the public interest, convicted juveniles are publicly named and shamed.

Over the same period, one of the most striking findings of several research projects involving young people and crime has been that there is an asymmetry between the high degree of civic obligation which the contemporary state expects to exact from young people, and the low degree of protection which it grants to them in return. For instance, while a majority of the young interviewees in one investigation into youth homelessness had been victims of crimes whose perpetrators would never be punished, whenever they themselves had been seen to deviate – from social mores, respectability, or the criminal law – they had received punishments out of all proportion to their initial wrongdoing (Carlen,1996). The findings of entirely different types of studies lead to similar conclusions (Brown, 1995; Loader, 1996). Yet, in recent proposals about the best way to tackle youth crime in what has optimistically been called 'the stakeholder society' – a concept whose popularity in the 1990s emanates, when all is said and done, from the belated realisation (and fear) of all political parties that the ever-widening gap between rich and poor poses a threat to social cohesion (see Dahrendorf et al., 1995; Field, 1996) – there has been little recognition of the fundamental conflict between the state's high expectations that young people should conform to the law of the land and the continuing immunity from punishment of the adults who criminally victimise them.

'Quality of life' is an important element in making people feel that they have a stake in society, and it is nowadays accepted by every main political party in Britain that quality of family life and parental supervision, together with regular paid employment, are crucial factors in determining whether or not young people commit offences (Home Office, 1997; Labour Party, 1997). But while the evidence that quality of family life affects children's propensity to get into trouble of one kind or another is overwhelming (Farrington and West, 1990), there is also some evidence that if young people feel they have an economic 'stake' in society they are less likely to commit (or persist) in serious crime (Carlen, 1989). And, the best recent proposals for 'defining in' the excluded young do indeed recognise the economic and social conflicts in which much crime is rooted. It is therefore frustrating to know that the very same politicians who are currently promoting supportive programmes for young persons are also continuing to encourage the courts to be indiscriminately and harshly punitive towards those of the presently excluded young who do not immediately change their itinerant and/or drug-taking lifestyles. It is this contradictory policy of 'support and punish' which, we argue, will not work.

An example of one such 'support and punish' approach is to be seen in the consultation document *Preventing Children Offending* (Home Office, 1997b) which proposes combining support for the deserving parents of delinquents prepared to accept help with their children in trouble, with penalties for those parents refusing any proffered help. Now, of course, carrot-and-stick strategies such as this reasonably adopt the classical assumption that the state's duty to protect should be balanced by the citizen's duty to fulfil social obligations (in this case those pertaining to responsible parenthood). What the government fails to recognise, however, is, first, that the social consciousness and incompetencies of many of today's young delinquents and their (often relatively young) parents are rooted in experiences of social exclusion from the citizenship benefits assumed in the classical model; and, secondly, that such exclusion has already had deleterious, and difficult to reverse, effects.

The need to recognise that the damage done by exclusion is real and lasting is urgent precisely because so many of today's excluded young have already (and most likely mistakenly) sought solace in parenthood. Consequently, they and their children are very likely to be the targets of the new proposals for the enforced counselling of delinquents' parents. Given the deep-rootedness of the conflicts between excluded youth and the older generations who have exploited them, it may well be that the 'counselling society' (which has become the glib flip-side of the 'risk society') will quickly reach the limits of its tolerance when confronted with the seeming recalcitrance of young parents suspicious of the new government's (conditional) benevolence towards them. The predictable results will be more exclusion, more fear of young persons and strangers, and more crime.

Instead, therefore, of engaging in coercive strategies which involve translating the still-relevant language of class conflict into the disarming language of stakeholding, citizenship or communitarianism, it might be more productive to recognise that the social damage wreaked by the class and inter-generation conflicts of the last two decades, together with the asymmetries of citizenship which characterise them, will take time to repair. It is, however, unlikely that any armistice for the conciliation of fractured community relations will be granted if the recently drafted 'community safety' proposals become law.

At first sight, the government's proposal that local authorities, working in collaboration with the police and others, be given a statutory duty to prepare Community Safety Plans (CSPs – see Morgan Report, 1991; Home Office, 1997c) appeared to express an holistic, communitarian approach to crime. 'Community safety' suggested both that crime prevention is about more than locks and bolts, and that policing is not only about crime but also about the general quality of neighbourhood life. Furthermore, the government proposed involving all major services – education, youth services, health, social services – in the preparation of CSPs. So far so good. The *bad* news was that the government also proposed introducing Community Safety Orders (CSOs – see Home Office, 1997d) whereby troublesome residents – individuals, groups or whole families – could be *excluded* from neighbourhoods.

The original proposal (Home Office, 1997d) was that applications for CSOs be made by either police officers or local authority officials to county, not magistrates', courts. Moreover, it would not be necessary for the subjects of CSOs to have committed a criminal offence; any 'anti-social behaviour' that 'disrupts the peaceful and quiet enjoyment' of a neighbourhood would do. The evidential test would be the civil one of 'the preponderance of the evidence' rather than the higher criminal test of proof 'beyond a reasonable doubt'. No victim need be produced; nor, indeed, would it need to be demonstrated that there was a victim – it would suffice for the police to produce evidence that the conduct 'would be likely to produce harassment'!

We accept that the CSO provisions have been proposed in response to real problems of neighbourhood and individual intimidation. What we take issue with is that instead of combatting intimidation through measures designed to build community solidarity, the government has chosen the easier (populist) and more dangerous route of impersonal, penal repression. The civil liberty objections to the lower evidential threshold are self-evident. More insidiously, the potentially holistic language of 'community safety' disarmingly masks a recipe for semi-institutionalised vigilantism.

Consider this scenario. A run-down neighbourhood with high youth unemployment has an ill-resourced secondary school which makes abundant use of exclusions. Noisy adolescents regularly gather in a particular location – a bus shelter or near a local newsagent – and they are abusive when asked by the shopkeeper and other residents to disperse. What is the average councillor likely to do when faced with pressure from local people made anxious by the behaviour of these youngsters? The government has stated that there will be no additional money to assist local authorities to prepare their CSPs. Reducing school exclusions will take time and resources and it is not clear where those resources will come from. There are no funds to restore the emasculated youth service. Long-term youth unemployment looks set to continue. None of the statutory services – police, social services, education, and so on – is capable, so they say, of investing more personnel to work the neighbourhood. Then ... Magic! The CSO offers a speedy solution which will quieten the complainants. Curfews, evictions and exclusions can, it is proposed, be made the condition of a CSO and a breach of whatever conditions are attached will be a criminal offence punishable by a sentence of imprisonment up to five years. This is a draconian and disproportionate sanction. Not only could a custodial sentence be imposed without any evidence that a criminal offence had ever been committed, but it could even be as long as one which is currently only awarded for a grave offence tried in the criminal courts. Just the job for dealing with wayward kids, 'siege families' (so called because they already feel alienated from hostile neighbours) or anyone else the neighbourhood has taken against!

As we write (December 1997) the Crime and Disorder Bill has been published. Regrettably, the only significant response the government has made to criticisms of its original proposals is to abandon the attractive, if misleading, 'community safety' disguise. The hard edges now stand exposed. CSPs have become 'Crime and Disorder Strategies' (CDSs, Clause 5) and CSOs are now Anti-Social Behaviour Orders (ASBOs, Clause 1). Practically all else remains the same and the two measures are to operate as an integrated whole. Part of the planning exercise on which local authorities and the police are now to embark will include procedural agreements as to who is to seek ASBOs against which persons or groups and under what circumstances. One possibility, the Home Secretary has suggested, might be that local authorities seek ASBOs in relation to council tenants, while the police deal with occupants of privately rented accommodation. ASBOs will thus allow all classes of troublesome persons – and not just tenants of local authority accommodation – to be cast out of neighbourhoods where their presence is deemed offensive. Contrary, therefore, to any holistic vision which the original 'community safety' concept initially appeared to offer, the ASBO will create a new form of exclusion, backed up by yet further resort to imprisonment. It could also be expected to imperil any newly emergent civil relationships based on mutual trust and respect with the debasing currency of threat and penalty.

So to conclude. We are not saying that fears about contemporary youth crime and other public incivilities are ill-founded. We accept that they are issues in urgent need of effective address. We *are*, however, saying that any policies which involve fast-tracking young persons or other already-excluded people into punishment are ill-judged; that custodial punishment should be a last, rather than a first, resort; and that, in any holistic conception of social regulation, redressing the balance between formal and informal social controls will be a prerequisite both to diminishing fear of crime and to cutting its actual incidence.

None of us need fear that crime will ever be unlimited. But the limits to crime are not to be found in the depths of imprisonment. Logically, of course, they inhere in the concept of crime itself. Sociologically, and more importantly, they are to be found in the reciprocal obligations that bind citizen to citizen and citizen to state. When those bonds are weakened by gross inequalities in life chances, they are seldom repaired, and too frequently sundered, by penal interventions. And that, quintessentially, is why it is so imperative to stop the rush to more and more punitive measures; why it is always, and already, time to regulate crime control itself.

REFERENCES

Audit Commission (1996) *Misspent Youth ... Young People and Crime*. Oxford, Audit Commission.

Barclay, P. (1995) *Joseph Rowntree Inquiry into Income and Wealth, Volume 1*. York: Joseph Rowntree Foundation

Brake, M. and Hale, C. (1992) *Public Order and Private Lives*. London, Routledge.

Brown, S.(1995) 'Adult Pasts and Youthful Presence: Community Safety, Age and the Politics of Representation'. Paper presented at the British Criminology Conference, Loughborough University, July,

Carlen, P. (1983) 'On Rights amd Powers:Some Notes on Penal Politics'. In D. Garlen and P. Young (eds), *The Power to Punish*. London, Heinemann.

Carlen, P. (1989) 'Crime, Inequality and Sentencing'. In P. Carlen and D. Cook, *Paying For Crime*. Buckingham, Open University Press.

Carlen, P. (1990) *Alternatives to Women's Imprisonment*. Buckingham, Open University Press.

Carlen, P.(1996) *Jigsaw – A Political Criminology of Youth Homelessness*. Buckingham, Open University Press.

Council of Europe (1993) *Report to the Dutch Government on the Visit to the Netherlands Carried out by the European Committee for the Prevention of Torture and Inhuman or Degrading Treatment or Punishment (CPT) from 30 August to 8 September 1992*, CPT/Inf(93)15, Strasbourg: Council of Europe.

Council of Europe (1997) *Space: Annual Penal Statistics 1995 Survey.* Strasbourg: Council of Europe

Currie, E. (1996) *Is America Really Winning the War on Crime and Should Britain Follow Her Example?* London, NACRO.

Dahrendorf, R., Field, F., Hayman, C. and others (1995) *Report on Wealth Creation and Social Cohesion in a Free Society.* London: The Commission on Wealth Creation and Social Cohesion.

Donziger S. (ed.) (1996) *The Real War on Crime: The Report of the National Criminal Justice Commission.* New York: Harper.

Downes D.(1988) *Contrasts in Tolerance: Post-War Penal Policy in the Netherlands and England and Wales.* Oxford: Clarendon Press.

Downes, D. and Morgan, R. (1997) 'Dumping the "Hostages to Fortune"? The Politics of Law and Order in Post-War Britain'. in M. Maguire, R. Morgan and R.Reiner (eds), *The Oxford Handbook of Criminology.* Oxford: Clarendon Press.

Field, F.(ed.) (1996) *Stakeholder Welfare.* London: IEA Health and Welfare Unit.

Giddens, A. (1991) *Modernity and Self-Identity.* Cambridge: Polity Press.

Home Office (1990) *Crime, Justice and Prtotecting the Public*, Cmnd. 965, London: HMSO.

Home Office (1991) *Custody, Care and Justice: The Way Ahead for the Prison Service in England and Wales*, Cmnd. 1647, London: HMSO.

Home Office (1996a) *Protecting the Public: The Government's Strategy on Crime in England and Wales*, Cm. 3190, London: HMSO.

Home Office (1996b) *Prison Statistics England and Wales 1995*, Cm. 3087, London: HMSO.

Home Office (1997a) *Prison Statistics England and Wales 1996*, Cm. 3732, London: HMSO.

Home Office (1997b) *Preventing Children Offending: A Consultation Document*, Cm. 3566, London: HMSO, March.

Home Office (1997c) *Getting to Grips with Crime: A New Framework for Local Action.* London: Home Office.

Home Office (1997d) *Community Safety Order: A Consultation Document.* London: Home Office.

Human Rights Watch (1995) *'Germany for Germans': Xenophobia and Racist Violence in Germany.* New York: Human Rights Watch.

ILO (1994) *The World Unemployment Situation: Trends and Prospects.* Geneva: International Labour Organization.

Labour Party (1996) *Parenting.* London: Labour Party.

Labour Party (1997) *Six Point Plan For Juvenile Crime and Disorder.* London: Labour Party.

Learmont Report (1995) *Review of Prison Service Security in England and Wales and the the Escape from Parkhurst Prison on Tuesday 3rd January 1995*, Cm. 3020, London: HMSO.

Loader, I. (1996) *Youth, Policing and Democracy.* Basingstoke, Macmillan.

Mayhew, P. and van Dijk, J. J. M. (1997) *Criminal Victimisation in Eleven Industrialised Countries: Key Findings from the 1996 International Crime Victims Survey.* The Hague: Ministry of Justice.

Morgan Report (1991) *Safer Communities: The Local Delivery of Crime Prevention Through the Partnership Approach*. London: Home Office.

Morgan, R. (1997) 'Imprisonment: Current Concerns and a Brief History since 1945'. In M. Maguire, R. Morgan and R. Reiner (eds), *The Oxford Handbook of Criminology*, 2nd Edn. Oxford: Clarendon Press.

Murray, C. (1997) *Does Prison Work?* London: Institute of Economic Affairs.

Pease, K. (1994) 'Cross-National Imprisonment Rates: Limitiations of Method and Possible Conclusions'. In R. D. King and M. Maguire (eds), *Prisons in Context*. Oxford: Oxford University Press.

Pitts, J. (1992) 'Juvenile Justice Policy'. In J. Coleman and C. Warren Adamson (eds), *Youth Policy in the 1990s*. London, Routledge.

Prison Reform Trust (1993) *Does Prison Work?* London: Prison Reform Trust.

Prison Service (1996) *Corporate Plan 1996–99*. London: Prison Service.

Rifkin, J. (1995) *The End of Work*. New York: Tarcher Putnam.

Rutherford, A. (1996) *Transforming Criminal Justice*. Winchester: Waterside Press.

Sim, J., Ruggiero, V. and Ryan, M. (1995) 'Punishment in Europe: Perceptions and Commonalities'. In V. Ruggiero, M. Ryan and J. Sim (eds), *Western European Penal Systems: A Critical Anatomy*. London: Sage.

Smith, D. (1997) 'Ethnic Origins, Crime and Criminal Justice'. In M. Maguire, R.Morgan and R. Reiner (eds), *The Oxford Handbook of Criminology*, 2nd edn. Oxford: Clarendon Press.

Tomashevski, K. (1994) *Foreigners in Prison*. Helsinki: European Institute for Crime Prevention and Control.

Tonry, M.(ed.) (1997) *Ethnicity, Crime and Immigration: Comparative and Cross-National Perspectives*. Chicago: University of Chicago.

van Swaaningen, R. and de Jonge, G. (1995) 'The Dutch Prison System and Penal Policy in the 1990s: from Humanitarian Paternalism to Penal Business Management'. In V. Ruggiero, M. Ryan and J. Sim (eds), *Western European Penal Systems: A Critical Anatomy*. London: Sage.

Walmesley, R., Howard, L. and White, S. (1992) *The National Prison Survey 1991: Main Findings*. Home Office Research Study no. 128. London: HMSO.

Western, B. and Beckett, K. (forthcoming) 'How Unregulated is the US Labour Market? The Penal System as a Labour Market Institution'. Princeton University.

Woodcock Report (1994) *Report of the Enquiry into the Escape of Six Prisoners from the Special Security Unit at Whitemoor Prison, Cambridgeshire, on Friday 9th September 1994*, Cm. 2741, London: HMSO.

Worrall, A.(1997) *Punishment in the Community*. London, Longman.

Young, P. and Halsey, A. (1995) *Family and Community Socialism*. London, Institute for Public Policy Research

Zimring, F. and Hawkins, G. (1991) *The Scale of Imprisonment*. Chicago: University of Chicago Press.

Zimring, F. and Hawkins, G. (1995) *Incapacitation*. New York: Oxford University Press.

Index